Reading James Joyce

Reading James Joyce is a ready-at-hand compendium and all-encompassing interpretive guide designed for teachers and students approaching Joyce's writings for the first time, guiding readers to better understand Joyce's works and the background from which they emerged. Meticulously organized, this text situates readers within the world of Joyce including biographical exploration, discussion of Joyce's innovations and prominent works such as *Dubliners*, *Ulysses*, and *Finnegans Wake*, surveys of significant critical approaches to Joyce's writings, and examples of alternative readings and contemporary responses. Each chapter will provide interpretive approaches to contemporary literary theories and key issues, including end-of-chapter strategies and extended readings for further engagement. This book also includes shorter assessments of Joyce's lesser-known works—critical writings, drama, poetry, letters, epiphanies, and personal recollections—to contextualize the creative and social environments from which his most notable publications arose. This uniquely comprehensive guide to Joyce will be an invaluable and comprehensive resource for readers exploring the influential world of Joyce studies.

A. Nicholas Fargnoli is Professor of English and Dean Emeritus of Humanities at Molloy University in Rockville Centre, New York. He is founder of the *Finnegans Wake* Society of New York and past president of the James Joyce Society. He has published on James Joyce, William Faulkner, and ethics.

Michael Patrick Gillespie is Professor of English at Florida International University. He has written books on film, literary theory, and the works of James Joyce, Oscar Wilde, and William Kennedy.

Reading Literature Today

Reading James Joyce
An Introduction
A. Nicholas Fargnoli and Michael Patrick Gillespie

For more information on this series, please visit: https://www.routledge.com/Reading-Literature/book-series/RLT

Reading James Joyce
An Introduction

**A. Nicholas Fargnoli and
Michael Patrick Gillespie**

NEW YORK AND LONDON

Designed cover image: James Joyce with a Magnifying Glass, 1939

First published 2023
by Routledge
605 Third Avenue, New York, NY 10158

and by Routledge
4 Park Square, Milton Park, Abingdon, Oxon, OX14 4RN

Routledge is an imprint of the Taylor & Francis Group, an informa business

© 2023 A. Nicholas Fargnoli and Michael Patrick Gillespie

The right of A. Nicholas Fargnoli and Michael Patrick Gillespie to be identified as authors of this work has been asserted in accordance with sections 77 and 78 of the Copyright, Designs and Patents Act 1988.

All rights reserved. No part of this book may be reprinted or reproduced or utilised in any form or by any electronic, mechanical, or other means, now known or hereafter invented, including photocopying and recording, or in any information storage or retrieval system, without permission in writing from the publishers.

Trademark notice: Product or corporate names may be trademarks or registered trademarks, and are used only for identification and explanation without intent to infringe.

ISBN: 978-1-032-12144-4 (hbk)
ISBN: 978-1-032-12142-0 (pbk)
ISBN: 978-1-003-22329-0 (ebk)

DOI: 10.4324/9781003223290

Typeset in Bembo
by Newgen Publishing UK

To Marge Melun, a woman of good character, wit, and kindness.

ANF

To my students at the Everglades Correctional Institution whose enthusiasm, curiosity, and insight into James Joyce's writings underscored for me the power and pleasure that his works offer.

MPG

Contents

List of Figures   viii
Acknowledgments   x

Introduction   1

1 Biography   11

2 Approaching *Dubliners*   26

3 Approaching *A Portrait of the Artist as a Young Man*   56

4 Approaching *Ulysses*   81

5 Approaching *Finnegans Wake*   125

6 Approaching the Minor Works   162

Chronology   176
Bibliography   179
Appendices   192
Index   210

Figures

1.1	Birthplace of James Joyce, 41 Brighton Square West, Rathgar. (Courtesy of the Irish Tourist Board)	12
1.2	Record of Joyce's election as the prefect of the Sodality of the Blessed Virgin Mary. (Courtesy of Belvedere College, Dublin)	14
1.3	Joyce (second row, center, wearing a mortar board) with the other cast members of *Vice Versa*. (Courtesy of Belvedere College, Dublin)	15
1.4	Joyce (right) with his college friends George Clancy (left) and John Francis Byrne (center). (Courtesy of the Croessmann Collection of James Joyce, Special Collections/Morris Library, Southern Illinois University, Carbondale)	17
1.5	Joyce with his son, Giorgio, in Triste. (c. 1915)	20
1.6	Joyce in the 1920s after one of his eye operations. His first attack of glaucoma occurred on the Bahnofstrasse in 1917 in Zurich when he was living in that city during World War I. A year later he wrote a poem of this experience titled "Bahnhofstrasse," which he included in *Pomes Penyeach*. (James Joyce Collection, General Collection, Beinecke Rare Book and Manuscript Library, Yale University)	22
1.7	Joyce in 1933	23
1.8	One of two original death masks of James Joyce by the Swiss sculptor Paul Speck resides at the Zurich James Joyce Foundation. (Courtesy of Fritz Senn)	24
2.1	The Gresham Hotel in Dublin, the setting of the final scene of "The Dead". (Courtesy of the Irish Tourist Board)	48
3.1	Clongowes Wood College, founded in 1814 by the Society of Jesus, is located west of Dublin in Sallins, County Kildare. (Courtesy of the Irish Tourist Board)	67
3.2	University College. (Courtesy of the Croessmann Collection of James Joyce, Special Collections/Morris Library, Southern Illinois University, Carbondale)	72
3.3	National Library, Dublin. (Courtesy of the Irish Tourist Board)	73

4.1	Slipcase and front wrapper for the first edition of *Ulysses*. (Philip Lyman, Gotham Book Mart)	82
4.2	Sandycove where the Martello Tower is located. (Courtesy of the Irish Tourist Board)	89
4.3	Leopold Bloom by Paul Joyce. (Courtesy of Paul Joyce)	92
4.4	A painting, by Flora H. Mitchell, of 7 Eccles Street, the address of Leopold and Molly Bloom in *Ulysses* (Courtesy of the Croessman Collection of James Joyce, Special Collections/Morris Library, Southern Illinois University)	93
5.1	Map of Phoenix Park, Dublin	132
5.2	Wellington Monument, Phoenix Park. (Courtesy of the Irish Tourist Board)	134
6.1	Title page for Joyce's first book. (Courtesy of C. W. Post Library of Long Island)	168
6.2	Card page and title page of *Pomes Penyeach*, Joyce's second volume of poetry. (Courtesy of C. W. Post Library of Long Island)	169

Acknowledgments

A great many individuals offered help and inspiration for this work, some directly and some by example. While its flaws remain ours, a number of its brightest spots come from others. We wish to thank in particular the following friends and scholars.

Chester Anderson, Margot Gayle Backus, Morris Beja, Bernard Benstock, Shari Benstock, Zack Bowen, Robert Boyle, William S. Brockman, Vincent Cheng, Kathleen Costello-Sullivan, Elizabeth Cullingford, Kimberly Devlin, Edmund L. Epstein, Harriett Fargnoli, Anne Fogarty, Bruce Koehler, Melvin Friedman, Kenneth Furton, Hans Walter Gabler, Luke Gibbons, Andrew Gibson, Paula Gillespie, Roy Gottfried, David Nochimson, Joel Greenberg, Michael Groden, Marianna Czeisel, M. Aishwariya, Bryony Reece, Cecile Gross, Murray Gross, Victoria Harding, Colleen Jaurretche, Declan Kiberd, Terrence Killeen, Sebastian Knowles, Sean Lapham, A. Walton Litz, Ana Luszczynska, Vicki Mahaffey, Asher Milbauer, Patrick McCarthy, Ira Nadel, Robert Newman, David Norris, Margot Norris, Christine O'Neil, Fran O'Rourke, Stephen J. Pantani, Timothy Gauss, Jean Michel Rabaté, Patrick Reilly, Marilyn Reizbaum, Mary Reynolds, John Rickard, Danis Rose, Michelle Salyga, C. George Sandulescu, Philip Sicker, Sam Sloate, Robert Spoo, Thomas Staley, James Sutton, Miriam Pilcher-Clayton, Weldon Thornton, Decherd Turner, Joseph Valente, Eamonn Wall, Florence Walzl, Harriett Nalty, and Phineas Chapman.

Introduction

At first glance *Reading James Joyce* seems like a title in search of a topic. Over the past 100 years, millions upon millions of people have read the works of James Joyce. His books have appeared not only in their original English versions, but they have been translated into more than 150 other languages. There are also hundreds, if not thousands, of critical guides to his works (two of which have been written by the authors of this study). Reading Joyce and writing about reading Joyce are occupations in which a great many people already engage. Nonetheless, there is ample anecdotal evidence that any number of readers still feel reluctant to take up that author's writings. Indeed, on many scholars' bookshelves *Ulysses* and *Finnegans Wake* enjoy the privileged position of secular Bibles. That is to say, they are displayed ostentatiously though rarely if ever opened.

The aim of this book is to reach those who have a genuine interest in Joyce's writings but for one reason or another feel hesitant to pick up his works. We do not believe that should be the case. Joyce is not a dilettante who writes in a self-consciously selective fashion. Rather, he is an author deeply concerned with human nature and one who continually struggles to find the language that makes his observations accessible to others. He drew intensely and insistently on his experiences in a world where he grew to manhood, and the specificity that he gives to 120-year-old descriptions of a city that no reader (even those who have lived in or visited Dublin) has ever seen. We do not think that Joyce meant these descriptions to frustrate those who come to his writings, but we understand that a fuller explanation of certain references and some elaboration on the narrative discourses can make engagement with the works more pleasurable. With this aim, we seek to bring readers to Joyce's canon and to help them comprehend how the diverse imaginative assumptions that shape the way that they look at literature can inform what they encounter in his works.

This book is not yet another variation on the meaning of Joyce's writings. Rather, by talking about the makeup of his writings within a broad context, we hope to help readers refine the assumptions that they bring to the writings and come to a better sense of how to judge the opinions that others have voiced. In the process we will highlight proven strategies for engaging

DOI: 10.4324/9781003223290-1

his canon as well as validate a wide variety of readings as legitimate responses to what Joyce has written.

With that in mind, this book is designed as an introduction to Joyce's writings, one that explores options for understanding by examining the mechanics and the consequences of reading his individual works. To that end, before looking at his writing, we feel it important to talk about the common and unique elements found in anyone's process of reading. In this way we aim to examine similarities in the approaches that most readers follow in taking up Joyce's works, and at the same time we seek to highlight the impact of our subjectivity on an individual understanding of each of his publications.

How We Read

We firmly believe that no one reads passively, as if our minds were empty vessels that a writer's words were meant to fill. Instead, we see reading as always involving the active engagement of an individual's imagination with that of the artist's. When we read, we create a comprehensible experience, giving meaning to the words before us. Reading engages ideas rather than reflects them, and it is important to stress that we understand the word *reading* itself as synonymous with interpreting and understanding. As we progress through our discussions of response to Joyce's writings, we will use those designations—reading, interpreting, and understanding—interchangeably.

We also acknowledge that reading employs words which, no matter what the language, are mutable, approximate, and ultimately uncertain. For the sake of expediency, people may assert that when one person exchanges words with another, the two convey and comprehend very specific concepts. In fact, no word or collection of words evokes exactly the same understanding in any two conversationalists, or in any group of readers, or even in the same individual looking at something at very different times in life. Instead, as Joyce says in *Finnegans Wake*, we "swop hats and excheck a few strong verbs weak oach eather yapyazzard" (*FW* 16.8–9).

If you dispute this premise, ask a group of people to define any common term, like beauty, and press each for an example that precisely fits his or her definition. The range and variety of their suggestions will prove the point we are making. Imagine if someone reads or views *King Lear* at 20 as someone's child, at 40 with young children of one's own, and at 60 with one's children grown, what the person comprehends is unique in each exposure. Although the words in the play never change, the individual's movement from young adulthood to old age insures that none of the interpretations will be like any of the others. What we are saying is that reading Joyce, or any other writer for that matter, can produce as many responses as there are readers, a desirable outcome revealing that literature is not circumscribed by one or a few meanings but alive with multiple interpretative possibilities.

Of course, one might assert that such assumptions challenge the validity of a book that offers observations on the process of reading Joyce's works. If everyone generates a personal point of view, there seems little to be gained from discussing the features that individualize those responses. In fact, we feel that the opposite to be true, particularly with writers like Joyce who engage our imagination from a range of perspectives. Like Shakespeare's Cleopatra whose infinite variety could not be withered or made stale by age, the mutability of Joyce's language promises each of us from one generation to the next new pleasure and insight with every reading. With this conception in mind, a book like ours aims to facilitate, without prescribing, ways of engaging those pleasures and insights by looking at the mechanics of the works and presenting guides to their construction. It remains to the reader the task of forming a unified impression of the compositions, something less difficult than might be imagined despite the persistent view among some that much of Joyce's writing is indecipherable and too demanding of one's time and efforts.

In fact, it is not what Joyce wrote that many find challenging but rather the way we read it. No matter what one's first impression, a careful study of his fiction, including his final work, *Finnegans Wake*, shows that Joyce, with occasional borrowings from foreign languages and some neologisms and puns that may make us roll our eyes, composed in English and used grammatically correct language. At the same time, aware of the multiplicity of meaning imbedded in every word and the complex variations that different individuals derive from those words, he tried to present a range of possible approaches through a variety of styles. As he once remarked to his friend Frank Budgen: "I have all the words already. What I am seeking is the perfect order of words in the sentence."

Because of his stylistic experimentation, the diversity and allusiveness of Joyce's works can seem daunting, and some may feel antagonistic toward an author whom they perceive as being intent upon showing them how little of what he has written they understand. In fact, while he integrated any number of different forms into his prose, Joyce always gave readers reference points to guide their interpretations. *Reading James Joyce* presents an overview of his writing that takes these aims into consideration and that gives readers a clear sense of how that composition process informs his works.

To that end, this volume highlights both clarity and multiplicity. We do not offer a template-like interpretive approach or privilege specific issues, to the exclusion of others. Rather, we come to his canon with the idea that simple approaches aid readers in comprehending a broad view of the narrative strategies that he, as one of the foremost Modernist and then post-Modernist writers of the twentieth century, introduced or elaborated. We want to outline the structure and construction of Joyce's writing, and leave interpretations to the readers. Nonetheless, we see the world as subjectively as do any other human beings, and so it will be useful to begin by laying out some of the assumptions that we have brought to our project.

Importance of Reading Joyce

Joyce ranks as the most important fiction writer in English of the twentieth century. His writing showed the appropriateness of themes and topics long considered too mundane or too vulgar for consideration in serious literature. At the same time, the construction of his works reoriented the stylistic expectations of readers beyond the conventional literary forms of traditional fiction.

With a degree of intense interest in ordinary detail surpassing authors like Charles Dickens or Honoré de Balzac, Joyce wrote about the quotidian routines of our lives and the disruptions and diversions that come through ordinary human behavior. He explored our most intimate experiences—copulation, masturbation, menstruation, urination, defecation, and countless others—with a frankness rarely seen in literature. Nonetheless, no matter how personal, how embarrassing, how flawed, or simply how unremarkable the behavior, Joyce never lost his respect for the humanity of any of his characters and never cast judgment against them, details that separate him from an author like Rabelais who gloried in vulgarity and used such descriptions as cudgels on his readers.

In addition, the styles—free indirect discourse, stream of consciousness or interior monologue, multiple and simultaneous perspectives, and a variety of others—that Joyce adopted, adapted, and in some cases created, give his works the power to resonate with a broad assortment of readers' outlooks. In his near obsessive view of the rhythms and details of ordinary middleclass life, Joyce used sophisticated constructions for insights into relatively familiar situations: his great achievement is the presentation of the complexity of the human character in a range of ordinary individual natures. When we come to see this diversity and lose the imperative to comprehend simultaneously all the perspectives that it suggests, we can experience the pleasure of his work. What at first may have seemed a confusing cacophony of views becomes an invitation to the reader to proceed in a selective fashion, engaging whatever one chooses on the multiple plains upon which narratives are simultaneously recorded.

From this arises the bifurcations that some feel between the innovative form of the writing and the paradoxical familiarity of the characters, situations, and actions that it represents. Even as his style captures the diversity, subjectivity, and nonlinearity of individual human perceptions, the content of this work dwells on thematic issues common to us all. It centers on the turmoil in ordinary lives—self-doubt, sexual desire, isolation, communal mores—animated by close examination, giving a humane view of characters balanced with a rigorous dissection of their behavior. It is Joyce's humane comedy that draws readers to his works time and again.

Critical Ways of Seeing

Criticism, and by extension critical theory, has been a topic of concern since Aristotle's *Poetics*. At least since the eighteenth-century figures like Joseph Addison, Richard Steele, and Samuel Johnson began to be paid regularly for telling people how to understand what they read. Certainly, the idea of a system offering definitive explanations to complex forms has a great deal of appeal, and particular critical theorists, that is those forcefully giving pre-eminence to a particular way of reading, have contributed to this view with implicit claims of authority that rivaled Pope's assertion of infallibility.

Before proceeding, let us dismiss the still prevailing canards that enjoyed wide circulation long before Jacques Derrida caused so much consternation by determinedly asserting the primacy of indeterminacy. We all read according to some methodical system or another, always governed by sets of assumptions that give validity to that particular way of seeing things. Those who consider theory to apply only to a select set of epistemologies that they have mastered (we use the term loosely) underscore their provincialism rather than the sophistication that they seek to project. Those who affirm that they do not use theory but rather simply read are admitting to an appalling ignorance of their process of reading.

In fact, any specific critical theory is nothing more or less than a summary of the assumptions that a particular perspective brings to a reading, interpretation or understanding, whichever we prefer to call it. Consciously or not, we all read according to some system that privileges particular perspectives and assumptions that coincide with our worldview or complement our sense of how literature should function. That is not meant to dismiss any or all of the formalized accounts of ways of coming to understanding. Quite the contrary, literary theories have great value because they foreground the specific assumptions upon which readers rely when they respond to literature. Regularizing these assumptions in a theoretical system enables one to grasp the perspectives forming the basis for particular conclusions. In acknowledging this method as a basis of our comprehension, we recognize that for any individual one set of assumptions may produce insightful and exciting conclusions, but no system has the all-encompassing power to present a definitive understanding, one that dismisses all others, of a particular work.

With this view in mind, we come neither to praise nor to bury critical theory. We simply wish to acknowledge its presence. The complexity and sophistication of Joyce's writing have enabled a range of perspectives to offer viable interpretations of his works for the past century. In the following synopses, we seek to present how important features in each theory highlight various ways of coming to a better understanding of Joyce's canon. Examples of more detailed applications are cited in this book's bibliography.

Biographical Criticism seems to many a logical starting point for any effort to understand Joyce's writing because in his process of composition he drew heavily on events from his own life and on the formative features of that portion of the Dublin world in which he grew to adulthood. This methodology does not propose a simplistic relationship of autobiographical facts to fictional representations. Rather, it believes that since the work originates from the consciousness of the author, understanding that author's life will illuminate the particular piece of writing that is under consideration. Although this can be a tricky position, sometimes leading to overgeneralizations, seeing Joyce's work in the context of his life can greatly enhance one's awareness of its subtle aspects, especially given the fact that one of his central characters,

Stephen Dedalus, lived the first 22 years of his life in a fashion similar to that which Joyce himself had undergone and that the other characters in his works are very similar to family members, friends, and acquaintances whom Joyce encountered in Dublin as he grew to manhood. (For an example of how this approach can be usefully applied, see Morris Beja's *James Joyce: A Literary Life*, cited in our bibliography.)

As already noted, formal experimentation dominated Joyce's literary output. As a consequence, *Stylistic Criticism* examines language from the structure of words to the constructions of narratives. (For a detailed explanation of the fundamental make-up of stylistic criticism, see Stanley Fish's *Is There a Text in This Class?*, cited in the bibliography.) This approach draws on linguistic theories as well as on theories founded on so-called close readings, but one would be mistaken to understand the three methods as synonymous. Stylistic criticism amalgamates and extends the other methods. It presents an organized critique of the way Joyce employs language, and it presents readers with important insights into the literal function of his composition process. Engaging Joyce's writing in this way focuses attention on his stylistic strategies and on their impacts on readers. A clear conception of this process will inevitably enhance one's understanding of broader elements of his writing.

Textual Studies is closely allied to stylistic criticism. Although the approach itself has been an established practice for centuries, its relation to Joyce studies grew out of the work leading up to the publication of *The James Joyce Archive* in 1979, a massive facsimile collection of Joyce's notes, drafts, and revisions held by research institutions in America, Ireland, and England. (For a detailed examination of this early work, see A. Walton Litz's pioneering examination *The Art of James Joyce: Method and Design in* **Ulysses** *and* **Finnegans Wake**, cited in the bibliography.) The reproductions made broadly available for study material formerly accessible only by extended visits to a staggering number of archives. The inchoate records of Joyce's composition process provided a range of readers the ability to form their own conceptions of how particular pieces of writing emerged in a fashion previously available only to scholars with the resources to support travel and research at a range of institutions. (Not unexpectedly a number of controversies arose as readers began to challenge the views of the heretofore privileged few able to undertake extensive examinations of various stages of Joyce's writings. For a cross section of these views, see "The Scandal of *Ulysses*" *New York Review of Books*, 30 June 1988 and the responses and rebuttals that continued in that journal for the next seven months.)

Some who wholeheartedly embraced the epistemology as a means to definitive readings quickly found that their close examinations often produced even greater ambiguity. Those with more realistic aspirations were satisfied by discoveries evidence of the complexity of Joyce's writings. In the end, textual criticism became an important though singular way of approaching the canon, often most useful when combined with other epistemological assumptions. (Hans Walter Gabler's essay on editing *Ulysses*, cited in the bibliography, gives a detailed look at how textual criticism can be applied to Joyce's writings.) Textual criticism can also extend to scrutinizing printed editions of Joyce's works where publishers may not have always been as attentive to what Joyce—one of the most meticulous of all writers—actually wrote.

Like textual criticism, *Genetic Criticism*, coming to prominence in Joyce studies in the final decades of the twentieth century, is most logically seen as a hybrid combination of textual and cultural studies. It concentrates on textual histories as a way of understanding the creative evolution of a particular work. Although that may seem an overly particular approach to many works, for Joyce's writing, crammed with allusions now often lost on contemporary readers, this methodology provides interpretive links otherwise unavailable. (For extended studies of genetic applications of Joyce criticism, see the Luca Crispi and Sam Sloate edition, *How Joyce Wrote* **Finnegans Wake**, cited in the bibliography.)

Psychoanalytic Assessments go back to the initial appearances of Joyce's writings coinciding to a heightened popular attention to the theories of Sigmund Freud. As interest shifted from Freudian to Jungian to the more recent conceptions of Jacques Lacan, the fascination in the conscious and subconscious or unconscious revelations imbedded in Joyce's fiction has remained strong, often long after the ideas themselves have lost credit among the psychoanalytic community. What stands as constant in this system of reading is an awareness of Joyce's evocative ability to cause the characters' thoughts and experiences to resonate with those of various readers. (A great many studies of psychoanalytic approaches to Joyce exist. For two examples covering most of the central issues, see the entries on books by Daniel Bristow, *Joyce and Lacan*, and Sheldon Brivic, *Joyce between Freud and Jung*, cited in the bibliography.)

In the last half century, a great many interpretive systems applied to reading Joyce have drawn on ideas presented in *Deconstruction*. In the 1970s Jacques Derrida and others who thought along the same lines liberated readers from the false quest of a definitive meaning by showing the indeterminacy, impermanence, and mutability inherent in language. While these observations in themselves do not offer particularly useful extended interpretations, nor were they meant to do so. However, they present a wonderful starting point for readers seeking a point for engaging the oscillating perspectives that permeate Joyce's fiction. Deconstruction's dual gift and curse of uncertainty have driven a powerful engine initiating complex, unstable examinations of the canon. (For further commentaries, see the collection of essays edited by Andrew Mitchell and Sam Sloate, *Derrida and Joyce*, cited in the bibliography.)

Feminist Criticism has presented strong commentaries on Joyce's canon from the time his writing began to be published, and it offered some particularly forceful readings in works that appeared over the past half century. While there is not an all-encompassing, unified approach to feminist analysis that fits the category, a number of critics examined Joyce's work with a sense of its representation of its attitudes toward female characters. In a number of instances this orientation incorporates various epistemologies: psychoanalytic,

Marxist, deconstructive, and others. (For a good, early view of the relation of Joyce and feminism, see Bonnie Scott's book, *Joyce and Feminism*, cited in the bibliography.)

Gender Studies, a relatively recently delineated critical methodology, anatomizes the complex attitudes of an individual's nature as represented through performative roles. It takes into consideration both the subjective values and the social attitudes that shape the construction of character along lines influenced but not prescribed by sex and sexuality. This approach finds ample material for study in Joyce's writing. From his earliest writings onward the willingness of Joyce to examine the most intimate biological functions and the most private emotional responses has provided the opportunity for epistemologies focusing on gender to offer significant insights. (For a good overview see the collection edited by Jolanta W. Wawrzycka and Marlena G. Corcoran, *Gender in Joyce*, cited in the bibliography.)

Queer Studies stands as a category intimately related to the methodology of gender studies but adamantly independent in its analytic premises. Its central assumption, often with a Lacanian tinge, is that homosocial and homosexual perspectives can illuminate a wide variety of characteristics and behaviors going well beyond individual sexual orientation. While we acknowledge the obvious danger of reading too much into a character's behavior by an emphasis on the queer eye—as Freud once said, "sometimes a cigar is just a cigar"—the suppleness of Joyce's representations are open to illuminating comments based on the assumptions of this approach. (Joseph Valente's collection of essays, *Quare Joyce*, cited in the bibliography, gives a good overview of the topic.)

Cultural Studies, like gender and queer studies, has come to the foreground of interpretive attention during the last few decades. At the same time, like both of the other methodologies, the assumptions upon which it bases its conclusions readily apply to the whole canon of our literature. It is an expansion of biographical criticism, putting the emphasis on community, social customs, and public interaction rather than on individuality. (*Cultural Studies of James Joyce*, edited by Cherly Herr and cited in the bibliography, gives a good overview of the topic.)

In Joyce's writing in particular, his minute rendering of Dublin in the early twentieth century gives ample opportunity for exploring the dynamics of social institutions, under heavy criticism by the modernist movement, on human interaction. Awareness of such conditions gives readers a sense of the environment in which and out of which Joyce wrote. Such perceptions do not in themselves explain Joyce's works, but they do contextualize the writings in a way that makes their orientations more accessible.

The distinctiveness of *the Irish Experience*—particularly in terms of the Colonial and post-Colonial attitudes of a predominantly white, Catholic populace—makes it a most useful form for framing Joyce's narratives. It is particularly efficacious in reminding readers that the tension between the imperialism of England and Ireland's response to it, always present if not always overtly noted, has much more complexity than one derives from a simple Manichean division of bad colonizers and good colonized. The varieties and levels of Irish accommodation and the successes and failures of English efforts at administration give a great deal of material for considering Joyce's writing from this perspective. (Emer Nolan's book, *James Joyce and Nationalism*, cited in the bibliography, touches on a number of these issues.)

In a broader view of the topic, *Postcolonial Studies* both fed on and ignored the central concerns of Irish studies. The latter, though acknowledging the scarring effect of English imperialism for over 750 years, concerns itself with cultural, social, and communal issues. Postcolonial interpretations, however, single mindedly pursue understanding from the perspective of the impact of English exploitation on the material, psychological, and spiritual elements of Irish life. A number of thoughtful critics have read Joyce from this point of view, but they would be among the first to acknowledge the partiality of any interpretation based on their assumptions. (See Vincent Cheng's book, *Joyce, Race, and Empire*, and Enda Duffy's, *The Subaltern Ulysses,* both cited in the bibliography, for a fuller discussion of the issue.)

There are, of course, many additional systems of reading Joyce that we have not mentioned here: Formalist, Marxist/Materialist, The New Historicism, Ethical, and more. Indeed, book-length studies, several of which are cited in the bibliography, have been done on alternative approaches without exhausting all of the categories. Our aim has not been to provide an exhaustive catalogue. Rather, we hope that by acknowledging the representative features of systems of reading that we have underscored the idea of diversity as the guiding principle to reading Joyce.

The underlying point of presenting these selected critical theories is to show that there are as many responses as there are readers. An awareness of a range of systems will help us sort out our own, but in no manner should they be seen as prescriptions for understanding. Nor, to recur to the idea that opened this section, should one expect to find in any epistemology the Holy Grail of interpretation that leads one to a pure and definitive sense of Joyce. We engage his writings because their perpetual mutability produces continuous surprise and pleasure with every reading.

Plan of this Study

Since we have written this work as a guide, we feel that it would be useful at its start to offer readers a clear idea of the book's organizing principles. As we have already noted, our aim is not to explain the meaning of Joyce's writing, for any such efforts inevitably limit its usefulness to one way of seeing the canon and would do little to contribute to alternative readings. Rather, we endeavor to lay out key points and central concerns in the process of understanding his fiction and thereby highlighting the individual interpretive decisions we make every time we read it.

Toward that end, after a summary of the Joyce's life, we will offer chapters on each of his major works of fiction: *Dubliners, A Portrait of the Artist as a Young Man, Ulysses,* and *Finnegans Wake*. We will also devote a chapter to what seems his less significant works—his poetry, his only extant play, and other miscellaneous writings—but which in fact are pieces crucial to understanding Joyce's artistic evolution and the development of his canon. We end with a chronology of Joyce's life, a bibliography of selected secondary sources, and eight appendices.

Each chapter follows the same form in its approach to a particular piece of writing. We begin with an outline of the artistic aims and habits of composition that Joyce followed in creating that work. We then look at the cultural context from which that composition emerged. After reviewing specific issues that engaged his attention when he was writing the work, we summarize the plotline and then offer two approaches to interpreting a selected portion from the book or collection under discussion. These alternative readings underscore the view that no single response to any of Joyce's writing is sufficient and that an awareness of a range of readings enhances individual understanding and pleasure. We end each chapter with a list of characters and suggested questions for further discussion.

A Final Note

We envisioned *Reading James Joyce*, with its encyclopedic-style entries running throughout the text, as a supplement to the individual's more focused study. We believe our book works best when it is consulted on an as needed basis. Though we would be flattered by anyone's decision to read our work from cover to cover, we expect that most experienced readers of Joyce's works will consult this volume with questions about a specific text, character, or even passage in mind. We have tried to anticipate this by making our entries as self-contained as possible. This inevitably produces some redundancy and to those with better memories than our own, which require near constant refreshing, we ask for your patience and understanding when encountering these recurrences.

We also see this as a guide for students approaching Joyce's fiction for the first time. Readers already familiar with his work may find a few new ideas that are useful to them. However, a great deal of what we say has been discussed for years among Joyce scholars. For us, this does not reflect a drawback of the study, but it rather underscores our sense that with the aid of proven concepts and tested theories even those taking up Joyce's works for the first time can experience a great deal of satisfaction from what they read.

The following standard editions of Joyce's works are the ones we cite throughout this volume:

> *Dubliners: Text, Criticism, and Notes*, ed. Robert Scholes and A. Walton Litz. New York: The Viking Press, 1996.
> *A Portrait of the Artist as a Young Man: Text, Criticism, and Notes*, ed. Chester G. Anderson. New York: The Viking Press, 1968.
> *Ulysses*, ed. Hans Walter Gabler et al. New York: Vintage, 1993.
> *Finnegans Wake*, New York: The Viking Press, 1944.

1 Biography

February 2nd marks Groundhog Day, Candlemas, and the eve of the Feast of St. Blaise. It is also the day in 1882 that James Augustine Aloysius Joyce was born. At the time of his birth, his family was living in what was then the south Dublin suburb of Rathgar at 41 Brighton Square, which in a quirk surprising to no one familiar with the Irish, is in fact laid out in the shape of a triangle.

Joyce was the oldest of ten surviving children of John and Mary Jane "May" Joyce (née Murray). In *A Portrait of the Artist as a Young Man*, when a friend asks Stephen Dedalus how many children his mother had, Stephen responds flippantly: "Nine or ten . . . some died." In reality there was little in the existence of either family to inspire glibness. The narratives of both *A Portrait of the Artist as a Young Man* and of *Ulysses* offer grim descriptions of life for the fictional Dedalus clan, particularly after the death of Stephen's mother. Although fiction is an unreliable reference for biography, doubtless many of the Joyce family's experiences mirrored the difficulties of their fictional counterparts. John Joyce's spendthrift habits, attraction to alcohol, and flagrant rejection of any financial, emotional, or parental responsibility made life in the Joyce household increasingly difficult, particularly after the early death of May Joyce.

Joyce would live his adult life abroad in various cities on the Continent, but during the years that he grew from infancy to manhood in Dublin, he was profoundly shaped by the city of his birth. In that formative period, the mores of a pervasive middleclass, urban, Catholic culture in a colonized country defined his perceptions of the world.

Dublin was at the center of England's relentless commercial exploitation of Ireland's resources and people. The British imperial mentality took for granted the circumscription of economic opportunities for the indigenous Irish population. Across the country the often-capricious decisions of absentee landowners and the monumental insensitivity of the Protestant Ascendancy who held all the economic and political power led to a sense of cautious conformity among many Irish. Seeing this diffidence to authority in any form, particularly among his fellow Dubliners, infuriated the young Joyce, and it eventually would become the target for a great deal of scorn in

DOI: 10.4324/9781003223290-2

Figure 1.1 Birthplace of James Joyce, 41 Brighton Square West, Rathgar. (Courtesy of the Irish Tourist Board)

his writing, including his political pieces that he wrote in Italian while living in Trieste.

Furthermore, years of observing this claustrophobic timidity sparked a determination in Joyce to achieve intellectual, spiritual, and emotional independence by escaping from such an environment. At the same time, these experiences, coupled with the insights derived from a formidable Jesuit education and wide-ranging personal reading habits, had a lasting impact on his artistic temperament and literary treatment of cultural, social, political, historical, theological, and religious themes throughout his works. Whatever rancor Joyce felt for his native land did not prevent him from using his experiences of growing up in Dublin as rich sources for his fiction. As his biographer Richard Ellmann records Joyce saying: "For myself, I always write about Dublin, because if I can get to the heart of Dublin I can get to the heart of all the cities of the world." Joyce reflects his Jesuit education here and the Aristotelean concept that the universal is contained in the particular.

In this respect, one could conceivably argue that when he eloped to the Continent with Nora Barnacle at 22 years of age, Joyce did more than take individual memories of Dublin with him. In his imagination he never left his native city, or at least he never left the world that surrounded him as he grew to maturity between 1882 and 1904.

Because of the feckless nature of his father, youth experiences were tinged with a riches to rags narrative arc that imbued Joyce's recollections of growing up with a good measure of cynicism. In his early years, Joyce's family enjoyed the benefits of a comfortable middle-class lifestyle, thanks largely to John Joyce's inheritance of property in Cork. In 1888 when James Joyce was six years old, his parents enrolled him in Clongowes Wood College, the exclusive Jesuit boarding school still in operation and located about 40 miles west of Dublin in County Kildare. Unfortunately, during Joyce's time at Clongowes, his father's profligacy greatly drained the financial worth of his Cork legacy. John Joyce's aversion to steady work and his attraction to alcohol increasingly strained the family's finances. As the income from the Cork properties dwindled, the Joyces could no longer afford to pay their son's school fees. After three years he was withdrawn from Clongowes.

After leaving Clongowes in 1891, James and his younger brother Stanislaus had a brief stint in a school run by the Christian Brothers on North Richmond Street (a location referenced early in the *Dubliners'* story "Araby") before they became scholarship-boys at a Dublin Jesuit day school, Belvedere College in 1893. Joyce rarely referenced this short period with the Christian Brothers later in his life, and he did not replicate that experience in *A Portrait of the Artist as a Young Man*. Stephen Dedalus after a brief hiatus from any organized education went from Clongowes to Belvedere College. (Belvedere College still operates at the top of North Great George Street, just a short block away from the James Joyce Centre that opened in 1996.)

At Belvedere, Joyce completed his primary and secondary education. He distinguished himself scholastically and won several academic prizes. He was popular with his classmates as a clever student whose wit could occasionally flummox some of his teachers. And, for a time at least he showed a commitment to his religious faith as evidenced by being made a prefect of the Sodality of the Blessed Virgin Mary. Sometime during his last year at Belvedere, however, he seemed to have abandoned the practice of Catholicism.

Evidence of what life must have been like in the Joyce family during those years is understandably thin and often subject to the vagaries of memory. As we have already suggested, *A Portrait of the Artist as a Young Man*, though certainly not an autobiography, can offer approximate views into the circumstances of the Joyce household. The opening of chapter five in the novel offers a grim description of the Dedalus domestic situation, and later in the episode Stephen indirectly points to the source of their difficulties as he sardonically recounts the failings of his father, with a dismissive mockery that recalls the quixotic career of John Joyce:

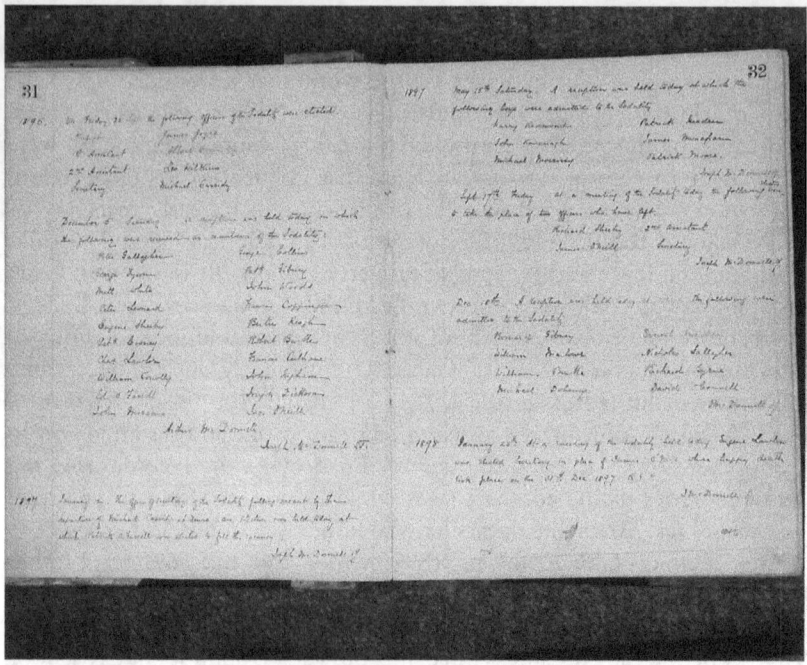

Figure 1.2 Record of Joyce's election as the prefect of the Sodality of the Blessed Virgin Mary. (Courtesy of Belvedere College, Dublin)

> A medical student, an oarsman, a tenor, an amateur actor, a shouting politician, a small landlord, a small investor, a drinker, a good fellow, a storyteller, somebody's secretary, something in a distillery, a taxgatherer, a bankrupt and at present a praiser of his own past.
>
> (p. 241)

The passage from *A Portrait of the Artist as a Young Man* where this quotation occurs also obliquely highlights a feature of Joyce's city life that had a marked impact on his fiction. As a young man eager to escape the clamor of his increasingly impecunious and always chaotic life, Joyce had few options. Without a disposable income, he could hardly meet friends in pubs, restaurants, or coffee shops. What he did instead was walk with them all over the city. As with Stephen and Cranly, Joyce and his friends strolled through Dublin, exchanging ideas and criticizing the world around them. In the process, Joyce inevitably developed an intimate knowledge of the thoroughfares of his native town. The intimate details of the urban landscapes that sharpen his narratives come from the experiences of these peregrinations. He would later brag that Dublin could be completely destroyed and then rebuilt with nothing more than the descriptions of it found in his fiction.

Figure 1.3 Joyce (second row, center, wearing a mortar board) with the other cast members of *Vice Versa*. (Courtesy of Belvedere College, Dublin)

After his graduation from Belvedere in 1898, Joyce matriculated at University College Dublin, his third school affiliated with the Society of Jesus. During his university studies, which focused on modern languages, Joyce became increasingly independent—intellectually, emotionally, spiritually, and, perhaps most importantly, imaginatively—from the social institutions that defined life in Dublin. By the time he completed his university training, Joyce had developed a worldview antithetical to that of many of his fellow Dubliners.

Biographers like Richard Ellmann have made a great deal of Joyce's dissatisfaction with Ireland and Irish institutions, and perhaps reflecting their own attitudes, have concentrated on what they see as his animosity toward Catholicism. In fact, one can offer no informed opinion, positive or negative, of Joyce's spirituality and religious sentiments. Nor, despite repeated and often acerbic criticisms recorded in his letters, one cannot speak with certitude about his personal attitude toward the Church and Catholicism. (When even Mother Theresa has admitted to moments of doubt in her own faith, it is all too evident that normal human vacillations make it challenging to ascertain with certainty the beliefs of almost any human being.)

Perhaps it is this very indeterminacy that makes some scholars continue to debate these ideas. That remains an intellectual choice to be defended by those who pursue the issue, but in point of fact we do not feel that personal belief. Nonetheless, no matter what interpretation critics choose to impose upon Joyce's beliefs, it would be a profound mistake for any reader to minimize the lasting impact that his disciplined, Jesuit education and his eclectic reading of Catholic philosophers such as the Dominican Renaissance philosopher Giordano Bruno and the Scholastic philosopher and theologian St. Thomas Aquinas had on the formation of his creative consciousness. Long after rejecting the legitimacy of the Roman Catholic Church's right to dictate how he should lead his life, Joyce continued to speak with pride of his Jesuit training.

One need only approach his canon with an awareness of the tenets of the *Ratio Studiorum*, a rigorous plan of studies for Jesuit education drawing upon the pedagogical philosophy of St. Ignatius, the Society's founder, to see how the intellectual curiosity, the independence of thought, and the vigorous articulation of ideas, so important to the Jesuits, stand at the center of all of Joyce's imaginative work. Joyce may have forsaken the forms and practices of Catholicism, but he never abandoned what he learned from it. In fact, throughout his literary works, he artistically exploited a sophisticated understanding of its theological concepts. Religious imagery, ritualistic practices, and theological analogies form thematic motifs and imaginative catalysts throughout his works.

It cannot be surprising then that Joyce's creative writing began while he was still under the direct influence of the Jesuits, for the breadth of knowledge and disciplined thinking that they advocated provided invaluable imaginative stimuli. In his mid- to late teens, Joyce wrote short prose pieces entitled *Silhouettes*, two collections of poems, *Moods* and *Shine and Dark*, occasional verse, and at least two plays, *A Brilliant Career* and *Dream Stuff*. All of these works, with the exception of a few fragments from *Shine and Dark* and *Dream Stuff* are now lost, yet the prolific creative energy to which they attest indicates how early Joyce committed himself to the pursuit of art.

During this same time, as he searched for ways to hone his craft as an author, he also began writing essays and book reviews. His first published piece, "Ibsen's New Drama," appeared in the prestigious English journal, *Fortnightly Review*, on 1 April 1900, when he was only 18. As a literary exercise in the summer of 1900, Joyce translated two plays by Gerhart Hauptmann, *Vor Sonnenaufgang* (Joyce rendered its title as *Before Sunrise*) and *Michael Kramer*. By 1901, he started composing the poems that he would later assemble for his first published work, *Chamber Music*.

After graduating with a Bachelor of Arts degree from University College Dublin in October of 1902, Joyce spent a brief period in Paris ostensibly there to pursue a medical degree. In fact, he lived a Bohemian existence while he immersed himself in the craft of writing. Joyce read eclectically at the Bibliothèque Nationale de France, carefully noted ideas meant to delineate his theory of aesthetics, and struggled to survive by writing book reviews, giving occasional language lessons, and getting sporadic financial help from home. In April of 1903, Joyce received word that his mother was dying of cancer. Although only 44 years old, May Joyce had been worn out from childbearing and by the peripatetic, impoverished life imposed upon

Figure 1.4 Joyce (right) with his college friends George Clancy (left) and John Francis Byrne (center). (Courtesy of the Croessmann Collection of James Joyce, Special Collections/Morris Library, Southern Illinois University, Carbondale)

the family by her irresponsible husband. After borrowing passage money, Joyce returned to Dublin to be with her.

After his mother's death in August of 1903, Joyce remained in Dublin for the next 13 months. During that time, he continued writing the verses of *Chamber Music* and began working on stories that would eventually be included in the *Dubliners* collection. He also wrote a long prose meditation "A Portrait of the Artist" and started a novel *Stephen Hero* that he would ultimately abandon for a more radical work on the same topic, *A Portrait of the Artist as a Young Man*. Over that period he also briefly taught at the Clifden School in Dalkey and lived for a short time in a Martello Tower with Oliver St. John Gogarty. (Both experiences are memorialized in fictional form in the first two chapters of *Ulysses*.)

Despite the considerable impact of the Dublin environment on Joyce's writing—as he said in the quotation noted above, all his fiction is set in that city and put in periods corresponding to the years of his growth to manhood there—he felt that the claustrophobic, conservative, Catholic, colonial atmosphere of the city was too much for his independent sensibilities and literary ambitions. Joyce determined to go to the Continent to become a writer. In October of 1904, he left Dublin with Nora Barnacle, a young girl from Galway. She had come to the city earlier that year, found work as a chambermaid at Finn's Hotel on South Leinster Street, and had met Joyce only three months before she departed from Ireland with him. To survive until he could make a name for himself as a writer, Joyce planned to teach English at one of the Berlitz Schools on the Continent.

As noted earlier, some time during his adolescence Joyce had left the Catholic Church, and from that period onward he fiercely resisted the discipline that it or any social institution for that matter sought to impose. This resistance was unambiguously stated in a letter to Nora about a month before the two left Dublin: "When I was waiting for you last night I was even more restless. It seems to me that I was fighting a battle with every religious and social force in Ireland for you and me" (*Letters II*.53). In fact, he and Nora did not marry until 4 July 1931, and only then it was done to protect the inheritance rights of their offspring.

Their first five months abroad must have recalled memories of Joyce's childhood for during that time the couple endured an impoverished, itinerant existence. They passed briefly through Zurich and Trieste before settling down in Pola (now the Croatian costal city named Pula) for four and a half months where Joyce gave English lessons at the Berlitz Language School. He eventually found a more stable teaching position in the Berlitz School in Trieste, a port city at that time on the edge of the Austro-Hungarian Empire. There, he and the by-now pregnant Nora were able to begin a more stable family life away from claustrophobic environment of conservative Catholic Ireland without the formality of marriage vows, something they never could have done in Dublin.

Five months after taking up residence in Trieste, Joyce and Nora's son, Giorgio, was born on 27th July in 1905, and two years later, on 26th July, Nora gave birth to their daughter, Lucia. With the exception of a bit more than a half year's residence in Rome from 1906 into 1907, the Joyce family lived an always chaotic and often penurious life for a decade in Trieste. Although Joyce continued to give language lessons, the family often had to rely upon the financial and emotional support of Joyce's brother Stanislaus who, in October of 1905, came to live with them in Trieste and began also to give language lessons through the Berlitz School. While providing much needed stability to the family, Stanislaus could be highly judgmental, particularly about his brother's spendthrift habits and heavy drinking.

Despite the often-stressful domestic conditions, surrounded by too many people crammed into inadequate space, Joyce worked steadily at his craft during his first decade abroad. While in Trieste, he managed to find a publisher for *Chamber Music* (which came out in 1907). In 1907 he composed "The Dead," completing the *Dubliners* collection that he had begun in 1904. (It appeared in print in 1915.) He discarded the half-completed naturalistic novel *Stephen Hero* that he began in Dublin, and he wrote *A Portrait of the Artist as a Young Man* in its place (serialized 1914–1915 and published in 1916). Joyce also contributed a series of articles, written in Italian, on Irish topics for *Il Piccola della Sera*, Trieste's daily newspaper (from 1907 through 1912), and he initiated a business deal with four Triestine investors to open Volta, Dublin's first movie theatre in 1909. (Joyce stayed in Dublin for a short time as its manager, but after he returned to Trieste the cinema ran into difficulties and ceased to operate in 1910). Finally, late in 1914 or early 1915, he began the composition of *Ulysses* and, by mid-1915, finished writing *Exiles*.

This type of hectic artistic activity is typical of his behavior throughout his life. Time and again, the family's strained finances required deft negotiations with tradesmen. And there were frequent changes in addresses when landlords tired of dunning the family for past due rents forced them to find other living quarters. But no matter what personal difficulties he had to face—lack of money, poor health, or chaotic family relations—Joyce retained a single-minded dedication to his art.

The outbreak of World War I in 1914 created even more domestic and creative challenges. Because Joyce held a British passport, he and his family were considered enemy aliens by the Austrian authorities. Joyce, Nora, Giorgio, and Lucia were compelled to leave the city and go to Zurich, seeking sanctuary in neutral Switzerland. Stanislaus Joyce was in a similar position. However, because Stanislaus was openly very vocal in his anti-Austrian political views, instead of being expelled from the city he was held in a detention camp.

From 1915 until 1919, Joyce and his family lived in Zurich. There he was able to earn some money by giving language lessons on an *ad hoc* basis. Joyce also received help from friends such as Ezra Pound and W.B. Yeats, and, for a time, he enjoyed the financial aid from Mrs. Harold McCormick (Edith Rockefeller) who admired his early writings. Her assistance proved to be temporary however, and she withdrew her support when Joyce balked at her suggestion that he submit to analysis by the noted Swiss analytical psychologist Carl Jung.

Despite all the stress, Joyce enjoyed his stay in Zurich and formed a lifelong attachment to the city. He wrote much of the first draft of *Ulysses* while he and his family lived there, and he made a lasting friendship with Frank Budgen who worked for the British Ministry of Information in

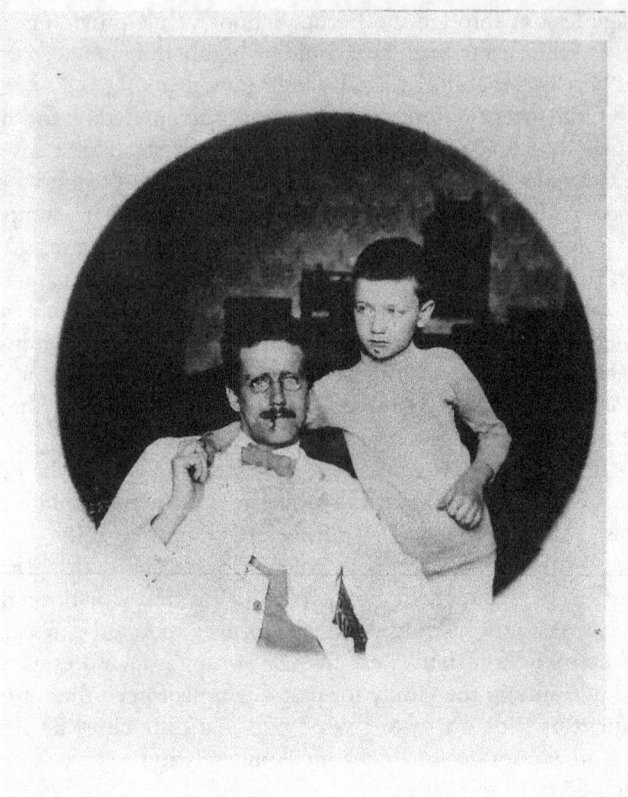

Figure 1.5 Joyce with his son, Giorgio, in Triste. (c. 1915)

Zurich and with whom he held long discussions about the composition of *Ulysses*. Joyce also came to know Claude Sykes, with whom he cofounded the amateur theatrical company, the English Players. When the company staged a performance of Oscar Wilde's *The Importance of Being Earnest*, Joyce who acted as the group's treasurer, got into a financial dispute with Henry Carr, a junior diplomat at the British Embassy. What should have been a simple misunderstanding escalated in claims, counterclaims, and finally legal action. Joyce eventually won his lawsuit, but he was only awarded negligible damages. His revenge came when, in the Circe chapter of *Ulysses,* he used Carr's name for a drunken British soldier. Overall, however, the Joyces greatly enjoyed living in Zurich and only left after the end of World War I when the cost of living became too expensive for them to bear.

The family returned to Trieste in 1919, the city they had left four years earlier. There, they found that Stanislaus, who had been released from internment, had developed decidedly independent views. In particular, he was now far less inclined than previously to taking on the role of propping up his brother and his brother's family. After a brief but contentious period in an apartment that had become the overcrowded living quarters not only of Joyce and his family but also of his brother, his sister Eileen and her husband, Joyce readily accepted Ezra Pound's suggestion that he and Nora and the children move for a short time to Paris so that he could find the peace and the quiet necessary to finish his novel.

The family arrived in Paris in July of 1920, and the city proved much more amenable to fostering domestic tranquility and imaginative creativity than did post-war Trieste. Joyce not only completed *Ulysses*, but he managed, with the steady financial, emotional, and spiritual support of an Englishwoman, Harriet Shaw Weaver, and the occasional help of a number of others who believed in his talent, to maintain a fairly stable household. Weaver's financial gifts began anonymously in May of 1917 and lasted throughout his life. Joyce eventually found out the name of his benefactor. Of equal importance, Joyce found much needed publishing assistance from an American expatriate, Sylvia Beach, who owned the Paris bookshop, Shakespeare and Company.

Although he felt *Ulysses* was ready for publication, Joyce had been having tremendous difficulty finding a way to get his novel before the public. Portions of the novel had appeared in the American journal, *The Little Review*, between 1918 and 1920. However, its serialization had ended when the United States Post Office charged the journals editors with distributing obscene material. A similar scheme for printing installments in the English magazine *The Egoist* proved to be no more successful. When Joyce tried to find a publisher for the full novel, no English firm would take it on because it feared the legal consequences of bringing out a work with so much controversial material in it.

Sylvia Beach stepped forward and agreed to publish *Ulysses* herself. She found a printer in Dijon (Maurice Darantiere) who spoke no English and had no concern for British or American legal hurdles, and the process began to move forward. However, Joyce could not stop writing and revising. During the course of going over page proofs, Joyce kept adding material, eventually increasing the work's length by one third. (The only way Darantiere could stop Joyce's additions was by telling the author that if he did not cease his emendations the book would not appear on his fortieth birthday.) Through it all Beach remained undaunted. She saw Joyce's numerous revisions as part of the creative process of a great artist, and tirelessly promoted the work both before and after its publication on 2 February 1922.

The novel drew immediate acclaim, and the notoriety of *Ulysses* made Joyce a Paris celebrity. Writers such as Sherwood Anderson, T.S. Eliot, Ernest Hemingway, F. Scott Fitzgerald, and Samuel Beckett flocked to the city to see him. Beckett, a fellow Irishman, became a close friend and the one of Joyce's strongest supporters for the rest of Joyce's life.

When writing *Ulysses*, Joyce had enlisted the help of a number of friends and family (particularly his aunt, Josephine Murray) to check facts and obtain information that he used to give his readers an intimate sense of the Dublin of 1904. His health had never been good. The eye problems that he experienced while he was finishing *Ulysses* would continue for the rest of his life. Now in the early 1920s not only difficulties with his vision but other health issues, perhaps exacerbated by his drinking, markedly decreased Joyce's physical ability to do the work of composition. Though he ultimately succeeded in his writings, Joyce's drinking and its effects should not be minimized. As a result of his health, to complete his final work, *Finnegans Wake*, a much broader and more complex allusive project, Joyce had an even greater dependence on others. He relied upon relatives, friends, and even casual acquaintances to research the innumerable references he wove into his composition, to record from dictation the chapters he was writing, and to reread the work to him as he laboriously revised his composition.

The logistical challenges of completing his final novel were compounded by the intensely divided critical responses to the project. The make-up of *Finnegans Wake* was so radically different from anything that had previously appeared, including the highly experimental *Ulysses*. Controversy arose as portions of what he then called *Work in Progress* appeared serially in various literary journals. Even among Joyce's friends and family opinions differed about its value. Ezra Pound and Joyce's brother Stanislaus, among others, bluntly told Joyce that he was wasting his talent, but Beckett, T.S. Eliot, Weaver, and other friends stood by him. In 1929 a group of friends published a collection of essays, *Our Exagmination Round His Factification for Incamination*

Figure 1.6 Joyce in the 1920s after one of his eye operations. His first attack of glaucoma occurred on the Bahnofstrasse in 1917 in Zurich when he was living in that city during World War I. A year later he wrote a poem of this experience titled "Bahnhofstrasse," which he included in *Pomes Penyeach*. (James Joyce Collection, General Collection, Beinecke Rare Book and Manuscript Library, Yale University)

Figure 1.7 Joyce in 1933

of *Work in Progress* seeking to rebut some of the fiercest criticism, though one could argue that its idiosyncratic make-up only added to the controversy. Through it all, including a period encompassed by his father's death in 1931, his daughter's progressive mental breakdown, and his grandson Stephen's birth in 1932, Joyce persisted. (Joyce commemorated these events in late 1932 with the poem "Ecce Puer," a document of greater biographical than artistic value.)

On 6 December 1933, Judge John M. Woolsey of the United States District Court, Southern District of New York, ruled to overturn the ban on importing *Ulysses* into the United States. He asserted that the book was too difficult to understand to be considered pornographic and obscene. Within two months, Random House published the first American edition of the novel on 25 January 1934. Since then, *Ulysses* has never been out of print.

During this same period Joyce continued working on *Finnegans Wake*. Much of the novel had already appeared in fragments from the late 1920s and through the decade of the 1930s, but it did not come out in book form until May of 1939. The process of composition had required a tremendous effort, and Joyce had great hopes for its success. However, before he could enjoy any respite, historical events overwhelmed Europe. World War II began on 1 September 1939.

After the Germans invaded France in 1940, Joyce, Nora, their son Giorgio, and their grandson Stephen felt compelled to leave the city. It was difficult to abandon their Paris apartment, and they were deeply concerned about the welfare of their daughter, Lucia, whose deteriorating mental condition had led to putting her in a sanitarium. After leaving Paris the family spent several months in rural France, mostly in Saint Gérand-le-Puy. As it became apparent to them that it would be necessary for the family to leave France, Joyce frantically tried to secure the necessary documents to allow them to take Lucia with them.

He ultimately failed, and when, in mid-December Joyce, Nora, Giorgio, and Stephen received permission to enter Switzerland, Lucia remained in Pornichett in Brittany where she had been staying with other patients

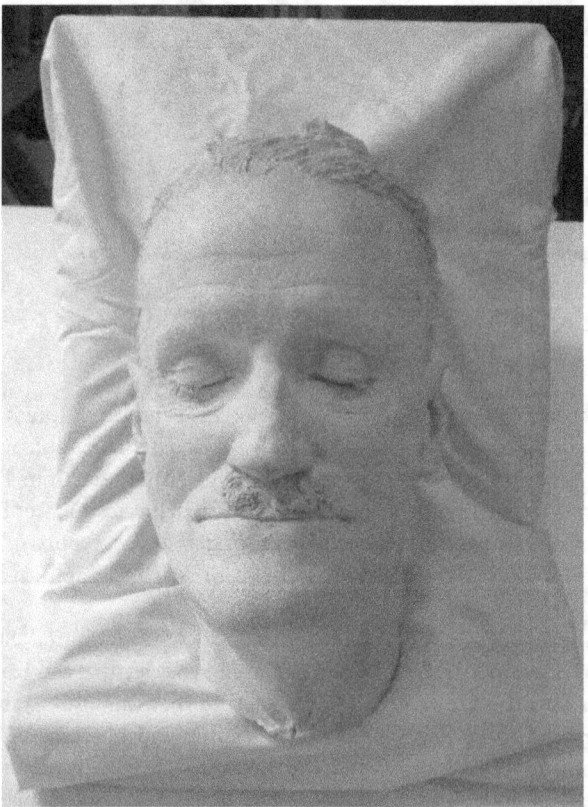

Figure 1.8 One of two original death masks of James Joyce by the Swiss sculptor Paul Speck resides at the Zurich James Joyce Foundation. (Courtesy of Fritz Senn)

evacuated from Paris. After two days in Lausanne, the family arrived in Zurich on the 17th of December 1941, and began to settle into life in the city that they had come to know so well during the previous world war. Unfortunately, Joyce's return to his beloved Zurich was short-lived. On 10 January 1941, Joyce became ill and went to a Zurich hospital. Doctors diagnosed his problem as a perforated duodenal ulcer. They recommended surgery, and initially it appeared to be successful. However, within three days his condition deteriorated and he died on the morning of 13 January 1941, less than three weeks before his fifty-ninth birthday. He is buried at Fluntern Cemetery in Zurich.

2 Approaching *Dubliners*

Dubliners is Joyce's earliest work of fiction to appear in print. Three short stories—"The Sister," "Eveline," and "After the Race"—were brought out in the late summer and fall of 1904 by the *Irish Homestead* a weekly Dublin newspaper edited by George Russell (Æ) and associated with the Irish Agricultural Co-operative Movement. Although he published nothing more separately, Joyce continued to compose stories over the next three years, collecting them under the edition's current title. However, despite a succession of tentative publishing agreements with several presses, in each case uneasiness over the content of some of the stories—use of the word "bloody" and the names of actual businesses in Dublin—delayed the appearance of the collection for a little over eight years. Finally, Grant Richards, the publisher who had first accepted *Dubliners* in 1906, put aside his objections to the certain material in the text and brought out the stories in June of 1914. Joyce's detailed account of the eight-year delay in publishing *Dubliners* appeared under the title "A Curious History" in *The Egoist* on 15 January 1914, with a brief preface by Ezra Pound.

Dubliners contains 15 stories of urban Irish life drawn almost exclusively from the world of lower middle-class, Catholic Dubliners. The stories initially offer accounts of maturation, moving from tales of childhood, through adolescence and early adulthood, to maturity. Then, they turn to examinations of public life: politics, entertainment, and religion. Finally, with the novella length story "The Dead" serving as a brilliant coda, the collection ends by revisiting the central concerns of the volume and offering a final, if ambiguous, comment on them. Because Joyce was only 25 years old when he completed the last story, unsophisticated readers might be tempted to view *Dubliners* as an apprentice piece. In fact, it stands as a stunning testament of an early talent that would continue to mature over the length of the artist's career.

Despite the years that have passed since their composition and even with their focus on the narrow demographics of a tightknit Dublin, lower middle-class, Catholic world, the stories themselves retain a vibrant immediacy that resonates with a variety of readers and makes them seem continuously contemporaneous. They continue to arrest one's attention with a stylistic complexity and a thematic sophistication that demonstrate creative abilities profoundly attuned to a range of human experiences expressed in forms that remain in touch with readers of any age and background. The stories of *Dubliners* succeed so well because their seeming specificity in fact reflects a timeless universality. As Joyce, late in his life, said to his friend Arthur Power about his process of composition: "I always write about Dublin, because, if I can get to the heart of Dublin I can get to the heart of all the cities of the world. In the particular is contained the universal."

Key Issues

In many ways, *Dubliners* serves as the perfect introduction to Joyce's writings. The quotation above reveals Joyce's lifelong fascination with his native city, and each of his short stories offers an intimate and sensitive introduction to some aspect of its intensely metropolitan, bourgeois ethos, seemingly commonplace but made unique by the rendition that Joyce gives it. The narratives contain enough references to customs, beliefs, and past events to give one a firm sense of the particular features distinguishing its urban setting of over a century ago. At the same time, the allusions to the Dublin milieu do not occur with the dizzying frequency and the tone of insider specificity that they follow in his later writings. In this way, the reader assimilates in manageable portions issues and styles that will recur throughout the canon.

One of the important benefits of the sustained presentations of the common topics and the recurring styles that arise in short stories comes from the opportunities that readers have to experience the range of formal perspectives and contextual attitudes developed by Joyce within his tightly defined imaginative ambiance. Like many writers, Joyce drew on events in his life from childhood to adulthood to create his stories. At the same time, he delineated incidents within the mundane world of his characters that would parallel those in the lives of any readers of every age and from every part of the world. What follows are synopses of the central concerns that made his narratives so intimately familiar to his readers.

Alcohol and its disastrous consequences, particularly in the form of alcoholism, are presented in a variety of situations being consumed by a range of people. However, despite this proliferation, alcohol rarely appears as a stimulus of comfort and conviviality. While he is content to show rather than proselytize, Joyce nonetheless represents drinking as a subversive force that blunts an individual's sense of responsibility and erodes the quality of life in countless families. **Tom Kernan** ("Grace") or **Farrington** ("Counterparts") are two examples among the many who illustrate the pain and misfortune that comes directly from this failing.

One can hardly be surprised that *Alienation*, a common topic in twentieth-century literature, features prominently in *Dubliners*, but its striking representations in Joyce's stories merit particular attention. In the collection, Joyce focuses not just on the feelings of a number of characters who experience marginalization. He probes the forces that, in both their particularity and their universality, contribute to individuals' often-conscious decision to isolate themselves. With characters like **Maria** ("Clay"), Joyce presents a figure nearly completely alone who keeps recognition of her state at arm's length through a steadfast denial of her circumstances. With others, like **James Duffy** ("A Painful Case"), Joyce examines the impulse to seek out and even embrace marginalization through a staunch unwillingness to modify their lives in any way that might overcome their isolation. Between these extremes he introduces a panoply of figures beset to one degree or another by feelings of alienation. Taken as a whole this range of examples produces a sense of loss that cannot fail to resonate with any reader who takes up the stories.

As one might expect from fiction set in Ireland, *Catholicism* is referenced directly in almost every story. However, Joyce avoids the reductive polarities that in the hands of other authors turn such allusions into clichés. Instead, Catholicism is examined as a cultural phenomenon rather than critiqued according to its mission as a theological system.

Certainly, narratives often allude to liturgical practices and biblical references. They even, as in the case of "Grace," provide a jumbled recapitulation of aspects of dogma. However, the emphasis always falls squarely on the cultural context of a society infused with Catholicism. The allusions mark the way liturgical observations—like Mass attendance on Sundays—provide a rhythm for the lives of Dubliners or show the integration of religion into social intercourse rather than affirm the strengths or weaknesses of individuals' beliefs. As one clearly sees in "The Sisters," "The Boarding House," or "Grace," although Catholic rituals are overt presences in many of the stories and the social authority of the Church is often emphasized, the faith of the characters, as opposed to habitual or superstitious responses, is something explored through their commissions and omissions but rarely through direct declarations of specific dogmas to which they subscribe.

Creativity, or more often than not frustrated creativity, represents a defining feature in many individuals. In some cases, it reflects frustrations or shortcomings tied directly to artistic endeavors. Joyce's characters—**Little Chandler** ("A Little Cloud") and **Gabriel Conroy** ("The Dead") are good examples of this. They strive to express themselves, more often in writing than in any other form, but they generally at best articulate only their sense of circumscribed imagination. In other cases, the narrative explores the usually frustrated efforts to behave in a fashion that will bring one's nature to a sense of fulfillment.

Duty was a concept easily understood by Victorians who maintained an implicit belief in the institutions that delineated one's public and private obligations. A long line of nineteenth-century novelists, from Janes Austen through Charles Dickens examined its centrality as a defining feature of the cultural context. For those in the Modernist world, the unquestioned belief in the efficacy of shaping one's life according to duty's guidelines no longer obtained. However, a lingering impulse to fulfill expectations regarding one's duty still exerted influence on early twentieth-century characters. Joyce understood the conflict between expectation and essence all too well, and depictions of the resulting confusion of individuals like **Eveline** ("Eveline") or Maria ("Clay") animate many of Joyce's stories.

Although recent epistemological emphasis on the applications of *Gender* to contextualize the features of narratives may make it seem to some a relatively recent concern, in fact, as an important aspect of identity, gender has always been an element in characters' developments. Joyce had a highly refined sense of how complex aspects of gender informed identity. One sees instances of this in every story, but three—"Araby," "A Mother," and "The Dead"—offer a number of good examples of its impact on the maturation of social roles, the delineation of family ties, and the definition of self. At the same time, a deft rendition of a reticence in a number of Joyce's characters to engage many of the features of their nature most closely related to gender underscores the tension between the gender roles that come more or less naturally to the characters and their inhibited expression formed by an oblique and tentative concern for the reception that might be accorded to manifestations of their gender roles within the content of daily Dublin life.

Identity, or, as more often is the case, incertitude about one's identity, deeply runs through all of the stories. Like the subcategory gender that it encompasses, identity is a pervasive yet illusive trait in many of the characters. From the unnamed boy in "The Sisters" to Gabriel Conroy in "The Dead," figures in Joyce's stories struggle to reconcile personal preferences with communal expectations to come to a clearer sense of self. Not all figures proceed with equal sensitivity to the process. Nonetheless, no matter the degree of individual awareness, all of Joyce's characters increasingly find themselves distrustful of the modes of behavior laid down by social institutions and at the same time feel at a loss as to where to turn for guidance.

In chapter five of *A Portrait of the Artist as a Young Man*, Joyce uses a discussion of Irish politics to make clear Stephen Dedalus' and one may assume by extension his own skepticism toward *Nationalism*. Throughout Joyce's writing, invocation of the term becomes an opportunity to critique the often-articulated principles of an Irish nation. While a good deal of idealism may have gone into their creation, as one sees its diverse manifestation in characters like **Joe Hynes** ("Ivy Day in the Committee Room"), **Kathleen Kearney** ("A Mother"), and **Molly Ivors** ("The Dead"), it shows that in its application all too human biases reshape ideals. In most instances, nationalism appears as a mode of clannishness employed to set its adherents apart from those acknowledging British colonial rule. Its form as presented in the stories of *Dubliners* appears as a highly subjective impulse not so much working for political change as claiming a moral high ground while producing no real tangible result beyond the creation of a secular religion.

A great many readers have already noted that *Paralysis*, the physical, emotional, or imaginative inability to act, is a central theme of *Dubliners* as Joyce himself clearly identified. Nonetheless, it is important to review how it recurs throughout the narrative as a constant threat to the stability and happiness of most of the characters. Joyce introduces it directly and forcefully in the opening paragraph of the first story, "The Sisters," and then it reappears, in one form or another throughout the collection. In some instances, as in the closing paragraphs of "A Painful Case," the condition of the character is readily recognized. In others, "Clay" for example, the character seems willfully unaware of the condition. In whatever degree it is manifest, the text makes clear that nature of Irish society greatly contributes to this condition.

In a collection with so much emphasis on alienation, it becomes easy to overlook the significance given in the narratives to *Relationships*. Nonetheless, whether dealing in accomplished fact or aspiration, a number of the stories outline the efforts of characters, like **Mrs. Sinico** ("A Painful Case"), to form satisfying bonds with others or, as is the case with Eveline, the inherent threat that individuals perceive in them. Whether exemplified by failed marriages, thwarted love affairs, or simply the fear of commitment, the concept of relationships stands as an insistent reminder of the near inevitability of isolation as the final fate of Joyce's characters.

In any account of the interactions of men and women *Sex* and *Sexuality* stand as inevitable themes. One may see them as a subcategory of many of the relationships delineated in the stories although the connection is not inevitable. What these themes do foreground, no matter how they are catalogued, is an impulse that recurs in many of the topics examined, a hesitancy of characters to challenge traditional behavior. Specifically, they show here that an unwillingness even to articulate or even recognize aspects of intimate human relations cause many individuals in the stories—Eveline ("Eveline"), **Bob Doran** ("The Boarding House"), James Duffy, and Mrs. Sinico ("A Painful Case"), for example—to stumble at expressing their needs or even to remain unaware specifically of what they were.

Style

The stories in *Dubliners* present early and ample compositional evidence of Joyce's innovative stylistic dispositions. While it may be true that the formal structure that he employed in these works follow are generally more conventional and less experimental than the style of later works, a few particular techniques are used most effectively, and they repay close attention. Awareness of these modes in their earliest application gives one a clearer sense of the development of the short stories and prefigures the more elaborate experimentation that will appear in later works.

Meticulous attention to detail and insistent emphasis on the routines of ordinary life inject a tone of *Realism* into Joyce's narratives. The narratives capture the ethos of Dublin's street life and the rhythms of the language of ordinary people with grace and dexterity. That in turn makes the world of his short stories immediately familiar to readers with no other awareness than these descriptions of Dublin at the turn of the last century. At the same time, striking innovative forms distinguish Joyce's writings from the works of most of his contemporaries.

As one runs through the titles in Joyce's collection, one can see a range of possible rhetorical labels to them. At the center of this linguistic multiplicity, acting as a key feature of the inversive meanings in so many passages, is his introduction of *Irony*. Although Joyce uses that technique to far greater effect in *A Portrait of the Artist as a Young Man*, in *Dubliners* his deft application serves to deflect the ponderous tone of self-righteous that always lurks around efforts at social criticism. The inherent double-sidedness of irony allowed for both intense scrutiny of various aspects of life in Dublin while it also permitted a distance from the views that resisted easy either/or categorizations.

A Deferral of Closure stands out as a feature that would become a definitive Modernist trait over the next few decades. When Joyce instituted it in 1904, the irresolution at the end of each story was a pioneering literary feature. From the inconclusiveness surrounding the motivations of **Father Flynn** and the awareness of the boy narrator in "The Sisters" to Gabriel Conroy's ambivalence toward his life at the end of "The Dead," none of the stories find the kinds of resolutions that one finds, for example, in the contemporaneous short stories of Henry James or Joseph Conrad. Although all three authors emphasized in their writing close examinations of intimate psychological issues, even the grimmest perspectives of the other show measures of certainty that Joyce's commitment to representing the inherent ambiguity of modern life would not allow.

The other distinctive form that characterizes many of the passages in *Dubliners* is *Free Indirect Discourse*. It is a narrative style that blurs distinctions between first and third person accounts by invoking perspectives similar to various characters without concretely linking the views to them. This gives the reader multiple perspectives of a particular observation that in turn underscore the range of possibilities for interpretation imbedded in the narrative. Although one can find examples of it throughout nineteenth-century English literature (the opening lines of Jane Austen's *Pride and Prejudice* are a striking example), few writers applied it with the relentlessness one finds in *Dubliners*.

The opening of "The Dead" offers a useful illustration of the diverse interpretive choices that this technique can offer: "Lily, the caretaker's daughter, was literally run off her feet" (p. 175) can reflect the view of a narrator using a tired cliché to begin the account and thus discounting the rigor of Lily's efforts, or it can be Lily herself, again using a cliché, but in this instance underscoring the fatigue and stress she felt by the demands of the arriving guests. As the reader becomes aware of the multiple perspectives imbedded in any scene, he or she develops a wide interpretive sense and a more complex understanding of the narrative, understanding that there is not a single or even a definitive way of reading *Dubliners* but rather the possibility of find a wide range of options for understanding the stories.

An Overview of the Stories

In a May 1906 letter to the man who would eventually publish the *Dubliners* collection, Grant Richards, Joyce, with all of the arrogant certitude of a 24-year-old writer, summed up the goal of his short story collection:

> My intention was to write a chapter of the moral history of my country, and I chose Dublin for the scene because the city seemed to me the centre of paralysis.... I have written for the most part in a style of scrupulous meanness and with the conviction that he is a very bold man who dares to alter in the presentment, still more to deform, whatever he has seen and heard.
>
> (*Letters*, I.134)

Certainly, a good deal of rancor informed Joyce's view of Ireland, and in a June 1906 letter to the same publisher he expanded upon this view:

> It is not my fault that the odour of ashpits and old weeds and offal hangs round my stories. I seriously believe that you will retard the course of civilization in Ireland by preventing the Irish people from having one good look at themselves in my nicely polished looking-glass.
>
> (*Letters*, I.63–64)

Yet, it would be a mistake to read these passages as exclusive summations of his view of Ireland. In a September 1906 letter to his brother Stanislaus, Joyce expressed a much less hostile attitude:

> Sometimes thinking of Ireland it seems to me that I have been unnecessarily harsh. I have reproduced (in *Dubliners* at least) none of the attraction of the city, for I have never felt at my ease in any city since I left it, except Paris. I have not reproduced its ingenuous insularity and its hospitality. The latter 'virtue' so far as I can see does not exist elsewhere in Europe. I have not been just to its beauty: for it is more beautiful naturally, in my opinion, than what I have seen of England, Switzerland, France, Austria or Italy.
>
> (*Letters*, II.166)

As he became accustomed to the exilic experience of a destitute author with a growing family, a range of viewpoints changed, not the least of which was a mellowing of his attitude toward the country he left. The wavering tone of the final passage offers a subtle reminder of the developing and maturing attitude that Joyce took toward the city that served as the centerpiece of his writing. The passages quoted above offer two searing summaries of the aims of the first 14 stories and a third view that seems to qualify those intentions with a need to present an alternative perspective. In fact, the dates of the letters' composition are important indicators of Joyce's evolving views of his themes and his cultural heritage, falling a year before he composed the volume's final story, "The Dead."

Joyce himself called this last work a coda. Taking their cue from that designation, many critics have seen in the tone of the final contribution to the collection a modification of the excoriating assessments appearing in the other stories. The degree to which this perspective can be usefully applied remains open to debate, but no matter how central one sees that disposition, it serves as a useful reminder of the complex and even contradictory attitudes inherent in all of Joyce's writing and of the ever-changing areas of interest that sustain a wide range of interpretive possibilities.

Certainly, Joyce's grand claims to be writing "the moral history of my country" fit the supposition that an as yet unrecognized writer would need to set bold aims for his work. However, one must also acknowledge in Joyce a creative honesty that never allowed this ambition to degenerate into reductive, clichéd portrayals of flat characters or predictable situations. From the start, Joyce's views were sharply focused, his observations subtly complex, and his goals dauntingly lofty.

To put those remarks further in perspective, one should keep in mind Joyce's growing affinity for ironizing even the apparently most sacred of artistic aims. In the closing lines of *A Portrait of the Artist as a Young Man*, Stephen Dedalus, with unselfconscious loftiness, intones rather ambitious creative goals: "I go to encounter for the millionth time the reality of experience and to forge in the smithy of my soul the uncreated conscience of my race" (p. 224). Careful readers have noted Joyce's gentle satirizing of Stephen's bravado throughout the novel's final chapter, and one could certainly justify seeing in these lines a gesture of atonement by the author for possibly going too far in the critiques of the Irish consciousness that run throughout *Dubliners*.

Certainly, Joyce rejected familiar patterns for fictionalizing Irish experience. In writing strictly about the contemporary experiences of lower middle-class Dubliners, the stories mark a sharp break from a century and more of Irish literature spent examining the lives of the aristocrats (like Sydney Owenson's *The Wild Irish Girl*), the landed gentry (for example Somerville and Ross' *The Real Charlotte*), or the peasant class that worked their farms (as in William Carleton's *Traits and Stories of the Irish Peasantry*). Instead, following the example of Charles Dickens and Guy de Maupassant, Joyce drew on selected aspects of city life, and in this realm he found a rich source of creative topics. At the same time, Joyce went beyond his literary antecedents in the theme and form of his stories. He incorporated a mixture of styles markedly different from the conventional narrative perspectives of the previous two centuries. In what he wrote about and in the way he wrote he adopted, and in fact pioneered, an approach would come to be called Modernist fiction—writing that shows a loss of confidence in social institutions, a reliance on the individual to set moral and ethical standards, and a sense of indeterminacy in representations of human interactions.

"The Sisters"

This was the first story that Joyce composed, and it begins the section that Joyce identified as devoted to childhood. It originally appeared in the 13 August 1904 issue of *The Irish Homestead*. As he did with many stories in the collection, Joyce would make some revisions on the narrative before it appeared in *Dubliners*. Nonetheless, even in its initial form, "The Sisters" shows none of the marks one would expect to see in a beginner's piece. It introduces readers to important themes—like paralysis and belief—that the narrative will develop over the course of the collection, and this early orientation allows one to understand these concepts that will later be reiterated through a variety of perspectives and often enhanced by styles like free indirect discourse that punctuate storylines throughout *Dubliners*.

"The Sisters" opens with the young boy who serves as the story's **unnamed narrator** keeping watch outside the house that the seriously ill **Reverend James Flynn**, the priest who had befriended the boy, shares with his sisters. The first sentence foregrounds the story's grim but understated tone in its oblique but emphatic suggestion of death: "There was no hope for him this time" (p. 9). Its definitive opinion, tinged by the uncertainty of what might follow a loss of hope, also underscores the contradictory nature of the boy's quest for understanding. At times in the story, he seems supremely certain while he appears completely baffled at other instances.

The narrative quickly turns to the boy's complicated attitude toward the priest's illness. While the unnamed narrator expresses both aloofness and concern, he very clearly articulates his determination to be the first outside the immediate family to learn of and then to announce Father Flynn's death. Both of these ambitions are frustrated when **Mr. Cotter**, a friend of the **aunt** and **uncle** (also not identified more precisely) with whom the boy lives, brings news to their house that the priest has passed away. The boy is not only irritated by Cotter's preempting the role of proclaiming the priest's death. He also feels unsure how to react to the unease that Cotter and his uncle display toward Father Flynn's character. In trying to understand the evasive suggestiveness of their conversation, the boy recollects the idiosyncratic views expressed by Father Flynn, in examples that also imply to readers the latter's possible loss of faith.

The next evening the boy goes with his aunt to the house on North Great Britain Street (now Parnell Street) where Father Flynn had lived with his sisters, **Eliza** and **Nannie Flynn**. The house is tawdry and gloomy. One of the sister's, Nannie, remains conspicuously silent. The other, Eliza, tries to blunt the strangeness of her brother's behavior by characterizing it as merely eccentric: "he was too scrupulous always" (p. 17). At the same time, she unconsciously undercuts her own efforts by recounting evidence of her brother's breakdown, telling of two other priests discovering her brother sitting "in his confession-box, wide-awake and laugh-like softly to himself" (p. 18).

The efforts of both sisters to ignore the seriousness of Father Flynn's emotional collapse give a sense of their fragile, claustrophobic world, but their determined vagueness also underscores the driving force of the story. With all that "The Sisters" reveals, it still studiously avoids passing judgment on Father Flynn. Rather, the story provides readers with ample material from which to form their own understandings. Perhaps the most intriguing aspect of "The Sisters" is the title. The women only appear in the final section of the narrative, and as yet no convincing critical explanation has yet to be offered for their place at the title of the story.

"An Encounter"

This second piece in the collection and the second in the childhood division of the collection. It was the ninth one composed, completed in September of 1905. Like "The Sisters," this story has an unnamed boy presenting a first-person narration emphasizing the events of a single day. With a narrator seemingly standing on the cusp of adolescence, its narrative takes up themes of sexuality, religion, and identity in a voice both curious and unenlightened, and unsurprisingly several potential publishers wished Joyce to drop it from the collection.

Two schoolboys, the **unnamed narrator** (who is generally considered to be the same boy who narrated "The Sisters") and **Mahony**, inspired by extravagant tales from cheap novels about the American West and by their own restless boredom, skip school for a day, "mitching" in Dublin slang. They meet at the Royal Canal on Dublin's Northside. From there, the boys walk along the North Circular Road, down to the city docks, and cross the River Liffey on a ferry. After a lunch of biscuits (cookies to Americans), chocolate, and raspberry lemonade, they laze about in a field near the Dodder River, unsure of what to do and ultimately giving up their plan to visit the Pigeon House, the well-known site of an electric generating plant and a drainage station on a breakwater on Dublin Bay.

While in the field, "**a queer old josser**" approaches them and strikes up a conversation with an undertone that reflects an obvious though unspecified sexual interest. The boys seem to have no clear sense of his pedophilic tendencies and the narrative never makes that inclination completely clear. Nonetheless, the two remain uneasy. Mahony runs off to chase a cat, leaving the strange man talking to the narrator about whippings and young girls. The narrator, growing increasingly uncomfortable, breaks away and calls to Mahony to join him. Mahony's return brings both relief and guilt "for in my heart I had always despised [Mahony] a little" (p. 28) The story ends on this line, leaving readers to come to their own conclusions about what has been encountered and what are the consequences.

"Araby"

This third story in the collection, and it was the eleventh composed, completed in October 1905. It is the last story in the section devoted to childhood, and, like the two preceding ones, it unfolds through a presentation of the impressions of an **unnamed narrator**. While internal evidence does not confirm that the same boy recounts events in these three stories, both the tone he adopts and the circumstances surrounding him in each account suggest that is the case.

"Araby" offers a seemingly unselfconscious account of the narrator's infatuation with the sister of a neighborhood friend, **Mangan**, a girl whom he has watched and followed but with whom he has hardly exchanged more than a few words. When **Mangan's sister**, the only way by which the girl is ever identified, mentions the Araby bazaar and laments her inability to attend it, the narrator rashly promises to go and to bring her back a present. In his mind, this pledge has become a romantic quest, but in his description, reality harshly interposes through details that make it clearly a prosaic experience.

While the narrator's fixation with Mangan's sister moves the action of the story, the boy's daydreams and recollections insistently intrude to broaden its scope. As the narrator walks with his aunt on a shopping trip, there is a sense of a questing imagination that endeavors to transform the banal surroundings that still has found no clear alternative. They underscore his own fascination with romanticism and, through his clear descriptions of his surroundings, they contrast his world of fantasy with the grim reality of the urban environment.

Although his thoughts keep returning to Mangan's sister, he gives few details to explain this fascination. The careful reader will discern that the narrator puts the emphasis not so much on the young girl and on what he feels for her but rather on the sentimentalized role that he seeks to actualize by his behavior. He unselfconsciously dramatizes the world around him, quite probably to blunt its harshness.

A mixture of familial tension and self-generated uncertainty heightens the boy's anticipation of his trip to the bazaar. On the Saturday that the boy had planned to attend the bazaar, his uncle returns home from work late and slightly the worse for drink. Consequently, the boy receives his pocket money with barely enough time to reach Araby before closing time. When he does arrive, many of the stalls have already been shut up, and he only finds tawdry goods still available for sale, hardly a worthy conclusion to the romantic journey he has felt he was on. A desultory exchange between a girl working at one of the booths and "two young gentlemen" with English accents gives an ironic rebuttal to the boy's romantic aspirations. The ending teases readers with a tone of bitterness that goes beyond adolescent frustration suggesting that it is a less idealistic, adult perspective that from the retrospection of several years describes the boy's feelings on leaving the fair: "Gazing up into the darkness I saw myself as a creature driven and derided by vanity; and my eyes burned with anguish and anger" (p. 35).

"Eveline"

The fourth story in the collection was the second that Joyce composed, and it begins the division of the collection relating to adolescence. It first appeared in the 10 September 1904 issue of *The Irish Homestead*. The discourse of "Eveline" shifts the narrative perspective from the unnamed first-person narrator of the first three stories to a third person point of view. At the same time, it inflects the detached perspective of the omniscient narrator with moments of free indirect discourse, a technique that suggests the consciousness of a character or even characters in the story without shifting the point of view. This gives readers a sense of contrasting ways of seeing the situation being described or experienced.

The story centers on the frustrations of **Eveline Hill**, a young woman whose life has become circumscribed by a range of tedious obligations: her work as a store clerk, her domestic responsibilities in the family household, and the need to take on a parental role in looking after her younger siblings, an informal position that she inherited on the death of her mother. When she meets **Frank,** a young sailor, Eveline sees the promise of an escape from her stifling existence. He opens her to the possibility of romance, adventure, and most of all freedom from the constrictions of her present life.

Her father's hostility toward the young man does not deter Eveline from making plans to break free of the constricted Victorian atmosphere of her life by eloping with Frank to Buenos Aires. Nonetheless, despite her attraction to Frank and this proposed new life, Eveline agonizes over her decision. She fluctuates between a sense of her duty to care for the family and a near desperate desire to find happiness away from the claustrophobic world of Dublin. In the end, although she accompanies Frank to the ship that would take her from the city, at the last minute she finds herself gripped by fear and uncertainty and cannot bring herself to accompany him up the gangplank onto the boat. The text does not make it clear whether this is an act of prudence or cowardice, and readers' response have covered a wide range of possibilities.

"After the Race"

This is the fifth story in the collection, the second in the section on adolescence, and the third in the order of composition. An early version appeared in the 17 December 1904 issue of *The Irish Homestead*. "After the Race" was the last story in the collection to appear in print before the publication of *Dubliners* in 1914. The background for the story comes from another piece of writing, a 7 April 1903 interview that Joyce conducted with the French racing car driver Henri Fournier that was published in the *Irish Times* under the title "The Motor Derby." (The interview has been reprinted in *The Critical Writings of James Joyce*.) Joyce gained access to additional background material for the story when Ireland hosted the fourth annual Gordon Bennett Cup race on 2 July 1903.

Although the Dublin setting of "After the Race" remains generally the same as that of the others in the collection, the demographic emphasis in the narrative shifts from the examinations of the lives of lower middle-class Dubliners to focus attention on aspirations of the *nouveau riche*. It chronicles the mindless prodigality of **Jimmy Doyle**, a self-indulgent young man whose father, originally an ordinary, suburban Dublin butcher, had become prosperous through a canny business sense that led to the ownership of a number of shops and some lucrative government contracts. With some pride,

Jimmy's father indulges his son's reckless behavior, which is dissolute but never quite reaching the level of scandalous.

The narrative begins with a description of the end of the unidentified motor race referenced in the title. It then follows Jimmy for the rest of the day as he entertains other racing enthusiasts, like **Charles Ségouin**, at his father's home, and the story ends with a late-night card game on the yacht of the American, **Farley**. In most instances, Jimmy acts as a passive observer, seemingly just content to be included in the group. The game ends as the day begins "in a shaft of gray light." Jimmy feels some remorse over the amount of money that he has lost, but he expresses no real sense of responsibility for his behavior. "He knew that he would regret in the morning but at present he was glad of the rest, glad of the dark stupor that would cover up his folly" (p. 48). Though the conclusion records Jimmy's sense of ambivalence, in the story's representation of vacuous materiality, its narrative comes closer than does any of the others to an unblinking social judgment.

"Two Gallants"

This is the sixth story in the collection, the third tale of adolescence, and the thirteenth in the order of composition, written over the winter of 1905–1906. It returns the narrative's focus to the observation of lower middle-class Dublin lives, and it introduces two characters, **John Corley** and **T. Lenehan**, who will each appear again, separately, in Joyce's novel *Ulysses*. Several of the preceding stories have explored the theme of isolation in Irish society, but "Two Gallants" presents a cold, unblinking view of the desolate lives of spiritually and economically alienated Dubliners.

The plot follows a relatively straightforward account of one man's desultory wandering around the city waiting for the other to return from an assignation. Early on, the narrative reveals Corley's plans to meet with a Dublin slavey (slang for an Irish female household servant) from a well to do household and spend the evening with her. Meanwhile, Lenehan, who has very little money, meanders around the Dublin city center to kill time as he waits for Corley to return. Lenehan finds a brief respite from his aimless peregrinations when he stops in a working-class restaurant off Rutland Square. During Lenehan's meal, the reader, through free indirect discourse, hears his laments over the insecurity of his life and his sense of alienation from all those who surround him. However, his ambitions go no further than finding someone to take care of his needs. (These revelations stand in sharp contrast to the upbeat attitude he feels he must outwardly maintain with Corley and anyone else whom he meets, for the parasitical Lenehan knows that he must always make himself agreeable to those from whom he hopes to gain something.)

At the end of the evening, Corley brings the young servant-girl back to the house on Baggot Street where she works and lives. He waits on the doorstep after she enters the house until she returns to put something into his outstretched hand. Only in the final line does the narrative reveal that she has given him a gold coin. (It is probably a twenty-shilling piece. Since the servant-girl probably earns around seven shillings per week in addition to being given room and board this is roughly the equivalent of almost a month's wages). There is no clear indication as to why she gives Corley the coin, whether the money comes from her savings, or if it is stolen from her employers. In any case, the two young men show no concern for its origin, but instead as the story ends, they smirk over the windfall.

"The Boarding House"

This is the seventh story in the collection, the last in the tales devoted to adolescence, and the fifth in the order of composition, finished on 1 July 1905. It was first published with the *Dubliners* collection in 1914. A year later it was reprinted, along with "A Little Cloud," in the May 1915 issue of H.L. Mencken's American magazine, *The Smart Set*.

The plot turns on the domestic melodrama, played out on a quiet Sunday morning in the parlor and one of the bedrooms of the domicile that gives the story its title. The animating question is how the landlady, **Mrs. Mooney**, referred to as the Madam by the young men in the house, will deal with the problem of her pregnant, unmarried daughter, **Polly Mooney**. Although the burden of resolution falls upon Polly's mother, there is never a doubt about her ability to bring the situation to a satisfactory conclusion. Through free indirect discourse, the narrative presents a detailed account of Mrs. Mooney's calculations regarding how best to secure "reparation" for the damage done to her daughter. (The narrative neatly suggests the commodification of Polly without directly making her a whore and her mother a procuress.) Mrs. Mooney's maternal concerns are practical and logistical, finding a way to offload the burden of Polly and her expected baby through a commitment from the father to marriage and to do so in time still to be able to attend noon Mass at the Catholic Pro-Cathedral just down the street.

The other principal characters take more limited views. Bob Doran, the roomer at the boarding house responsible for Polly's condition, thinks strictly in terms of the social impact: how various parts of Dublin society would respond to news of what he has done. While he is not anxious to marry, he fears the loss of position if a scandal broke out. Polly herself, despite the sexual aggressiveness that contributed to her situation, shows only a vague concern about the consequences of her pregnancy. She appears more than content to follow her mother's lead and so to leave it to others to sort out matters.

Overall, the story very neatly captures the oppressive atmosphere of city's various social institutions—family, religion, and commercial—but it carefully avoids typing any of them. This is not a diatribe against social hypocrisy, moral laxity, or emotional cowardice. It does not offer polarized, Manichean characterizations of individuals caught up in the drama. Rather, it encapsulates how all the figures involved are circumscribed by the collective mores and restrictive economic conditions from which they feel they have no ability to escape.

"A Little Cloud"

This is the eighth story in the collection. It begins the section dealing with maturity. And, it was the sixth in the order of composition, written in early 1906. "A Little Cloud" was first published with the other *Dubliners* stories in 1914. A year later it was reprinted, along with "The Boarding House," in the May 1915 issue of H.L. Mencken's American magazine *The Smart Set*. In a 1906 letter to his brother Stanislaus, Joyce expressed his delight in this story when he wrote that "a page of A Little Cloud gives me more pleasure than all my verses" (*LettersII*.182).

Joyce drew the story's title from a Biblical verse: "And it came to pass, at the seventh time, that he said, Behold, there ariseth a little cloud out of the sea, like a man's hand," (1 Kings 18:44). The line alludes to an incident in the prophet Elijah's triumph over the adherents of Baal. Although, like many of the titles in the collection, its immediate link to the events of the story can seem tangential, it does suggest an ironic grandeur to the meeting of the timid **Thomas Malone**, a man still more known by his nickname Little Chandler than by the one he was given, and his bombastic expatriate friend **Ignatius Gallaher**.

In vignette form, "A Little Cloud" presents a sardonic sketch of how Joyce's own life might have unfolded had he and Nora not left Ireland in 1904. Though Little Chandler is situated in a comfortable middle-class life, employed as a law clerk, married, and with a child, he still harbors vague poetic ambitions. The catalyst for the story's action and for the eruption of Little Chandler's subsequent discontent is a social encounter with Gallaher, a former Dublin journalist now living in London.

The two men meet for drinks after Little Chandler finishes a day of work, and Gallaher's stories of life in London make Little Chandler feel that his own creative aspirations are little more than timid daydreams. Gallaher's bombastic self-confidence and his patronizing view of the sort of life that Little Chandler lives acts as a none too subtle dismissal of all that his friend has achieved. When Little Chandler returns home, slightly befuddled by the whiskeys he is unaccustomed to drinking, his wife's scolding dismissal leaves him with an exaggerated sense of bitterness and failure. "He listened while the paroxysm of the child's sobbing grew less and less; and tears of remorse started to his eyes" (p. 85). Whether he laments his inability to fulfill ordinary domestic duties or resents the quotidian life that he now lives is left to the individual reader to determine.

"Counterparts"

This is the ninth story in the collection, the second in the section on maturity, and the sixth in the order of composition, finished on 12 July 1905. Like its immediate predecessor, "Counterparts" deals with a lack of self-esteem. The distinction, however, is that its central character is by no means as economically successful as Little Chandler, and he is much more brutal in his expressions of resentment.

That central character, Farrington, is known only by his surname. Like Little Chandler, he works as a clerk in a law office. However, he is older than Chandler by ten years or so, strikingly less intelligent, much less conscientious, and considerably more truculent. An unintended witticism by Farrington embarrasses his employer, **Mr. Alleyne**, leads to a public reprimand and the clerk's groveling apology. After what he considers to be an unjustified humiliation, an enraged Farrington decides to soothe his wounded feelings by indulging in a night of dissipation. Without the money to finance his drinking, Farrington pawns his watch, a sign of both his desperation and his irresponsibility, and sets off.

During the pub crawl that follows, Farrington offers increasingly hyperbolic accounts of his exchange with Alleyne, given a chorus of approval by the varying men for whom Farrington is buying drinks. Nonetheless, he seems to derive little satisfaction from this debauch, and in Mulligan's pub, near the end of the evening, he first fails to impress a young actress who teases him and then loses an arm-wrestling match to a younger man for whom Farrington has bought drinks. After it all, his sense of humiliation remains undiminished by the alcohol he has consumed.

When the defeated, drunken Farrington returns home, he takes out his frustration over the failures in his life by beating his son **Tom**, ostensibly for letting the fire go out. Joyce was fully aware of the inevitable mindless brutality of the world he describes, yet he sees environment as much to blame as individual temperament. As he notes in a 13 November 1906 letter to his brother Stanislaus, "I am no friend of tyranny, as you know, but if many husbands are brutal the atmosphere in which they live (vide Counterparts) is brutal and few wives and homes can satisfy the desire for happiness" (*Letters*, II.192).

"Clay"

This is the tenth story in the collection, the third in the section on maturity, and the fourth in order of composition, completed in early 1905. The story was originally entitled "Hallow Eve," connecting the sense of misrule associated with Halloween to the events in the story. As in "Eveline," "The Boarding House," "A Little Cloud," "Counterparts," "A Painful Case," and "The Dead," "Clay" offers an account of a life of quiet desperation, but its central character responds to her situation with a method of coping very different from the strategies employed by figures in other stories. Rather than expressing the impotence of Bob Doran, the fear of Eveline, the resentment of Little Chandler, or the rage of Farrington, Maria turns a blank face toward the grim and empty features of her life.

Maria is a scullery maid at the Dublin by Lamplight Laundry, a Protestant establishment that provides shelter for reformed prostitutes. In return, they work in the laundry, cleaning the clothes of others. Maria, however, is not a former sex worker. Rather, she is a superannuated nanny who had found a position in the laundry after the Donnelly children—Alfy and Joe for whom she had cared—had grown into adulthood and had families of their own.

The narrative recounts Maria's visit to one of the brothers, **Joe Donnelly,** and his family to attend a Hallow's Eve celebration. In detailing her trip from the Ballsbridge laundry to the Donnelly home in Drumcondra, the story highlights Maria's fussiness, her flightiness, her strained financial condition, and the isolation she now feels from those around her, who politely patronize her. After a drawn-out shopping trip to purchase a plum cake for the party, Maria becomes flustered by a drunken gentleman on a tram and leaves the package with the cake behind. At the Donnelly household Maria is welcomed, but she is then spoken sharply to by Joe when she attempts to mediate a feud he has with his brother. As they all turn to playing saucers (a game of divination of the players' futures), a thoughtless allusion to mortality leads to some embarrassment, and the ending with Maria's botched rendition of her **party piece,** "I Dreamed that I Dwelt," gives a tone of bathos to the final lines. While there is an aura of simplicity to the story, an undercurrent of unacknowledged frustration and disappointment gives a grim sense of the life of lower middle-class Dublin spinsters.

"A Painful Case"

This is the eleventh story in the collection, the final one devoted to maturity, and the seventh in order of composition. Joyce wrote it in July of 1905. It is the final study of an individual examining the emptiness of his or her life, and it takes a view far harsher and more desperate than any expressed in the stories that preceded it. While the other stories in varying degrees acknowledge the failure of the central characters to gain esteem in the eyes of the community, this story shows the bitter consequences of someone who has attempted to avoid such disappointments by holding himself aloof from society. "He had neither companions nor friends, church nor creed" (p. 109). (Some may argue that Gabriel Conroy in "The Dead" undergoes similar self-scrutiny, but as the gathering at the Morkan sisters' house establishes he is surrounded by family and friends and voices his strong commitment to communal values. Further, there is much to suggest in the narrative that Conroy's insights lead to increased compassion for those around him and negates his transitory sense of emptiness.)

The central figure of "A Painful Case," **James Duffy,** lives a solitary life by choice. He spends his time, when not working as a cashier in a private bank, reading, listening to music, and brooding. One evening at a concert in Dublin, the woman seated next to him, **Mrs. Emily Sinico**, strikes up a conversation with him. After coincidentally meeting again at another musical event, the two form an acquaintance that steadily moves toward a greater intimacy that Duffy had previously known.

Mrs. Sinico's husband is the captain of a merchant ship that regularly sails between Dublin and Holland. These absences and the incompatibility of his temperament and his wife's suggest to the reader reasons for Mrs. Sinico to pursue her friendship with Duffy. Her ultimate motives remain unstated, but the closeness of the two progresses steadily. As she becomes more overt in signaling her desire for greater physical intimacy, Duffy feels that he cannot sustain the friendship and abruptly breaks it off.

Four years later, while glancing at a newspaper over a solitary dinner, Duffy sees a story announcing the death of Mrs. Sinico. Reading further, he learns that she has been killed at a railway crossing. According to the newspaper account, at the coroner's inquiry that followed, testimony by **Captain Sinico** and by their daughter, **Mary**, suggests that long-term alcoholism was a factor in the accident. Duffy is shocked by the death and initially feels revulsion rather than sympathy. As the sad news sinks in, he continues to dwell on Mrs. Sinico's death. While it is not clear whether or not he begins to comprehend his complicity in the tragic affair, a reader cannot ignore the suggestion that a sense of desolation and of alienation overwhelms him. At the same time, in keeping with the pattern of the collection, Joyce does not give a definitive sense of his feelings. The story ends on an emphatic yet unelaborated note: "He felt that he was alone."

"Ivy Day in the Committee Room"

This is the twelfth story in the collection and the eighth in order of composition. Joyce completed it in the late summer of 1905. It marks a shift in the narrative's attention from the personal lives of Dubliners to examinations of the public sphere. One might intuit the central themes of alienation and hopelessness in the exchanges between characters in this story, but greater scrutiny is given to the way a social institution, like nationalism, can be used to insulate these same individuals from a clear sense of the desperation that informs many of their interactions with the community.

"Ivy Day," 6th October, is the anniversary of the death of **Charles Stewart Parnell**. In an ironic twist it is being observed by men congregating in the shabby political headquarters in Dublin's Royal Exchange Ward of a Nationalist candidate for local office, **Tricky Dicky Tierney**. This group of men, underemployed and with loose political affiliations, are gathered in the committee room waiting to be paid for their efforts at canvasing the area for votes for Tierney. There is much grumbling among them about the political vicissitudes that have thrown them together, about the nastiness of the weather, and about the meanness of their employer, Tricky Dicky. In keeping with this tone, **Old Jack,** the building's caretaker, offers cranky, desultory complaints from about how different things now are from the good old days.

The arc of the narrative—a depiction of ill-tempered, under-employed, middle-aged men who are openly dissatisfied with the world they inhabit—may seem clichéd. However, within its representations, the story evokes the unvoiced pain of individuals living in isolation while justifying their condition with a sense of grievance over the unfairness of life. A good deal of cynicism, particularly toward politicians, permeates their discussions, though that is tempered in some by nostalgic recollections of the efforts of Parnell and the Home Rule Party. The account ends with a commemoration of Ivy Day as Joe Hynes recites a maudlin poetic tribute that he had composed in honor of Parnell, depicting him as a political martyr with Christ-like attributes.

These final pages turn on a daring gambit. The mawkishness of Joe's poem is rendered even more cloying by the apparent deep appreciation felt by his audience. Sentimentality is presented as a drug that blunts impotence, despair, and cynicism as the dominant feelings. One might easily dismiss their emotional reaction had the narrative not already shown how skeptically the viewed most political efforts. Without a definitive signal from the narrative, the reader is left to discern whether bitterness or delusion stands as the better response to their suffocating environment.

"A Mother"

This is the thirteenth story in the collection. It was the tenth in order of composition, completed in late September of 1905. It is the second in the fourth and final division of the novel, public life. It has some parallels to "The Boarding House" in its examination of the Dublin world from the perspective, not always flattering, of a dominant female, **Mrs. Kearney**.

However, clear social and economic differences between the two women and the contrasting private and public nature of their concerns lead their narratives to develop very different aims. Mrs. Mooney, a single mother who supports herself by running a boarding house must be concerned with public opinion so that there is no ill-effect on her business, but her central interest is the domestic security of her daughter and expected grandchild. Mrs. Kearney has no such private worries regarding economic security or the reputation of her daughter **Kathleen**, so her energies are devoted nearly exclusively to a drive for public esteem. Unlike Mrs. Mooney, her concerns emphasize a yearning for social status in and of its own sake rather than reflecting an abhorrence of social condemnation that might in turn lead to an economic impact on her business.

There are perhaps some domestic parallels in the marital lives of both women, though the extent of the similarities is minimal. Mrs. Mooney's unhappy marriage was to a failed butcher whose violent behavior has had to be restrained by the intervention of the parish priest. Mrs. Kearney, though at heart a romantic, has given in to pragmatism. When she perceived that people were beginning to talk about her remaining single, she married an older man peremptorily and petulantly. "Miss Devlin had become Mrs. Kearney out of spite" (p. 136). **Mr. Kearney** is a successful bootmaker who is able to provide a secure life for his family and who rarely if ever questions his wife's decisions. This leaves Mrs. Kearney free to pursue a measure of social acclaim by promoting the singing talents of her daughter, Kathleen, and by using enthusiasm for the Irish Literary Revival as a vehicle to that end. In consequence, Mrs. Kearney is working with **Hoppy Holohan**, the assistant secretary of the *Eire Abu* society, to organize a concert at which her daughter will perform.

Ticket sales for the concert do not meet expectations, and so on the night of the last performance the organizers declare that the remuneration promised for Kathleen's performance must be scaled back while other performers received what they were originally promised. Mrs. Kearney, more concerned with the inequity than the actual monetary amount, is outraged and refuses to allow her daughter to sing. The story ends with the deeply offended Mrs. Kearney leaving the concert hall, while the others present either sneer at her or maintain an embarrassed silence. Although the peremptory, domineering nature of Mrs. Kearney may make her an easy target for dismissal, Joyce also offers a keen sense of the frustration of an intelligent, strong-willed woman trying to find fair treatment in a carelessly patriarchal world. It remains for each reader to come to a sense of what Mrs. Kearney does or does not deserve.

"Grace"

This is the fourteenth story in the collection and the final one in the section on public life. Joyce completed it late in 1905, and it was the twelfth in order of composition. It concerns a fall, both literal and metaphoric, and a redemption, or at least the appearance of one. While it is easy to see the story as a parody of Catholic ritual and moral insincerity, perhaps underscored by selective allusions to the *Divine Comedy* as well as to fragmented and often ill-informed allusions to various beliefs and liturgies, that view would miss much of the subtlety. While "Grace" gently lampoons the unthinking hypocrisy of many of the men involved in the salvation of Tom Kernan, it takes a much more significant role in its examination of the importance of public performance to the identity of the middle-class Dubliners.

The opening lines of the story describe the consequences of an inebriated Kernan tumbling down the steps leading to a pub's toilets. Great confusion results, and **Jack Power**, a friend and member of the Royal Irish Constabulary, intervenes and prevents Kernan's arrest for public drunkenness (an occurrence that would be seen in claustrophobic Dublin as a disgrace far greater than it would be considered in today's more lax social climate). Later, Power and other friends including **Martin Cunningham** and **C.P. M'Coy** (all of whom will reappear in the narrative of *Ulysses*) visit Kernan who is recuperating at his home to convince him to attend an evening of spiritual reflection conducted at St. Xavier's Church by **Father Purdon**, a Jesuit well-known for his informal approach to conducting such services.

During the visit to Kernan's sickroom, a number of his solicitous comforters hold forth on various aspects of Catholic liturgy, religious dogma, and Church history. The result of these disquisitions is a jumble of facts, superstition, and misinformation that gives a buffoonish aura to their efforts.

While these displays give ample evidence of the men's faith as mechanical, ill-founded, and invoked publicly only when useful in a specific situation, a measure of sincerity seems to inform all of these gestures.

Reader's receive the subtle suggestion that Kernan, despite his conversion to Catholicism in order to marry, is not markedly different from the men who come to console him. Their efforts in getting Kernan to attend the evening of recollection do not appear to be anything so dramatic as an intervention on his drinking. Rather, they seem to offer the opportunity for Kerman to make a mild public propitiation, a gesture of acknowledgment of poor behavior and an open recognition of society's standards. The story ends as the ceremony begins, with the behavior of the cohort of men in attendance at St. Francis Xavier's emphasizing their sense of the importance of appearance over the need for expression of genuine contrition.

"The Dead"

This is the fifteenth story of the collection and the last one that Joyce composed. It was written in 1907, a year after the other stories had been finished. It is also the longest in the book, and many critics consider it a novella. It will be the subject of the alternative readings section of this chapter.

The story divides, fairly naturally, into two parts. The first section gives an account of the annual Christmas gathering on the **Feast of the Epiphany**, hosted by the Morkan sisters, **Julia** and **Kate**, and by their niece, **Mary Jane** at their house on Isher's Island (though in fact the area is not an island but a street bordering the south bank of the River Liffey). The central character, Gabriel Conroy, a nephew of Julia and Kate, has come to the party with his wife, **Gretta**. They meet a cross section of Dublin society there with many of the middle-class attitudes and prejudices that have been depicted throughout the fourteen previous stories. Much of the conversation centers on music, reflecting the background of the Morkan sisters and of Mary Jane who earn a living giving a variety of vocal and instrumental lessons.

Characters like the drunken **Freddy Malins** and the bombastic **Mervyn Browne** offer a form of bathetic comic relief. At the same time, through accounts of the guests' conversations and in Gabriel's after-dinner speech, the narrative offers a more congenial sense of Irish hospitality than has been shown in any of the other stories. On balance, Joyce deftly avoids slipping into either satire or sentimentality. An old friend of Gabriel's, Molly Ivors, presents a contrast between her fervent Nationalist views as she chides the cosmopolitan Gabriel for his lack of enthusiasm for Irish tradition and culture.

As the party comes to a close, the noted tenor, **Bartell D'Arcy**, sings "The Lass of Aughrim." Gabriel is deeply moved when he observes his wife's rapt interest in the performance. This seemingly trivial moment sets in motion recollections that will drive the action of the remainder of the story.

The second portion of "The Dead" focuses on Gabriel and Gretta and on the influence of the past. They have arranged to stay at the Gresham

Hotel in Dublin's city center to avoid a long, late-night winter trip home to Monkstown, a neighborhood located in what is now Dun Loaghaire, a seaside town to the south of Dublin. The narrative makes clear that on the way to the hotel, Gabriel begins to feel strong sexual desire, and he presumes that his wife does as well.

In their hotel room, Gabriel is on the point of initiating intimacy when Gretta tells him that the song D'Arcy sang has reminded her of a now dead young man, **Michael Furey**, who had loved Gretta years ago when both lived in Galway. She speaks with great tenderness of the time that a mortally ill Furey had left his sickbed to stand outside Gretta's window and sing "The Lass of Aughrim" for her. Gabriel is taken aback by her revelation and chagrined by his misreading of the situation.

After Gretta has fallen asleep, Gabriel broods over the love that Furey had for his wife, and he feels a great emptiness that in his own life has not felt a similarly profound love. The final paragraph records Gabriel's thoughts about his current condition, but it leaves the reader to resolve the question of whether Gabriel has come to a more open sense of possibilities or has slipped into profound despair. The final lines of the story underscore the depth of Gabriel's feelings, but they leave the reader to their interpretation: "His soul swooned slowly as he heard the snow falling faintly through the universe and faintly falling, like the descent of their last end, upon all the living and the dead" (p. 224).

Alternative Readings of the Second Portion of "The Dead"

"Nostalgia and Rancor at the Gresham Hotel"

The second half of "The Dead" focuses on the actions of Gabriel Conroy and his wife Gretta after they have left the Morkan sisters' Christmas party to go to the Gresham Hotel where they have arranged to stay overnight rather than make a late-night journey back to their Monkstown's home. While desire is a prominent feature of this portion of the narrative, two other attitudes dominate its tone: nostalgia and rancor. These feelings sum up the solipsism of both husband and wife, and underscore the responses that many Dubliners, no matter what their domestic circumstances, make to the threat of alienation.

Shortly before leaving the Morkan's party, Gabriel watched Gretta standing on the staircase to the second floor and listening to the tenor Bartell D'Arcy sing "The Lass of Aughrim." The spellbound look on Gretta's face has aroused Gabriel's sexual appetite, and, as they cross the city in a cab, he is anxious to satisfy his desire. Gretta, on the other hand, is oblivious to all his feelings.

In the hotel room, Gretta does not respond to Gabriel's tentative advances. Instead, she speaks of the strong emotional connection that she has to the song that D'Arcy sang. She tells Gabriel that, when she was still a young woman living in Galway, a seventeen-year-old boy named Michael Furey had become infatuated with her. Hearing "The Lass of Aughrim" has brought back nostalgic recollections of the night that the young man, despite being quite sick, came to the garden of her grandmother's home and sang to her. Gretta subsequently left Galway to go to a convent school in Dublin, and later learned that Michael Furey had succumbed to his illness.

Gretta would not be the first wife to be unaware of a particular moment of her husband's sexual desire. Nonetheless, there is certainly a measure of self-absorption that enshrouds her, not simply in revealing her sentimental recollections but in giving a melodramatic cast to her memories: "I think he died for me" (p. 220). After telling the story of Michael Furey's serenade, Gretta bursts into sobs, and then, with Gabriel, now "shy of intruding on her grief" (p. 222) she falls asleep.

Though Gretta has been impervious to it, throughout her account of her relations with Michael Furey, Gabriel has felt bitterness and anger. The immediate cause of is frustrated sexual desire, but there is also a measure of jealousy and even envy as he thinks of the seemingly idyllic relationship between Gretta and Michael. While Gretta sleeps, Gabriel thinks of his own circumscribed emotional life. "He had never felt like that himself towards any woman but he knew such a feeling must be love" (p. 223).

The story ends ambivalently. As Gretta sleeps, Gabriel comes to terms with her sentimental recollections of Michael and with his own emotional emptiness. As snow begins to fall, Gabriel thinks of its universality, "snow

Figure 2.1 The Gresham Hotel in Dublin, the setting of the final scene of "The Dead". (Courtesy of the Irish Tourist Board)

was general all over Ireland," but the conclusion gives no clear sense whether Gabriel has achieved an emotional breakthrough and now disposes himself toward feeling love. Neither does it give any insight into Gretta who, without any concern for her husband's feelings, has told Gabriel about the deep affection she still feels for the memory of a young boy who has been dead for decades.

A pessimistic interpretation would have the title apply to the living as much as to the dead, those who have become little more than detached spirits because of emotional solipsism. An optimistic view would see in the final pages a moment of enlightenment for Gabriel who now has the insight that will greatly enhance his humanity. Joyce does not push one interpretation over the other but rather has the confidence to allow his readers to find their own way.

"Thematic Summation in 'The Dead'"

The last part of "The Dead" offers a thematic climax not only to this short story but also to the fourteen that precede it. The introduction in "The Sisters" of how tribal loyalties and tensions define the relationships in any family anticipates the catalytic effect of relationships that extends throughout the volume to the Morkan sisters. In this fashion, "The Dead" becomes the final reflection on various themes found throughout *Dubliners*, in particular those of loss and death.

At the same time, in this last look at common themes, Joyce allows himself the freedom to reconsider many of his views. The auditory imagery of the words *faintly* and *softly*, found in the opening paragraph of the first story and then rhythmically reappearing in the last paragraph of "The Dead," seems to offer an aural connection and verbal unity to the collection. The focus on Irish hospitality in "The Dead," however, presents characters in *Dubliners* in a social light much different from and much more pleasant than that found in the previous stories. Nonetheless, the question remains: once the festivities end, does this last portion of the story lapse back into the collection's themes of alienation, loss, and death? A recollection of what has gone before gives one a clearer sense of how to judge this question.

Gabriel's own words spoken during his dinner speech ironically adumbrate his fate at the end of the story. Speaking in a tone softly modulated as though he were the celebrant at the moment of anamnesis in the Eucharistic prayer during the liturgy of the mass, Gabriel reminds those gathered round the sumptuous dinner table—an altar of good gifts and offerings by the Morkan sisters—to call to mind "thoughts of the past, of youth, of changes, of absent faces that we miss here tonight" (p. 204). He then continues with a warning that unwittingly he himself will bitterly heed in the closing pages of the story. Though at times life confronts us with sorrowful memories, "were we to brood upon them always," Gabriel cautions, "we could not find the heart to go on bravely with our work among the living" (p. 204).

In their room at the Gresham Hotel, Gabriel for the first time hears from Gretta the story of Michael Furey, whom she believes died for her. The sad memory of Michael's death seizes Gabriel with terror and momentarily paralyzes him. As though symbolically burying himself under the bed sheets—the dual cerements for the dead and for the passionless life he has lived—Gabriel acutely realizes the inevitability and definitiveness of mortality and the need for passion to sustain his life. "His own identity," the narrator tells us, "was fading out into a grey impalpable world: the solid world itself . . . was dissolving and dwindling" (p. 223). His sense of loss on several levels is apparent, but it could also be a foreshadowing of a change of heart, a spiritual metanoia, to sustain him in discovering new possibilities that stem from a renewed life, a life without prolonged brooding. Perhaps the hopelessness and its allusion to the first three stanzas of Canto III of the *Inferno* with which *Dubliners* begins—in particular to the line: "Abandon all hope, you who enter."—is muted here in Gabriel's thoughts.

A shift in mood also occurs on the very last pages of "The Dead," and it reflects a poetic sentiment that radically modifies the narrator's use of free indirect discourse in the opening lines of the story. This poetic sentiment is not concerned with Gabriel's cultivated, and at times pompous, language. It bypasses his diction to reflect his heightened emotional state. If at this point the narrative voice is interpreted to be sympathetic toward him, it too seems to offer hope. But readers can only speculate on what the next day will bring and on whether Gabriel finds "the heart to go on bravely" with his work and relationship with Gretta.

Topics for Further Discussion

1. How does the concept of paralysis inform different stories in the collection?
2. Do the stories show love or antipathy for the city of Dublin?
3. Is the narrative tone consistent throughout the collection?
4. Could one argue that the first three stories of *Dubliners* are told by the same narrator?
5. Is it possible that the third story, "Araby," is being told by that narrator as an adult reconsidering the events of his childhood?
6. What characters have experiences that relate to those of contemporary readers?
7. How necessary to the understanding of the stories is some background in Irish history, Catholic beliefs and rituals, or the mores of Victorian society?
8. Is *Dubliners* a collection of short stories or a novel where characters are united by the way Dublin shapes their lives?
9. Does Joyce's approach to writing fit any popular label—Traditionalist, Modernist, post-Modernist?
10. How well does "The Dead" fit into the collection?
11. Should "The Dead" be read as a stand-alone story?

A Glossary of Characters

Mr. Alleyne—the employer of Farrington in the story "Counterparts." When Farrington inadvertently makes a remark that embarrasses Alleyne, the latter forces him to apologize before the entire office.

The Aunt—the unnamed relative who cares for the boy narrator at the center of "The Sisters," "An Encounter," and "Araby."

Mervyn Browne—one of the guests at the Morkan's Christmas party. Though he is not terribly witty, he spends the evening holding forth on any topic that comes to hand. He bullies Freddy Malins unmercifully. And then, after drinking too much, Browne falls asleep before the party ends.

Little Chandler (Thomas Malone Chandler)—the central character of "A Little Cloud." He is a self-pitying law clerk and would-be poet. The final scene of the story makes clear that his wife has far more concern, and respect, for their child than him.

Gabriel Conroy—the central figure in "The Dead." He is nephew to Kate and Julia Morkan and cousin to Mary Jane. At their annual Christmas gathering, he is called upon to give an after-dinner speech over which he agonizes. In the second part of the story, the revelation of his wife's girlhood lover, Michael Furey, causes him to reassess his emotional life.

Gretta Conroy—the wife of Gabriel Conroy and a catalytic figure in "The Dead." Although she has a relatively minor role in the first half of the story, her recollections of Michael Furey, an admirer from her girlhood, and her obliviousness to her husband's feelings stand as the story's turning point.

John Corley—one of the two principal characters in "Two Gallants." As the son of a police inspector, Corley comes from a solid middle-class background, though his coarse hedonism belies it.

Mr. Cotter—a friend of the uncle of the unnamed narrator in "The Sisters." Cotter's heavy-handed innuendoes cast doubt on the moral probity of Father Flynn.

Martin Cunningham—a character in "Grace." He is among the men who visit Tom Kernan during the latter's convalescence after falling down a pub's stairs, and Cunningham is the strongest advocate for Kernan's joining a group of friends for an evening of religious reflection at St. Francis Xavier's Church.

Bartell D'Arcy—a well-known Dublin tenor. As a guest at the Morkan sisters' Christmas gathering, he first refuses to entertain the company but later, as people are leaving, he sings "The Lass of Aughrim," the song that has such a great effect upon Gretta Conroy.

Joe Donnelly—he appears in the story "Clay" as the current head of the Donnelly household whom Maria visits on Halloween. He is bombast and insensitive and, based on Maria's concerns, apparently a heavy drinker.

Bob Doran—the lodger in "The Boarding House" who is responsible for getting Polly Mooney pregnant. As a result, Mrs. Mooney, the landlady, browbeats him into marrying her daughter.

Jimmy Doyle—the central character in "After the Race." He embodies the aspirations of his indulgent, social-climbing father through careless living and a sense of embarrassment over his origins.

James Duffy—the central character in "A Painful Case." He is a cashier in a private bank with misanthropic tendencies. He meets Emily Sinico at a concert, and they begin an unlikely friendship. Duffy ends their acquaintance when Mrs. Sinico makes it clear that she seeks intimacy beyond simple friendship. When, a few years later, Duffy learns of her death he can initially feel only disgust, but that turns to a sense of his profound isolation.

Farley—the wealthy American on whose yacht Jimmy and others play cards in the final scene of "After the Race."

Farrington—the main character in "Counterparts." He is an only marginally competent law clerk who pawns his watch and goes on a drinking spree after being humiliated by his employer, Mr. Alleyne.

Tom Farrington—the young son in "Counterparts" upon whom Farrington, his father, vents his rage at the end of the story.

Eliza Flynn—one of the two women who provide the title for the collection's first story. "The Sisters." With her sister Nannie she runs a shop and cares for their retired priest brother, James. At the end of the story, she attempts to justify her brother's increasingly bizarre behavior.

Rev. James Flynn—the priest whose death is reported in the opening of "The Sisters." Although he never actually appears, a number of characters recall various aspects of his behavior. He is alternately shown as a kind mentor to the boy who narrates the story, a somewhat befuddled invalid, and a deeply troubled man who seems to have lost his faith in God. No single account gives the complete picture, and several offer contradictory views.

Nannie Flynn—one of the two women who provide the title for the collection's first story, "The Sisters." With her sister Eliza, she runs a shop and cares for their retired priest brother, James. Although her actions in the final scene of the story are carefully recorded, she has no dialogue.

Frank—the young man, presumably a sailor though some critics have called that into question, who wishes to elope with Eveline Hill in "Eveline."

Michael Furey—the young man who was in love with Gretta Conroy when she was a young girl in Galway. His early death makes a romantic impression that Gretta carries with her and that she reveals to her husband, Gabriel, at the Gresham Hotel after the Morkan's Christmas party.

Ignatius Gallaher—a former Dublin newspaper man who has become a successful journalist in London. He has drinks with Little Chandler in "A Little Cloud," making the latter acutely aware of the claustrophobic elements of his life.

Eveline Hill—the title character of "Eveline." She is a young woman trapped in a dreary life working in a shop and caring for her siblings. She clearly feels restless and dissatisfied, but ultimately she lacks the courage to break away from familiar surroundings.

Hoppy Holohan—the assistant secretary of the *Eire Abu* society. In "A Mother" he is the man responsible for arranging the concert that is at the center of the story.

Joe Hynes—a newspaper reporter who appears in "Ivy Day in the Committee Room." He recites the sentimental poem that he has composed, "The Death of Parnell," at the end of the story.

Molly Ivors—a minor character in "The Dead" who chastises Gabriel Conroy for his lack of Nationalist feeling.

Old Jack—the aged, embittered caretaker of the offices where the men of "Ivy Day in the Committee Room" gather to wait for payment for their political canvasing efforts.

Mary Jane—the unmarried niece of Julie and Kate Morkan who offers music lessons. She appears in "The Dead" as one of the hosts of the annual Christmas party.

Kathleen Kearney—a pianist, singer, and enthusiastic supporter of the Irish Literary Revival. She appears in "A Mother" as the docile child who is dominated by her strongminded mother.

Mr. Kearney—a successful bootmaker by trade who is the henpecked husband of the title character in "A Mother."

Mrs. Kearney—the title character of "A Mother." She is a willful and aggressive person who is not afraid to challenge any authority that she cannot bend to her wishes. Nonetheless, in the end she is frustrated by the patriarchal order that dominates the perspectives of both the men and the other women in the story.

Tom Kernan—the central character in "Grace." His drunken fall down the steps leading to a pub lavatory and his subsequent convalescence cause a number of men to visit him and encourage him to reform by attending an evening of reflection at St. Francis Xavier's Church.

T. Lenehan—a hanger-on who is Corley's companion in "Two Gallants." Despite his affected nonchalance, Lenehan spends most of his time ingratiating himself to those who can pay for drinks and give him money. He draws on a store of coarse humor, ribald gossip, and horse racing tips to gain the approval of others.

C.P. M'Coy—one of the men in the story "Grace" who visits Tom Kernan to convince him to attend an evening of reflection at St. Francis Xavier's Church.

Mahony—the schoolboy who skips classes with the unnamed narrator of "An Encounter." He pretends to be named Murphy to hide his identity from the "queer old josser."

Freddy Malins—one of the guests at the Morkan's Christmas party in "The Dead." He arrives inebriated and becomes a source of concern and embarrassment for his mother and the butt of amusement for Mervyn Browne.

Mangan—he is a friend of the unnamed narrator of "Araby." It is his sister who inspires the narrator to go to the bazaar that gives the story its title.

Mangan's Sister—a girl who appears in "Araby" and is never identified by anything more than this designation. She becomes the focus of the unnamed narrator's infatuation.

Maria—the central character in "Clay." Though at present employed at the Dublin by Lamplight Laundry, she had at one time cared for Joe Donnelly and his brother Alfie when they were children. She visits Joe's family to celebrate All Hallows Eve.

Mrs. Mooney—the landlady in "The Boarding House" and the dominant personality of the story. Her unflinching determination forces Bob Doran to marry her pregnant daughter.

Polly Mooney—the young girl in "The Boarding House" made pregnant by Bob Doran. Their sex is consensual though it is unclear whether it was part of a ploy to get Polly married or simply the result of animal appetites.

Julia Morkan—the aunt of both Gabriel and Mary Jane of one of the hosts in the annual Christmas party at the heart of the first portion of "The Dead." Her rendition of the song "Arrayed for Bridal" underscores the custom and hospitality embodied by their party. At the same time it is seen by Gabriel and others as a poignant reminder of the passing of an age.

Kate Morkan—the aunt of both Gabriel and Mary Jane of one of the hosts in the annual Christmas party at the heart of the first portion of "The Dead."

Charles Stewart Parnell—an actual political figure who worked to achieve Irish Home Rule but was driven from power over his adulterous relationship with a married woman, Kitty O'Shea. He became a secular martyr in the eyes of Irish Nationalists.

Jack Power—the man in "Grace" who rescues Tom Kernan after the latter's fall down the staircase in a pub and who is among the men who later visit

Kernan to convince him to attend an evening of reflection at St. Francis Xavier's Church.

Father Purdon—the Jesuit priest in "Grace" who conducts the evening of reflection at St. Francis Xavier's Church.

Queer old josser—the unidentified man who accosts the truant young boys in "An Encounter" as they lie in a field near the Dodder River.

Charles Ségouin—the owner of the French race car in "After the Race" and one of the winners in the card game at the end of the story.

Captain Sinico—the seafaring husband of Emily Sinico in "A Painful Case." His frequent absences and general indifference to his wife contribute to her restlessness and eventual decline.

Mrs. Emily Sinico—a central character in "A Painful Case." She is a cultured woman in an unfulfilled marriage who becomes friends with James Duffy through their mutual love of music. When she seeks a more intimate relationship with Duffy, he rebuffs her. This in turn leads to increased drinking and a death that may have been accidental or suicide.

Richard "Tricky Dicky" Tierney—a politician and pub keeper who, in "Ivy Day in the Committee Room," has hired men to canvas the Royal Exchange Ward for votes for him. He never appears in the story, but a number of men disparage his character.

The Uncle—the unnamed relative who cares for the boy at the center of "The Sisters," "An Encounter," and "Araby."

The Unnamed Narrator—while there is no clear connection confirming the link, he seems to be the young boy who narrates all of the first three stories in the collection: "The Sisters," "An Encounter," and "Araby." The boy has an adolescent understanding of the world, in some cases extremely insightful and in others quite naïve. However, the narratives give a sufficiently precise picture of him to allow readers to make an informed interpretation of his nature.

Selected Annotations

Gifford, Don, and Robert J. Seidman. *Joyce Annotated: Notes for **Dubliners** and **A Portrait of The Artist as a Young Man***. 1967; 2nd edition, Berkeley, Los Angeles and London: University of California Press, 1982.

Jackson, John Wyse, and Bernard McGinley, *James Joyce's Dubliners: An Illustrated Edition with Annotations*. New York: St. Martin's Press, 1993.

Scholes, Robert, and A. Walton Litz. eds. ***Dubliners**: Text, Criticism, and Notes*. New York: The Viking Press, 1996.

3 Approaching *A Portrait of the Artist as a Young Man*

Although the incomplete *Stephen Hero* was the first novel that Joyce began, *A Portrait of the Artist as a Young Man* is the first one that he published. Initially, it appeared in serialized form in the British journal *The Egoist*, from February 1914 to September 1915. The Imagist poet and expatriate Ezra Pound, who, in his anthology *Des Imagistes*, had published one of Joyce's poems from *Chamber Music*, and the financially independent English woman Harriet Shaw Weaver, who would become a longtime patron and close friend of Joyce and his family, had strongly endorsed the work's appearance in the journal.

After its serialization, Weaver endeavored with little success to enlist an English publisher for the novel. Finding a printer willing to do the job was the central impediment she faced because English law at that time held that the printer is as liable as the writer and publisher for material in a book. Restrictive Victorian values were still strong enough to discourage any British printer from taking on the task. (As noted in the previous chapter, Joyce had experienced the same reluctance when he sought the publication of *Dubliners*.) To skirt the problem, Pound suggested having the novel published in the United States and copies imported to England. The strategy worked, and *A Portrait of the Artist as a Young Man* appeared under the imprint of the American publisher B.W. Huebsch on 29 December 1916.

The novel was derived from two diverse sources although it stands as markedly differed from either. On a commission from the Irish journal *Dana*, Joyce composed "A Portrait of the Artist," a brief prose sketch that combined fictional narrative with philosophical exposition. It aimed at presenting the impressions of the emerging aesthetic consciousness of an unnamed young man, but it was not well received when he submitted it in early January 1904. One of the editors of *Dana*, W.K. Magee, offered a brief but bluntly critique saying, "I can't print what I don't understand." (For further details, see "A Portrait of the Artist" in the Minor Works chapter of this book.)

Shortly after this rejection, on his twenty-second birthday, 2 February 1904, Joyce began a novel, *Stephen Hero* using and expanding upon a good amount of the material that had gone into his rejected essay and following a story line that parallels the author's own experience in growing up in Dublin. (A number of critics have seen the obvious echoes of Joyce's own

DOI: 10.4324/9781003223290-4

life in both *Stephen Hero* and the subsequent work *A Portrait of the Artist as a Young Man*. However, there is widespread agreement that only the most naïve readings would equate these fictions with autobiographies.)

Stephen Hero traced the early life of Stephen Daedalus as he grew to manhood in late nineteenth-century Dublin. It had all the formal hallmarks of a conventional narrative of the era, chronicled in plodding detail. Though only a fragment of the manuscript has survived, the textual evidence it provides shows that Joyce planned to write a *Künstlerroman*, a work about the development of an artist. The evidence also suggests that its highly conventional form indicates an attempt by an author not yet free of the expectations set by works in this genre that preceded it. It may have been just as tedious to write as the surviving fragment is to read. In any case, Joyce abandoned work on the novel in June or July of 1905. (For further details, see *Stephen Hero* in the Minor Works chapter of this book.)

It would be logical to presume that because he wrote many of the *Dubliners* stories while still working on *Stephen Hero*, he may have become dissatisfied with the conventional form of the latter work, particularly when compared with the stylistic achievements of the short stories. Despite this frustration with the form of the novel, Joyce did not abandon his plan for delineating the creative evolution of a young writer. The main themes of the two earlier pieces gave Joyce the contextual grounding he needed to renew the project, and his maturing formal skills enabled him to adopt a far more sophisticated form of expression than that which had characterized *Stephen Hero*. He began *A Portrait of the Artist as a Young Man* in 1907 shortly after finishing "The Dead," the final story in the *Dubliners* collection. Completing these accounts of the diverse aspects of lower middle-class Dublin life allowed him to return to the project of tracing a writer's artistic growth from infancy to adulthood.

A Portrait of the Artist as a Young Man radically breaks from the conventional narrative structure adhered to by most nineteenth-century novelists and develops its themes and discursive style in an innovative fashion. Viewed in tandem with the two related works that preceded and inspired it—"A Portrait of the Artist," and *Stephen Hero*—*A Portrait of the Artist as a Young Man* underscores the evolution of Joyce's imaginative talent and the emergence of a stylistic dexterity that allowed such radical revision. Not only does the novel illustrate the monumental difference in Joyce's writing compared to the *Stephen Hero* fragments, but it also distinguishes itself from the works of his contemporary novelists. (For example, *The Voyage Out*, Virginia Woolf's first novel that appeared in 1915, has of course a great many strengths, but it exemplifies the traditional form of writing from which Joyce was breaking away.) The novel that resulted from this reconfiguration has come to be seen as a prototypical example of Modernist fiction. (For our working definitions of Modernism and Postmodernism, see Appendix IV.)

In foregrounding concern for the development of the consciousness of its central character, Joyce's narrative commits himself to an extended, personal, and critical look at the growth of the individual artist. The novel meticulously traces the emotional, spiritual, imaginative, and creative maturation of Stephen Dedalus, who gradually comes to resist the impact of the cultural ethos on the formation of his character, attitudes, and behavior. Through its unflinching representations of every aspect of the young artist's life and its aggressive challenges of the efficacy of most social institutions of the period, Joyce's novel broke from the conventions that dominated Irish fiction during the previous century.

While the thematic concerns of this novel echo those expressed in the two works that shaped it, as noted above, the stylistics shifts in *A Portrait of the Artist as a Young Man* mark a radical change in the form of Joyce's writing when contrasted with that which he employed in "A Portrait of the Artist" or in *Stephen Hero* and distinguish it as a paradigmatic work of twentieth-century literature. Evidence of the distinctive approach to style that characterized his creative endeavors appears throughout the stories in *Dubliners*, and it is easy to suppose that the process of their composition forever changed his approach to writing. *A Portrait of the Artist as a Young Man* shows this form, radically different from that of its Victorian and Edwardian predecessors, now inculcated into the mature process of composition that would distinguish all his subsequent prose fiction. In the following sections, we elaborate on these central features of the work.

Key Issues

In the short stories of *Dubliners*, Joyce examined in detail a series of fundamental issues touching on religious belief, nationalistic dispositions, familial loyalties, and other cultural and social forces that had an impact of the formation of the identities of a broad spectrum of middle-class urban characters. In story after story, he dissected the specific communal elements that characterized the world in which these individuals resided. In the process of showing the effects of these commonly held beliefs, practices, and expectations on individuals, Joyce's narratives gave a robust picture of the social ethos shaping Dubliners at the turn of the twentieth century.

Further, they illustrated the difficulties that individuals encounter when trying to escape the influences society has on them. At the same time, although he presented the desperateness of their situations with unflinching clarity, he also showed most of the characters in the short stories making no attempt to seek independence from the demands of society. Rather, almost without exception, his characters seem to be searching for ways to come to accommodations within the environment in which they find themselves.

In *A Portrait of the Artist as a Young Man*, Joyce takes as a given the fractured condition of the Irish social institutions that he had exposed and excoriated in the *Dubliners* stories, and so the impact of their defects across society receives less direct and extended attention. Instead, his narrative examines the challenges posed by this dysfunctional system to the formation of the identity of an individual with an independent nature that resisted the pressures toward conformity. By highlighting the struggle of the novel's central character, **Stephen Dedalus**, to come to a full understanding of who he is in relation to what he views as the suffocating world that those institutions define, Joyce builds on the social criticism of his earlier work while allowing readers to focus attention of the dynamics of the growth of an artistic temperament.

Identity is a topic already quite familiar in Joyce's writings. It certainly featured as an important issue in many of the stories in *Dubliners*. However, the collection's character examinations concentrate on figures whose natures are already fully formed and that are dominated by the inexorableness of the events surrounding environment. The condition of resignation to an oppressive and seemingly inescapable environment that runs through *Dubliners* changes to determined rebelliousness over the course of *A Portrait of the Artist as a Young Man*.

Indeed, it is the possibility for developing in an alternative fashion that drives the arc of the narrative. The central character's growing resistance to these forces comes to a definitive conclusion in the novel's closing chapter. There we see Stephen turning irrevocably away from the communal ideals that surrounded him throughout his childhood and striving to find the means to define himself independent of the expectations of society.

This focus makes the construction of identity a central theme of the novel as Stephen Dedalus endeavors to come to a sense of himself first within and ultimately outside the context of late nineteenth- and early twentieth-century Ireland. Significantly, however, the narrative does not fall into the simplistic dichotomy, often advanced by some less talented Modernists, of representing any aspect of society as irredeemably bad and any individuality as unquestionably good. Joyce instead sees both the attractions and the dangers of dominant social attitudes, and he deftly underscores the challenges posed by these often-contradictory feelings as Stephen navigates through the process of the development of his nature.

Most significantly, yet nonetheless perhaps most easily overlooked, is the complexity of Stephen's relations with the specific social institutions against which he rebels. The narrative quite clearly delineates how he comes to see the expectations of family, church, and nation circumscribing his development. At the same time, Joyce writes far too well to describe these forces in a simplistic fashion. The social codes they seek to enforce are ultimately inimical to Stephen, yet, at various moments in the narrative, each institution provides him the support and nurturing he needs to continue to grow and eventually to break free of their influence. It is useful, consequently, before moving on, to consider the particular effect of each on his transformation.

The complexity of Stephen's view of Ireland is underscored in the novel's final lines. There, he does not declare his determination to abandon his country. Rather, he commits himself to working toward its reconfiguration: "I go to encounter for the millionth time the reality of experience and to forge in the smithy of my soul the uncreated conscience of my race" (p. 224). Thus, despite the insistent assertions of Stephen's psychological independence from the environment that surrounded him as he grew to manhood, readers need to be attentive to the impact and even the value he still places on certain elements within the largely rejected communal world of Irish society to understand the significance of the break that Stephen struggles to make over the course of the narrative.

As it did for many of the characters in *Dubliners*, Family stands as a powerful force in Stephen's development. The novel opens with a deeply personal yet at the same time a disarmingly charming look at the interaction of a parent and child through an embellished story of ordinary life depicting the interactions of baby tuckoo and the moo cow. It closes with Stephen Dedalus' seemingly offhanded yet subtly personal comment that his mother is packing his clothes as he prepares to leave home for the Continent. Sandwiched between these events are the successive incidents—both joyful and traumatic—that mark an individual's movement from childhood to adulthood. They capture the support, the conflicts, the inhibitions, and the consequences of family life, particularly as they are shaped by a doting mother and a selfish, irresponsible, and often unstable father.

From the start, Stephen has a unique place in the family as the privileged eldest child. While he certainly suffers, along with his brothers and sisters, as the economic fortunes of the family deteriorate through the fecklessness of his father, **Simon Dedalus,** Stephen never loses that sense of his exceptionality. This will give him self-confidence when facing challenges from the outside world at Clongowes Wood College and later at Belvedere College and at the same time cause him to bristle at the gentle chiding of his pious mother, **May Dedalus**, despite his deep love for her, when she exhorts him to live according to the expectations of the Catholic faith. A duality of feelings of connection and independence propel his process of maturation. In consequence, although the narrative clearly delineates Stephen's rebellion and does not stint in its representations of the human failings of family members, there is no ambiguity about the material privileges that shaped his early life or about the impact of the love that he continues to enjoys

Religion, particularly when represented by elements of the Catholic Church, can be an easy target for derision from contemporary readers who readily presume it to be nothing more than a trope for an oppressive and (ironically) a soul numbing force. Certainly, as a human institution Catholicism has been riddled with individuals demonstrating in their behavior or their thinking every human flaw imaginable. In the narrative this takes the form of an all too human willingness to impose rules while forgetting the motivating force behind them. At the same time, throughout the discourse of the novel Stephen shows himself increasingly attuned to that distinction between theology and administration.

Because of Stephen's own sophistication, the narrative does not show Catholicism as an inherently evil establishment. Rather, on the one hand, it highlights an institution capable of nourishing and supporting an individual providing one with a clear sense of values and direction. At the same time, it delineates an institution that cultivates conformity and demands from all its adherents an unswerving adherence to its discipline. It can have at various times an invigorating as well as a deadening effect on the imagination. Thus, assessments of Catholicism's effect on Stephen's development—from Stephen's early pieties to his ultimate rejection of the obligation to perform his Easter Duty—necessarily should take into consideration both the positive and the negative ways that it sought to form his consciousness.

Irish Nationalism also unfolds as a force exerting mixed benefits on Stephen's life, though, particularly after the first chapter, its positive qualities are much less celebrated. Initially, nationalism offers perspectives of public life that help Stephen define himself. However, in short order—dramatically illustrated through the confrontation of Simon Dedalus and **Dante Riordan** in the Christmas Dinner scene in chapter one—the forceful examples of the diverse ways that individuals react to the complex demands of Nationalism that recur throughout the narrative rebut any simple interpretation of its influence.

As a caveat to any discussion of Irish nationalism, it is useful to keep in mind that, at the time the story takes place, Ireland is still a colonized country, with many Irish vocally expressing strong sentiments for achieving independence from England. However, the narrative represents nationalism as much more complex than a delineation between resistance to the role of colonized or submission to the will of the colonizers. Factions within the Irish nationalist movement are shown having animosities toward one another as strong as those direct toward the British, particularly when religious views mix with political ones.

As demonstrated from the first to the final chapter of the novel, the more strident advocates measure the sincerity of national feeling by an individual's willingness to oppose English domination, and those who do not join in vigorous resistance have their legitimacy questioned. (Joyce has already explored this sort of clash in "The Dead" when Molly Ivors rebukes Gabriel Conroy's disinterest in activism.) For Stephen Dedalus, as he tells **Davin**, a close friend and ardent nationalist, in chapter five, such dichotomies elide the weaknesses of the institution. The reductiveness of such approaches makes nationalism prove to be the easiest of the nets to fling off. At the same time, it remains an important issue for understanding how the central character comes to a sense of personal identity.

As is the case with *Dubliners*, by the end of *A Portrait of the Artist as a Young Man* readers will have a clear sense that the *Culture* that surrounded Stephen Dedalus from his birth affects him, but its secondary importance within the narrative arc may make specific features more difficult to delineate. Admittedly, to a degree, some delineation of culture can be seen in Stephen's reflections on dominant social institutions like family, church, and state. However, even within a relatively homogeneous society, as the narrative insistently demonstrates, their amalgamated influences can vary significantly from individual to individual.

Consistently, the impact of the Dublin ethos on individuals signals the way the central characters come to understand how to behave within their world. At the same time, such reactions are neither uniform across the society nor consistent within the individual. (The long conversation that Stephen has in chapter five with his friend **Cranly** provides a good illustration of this condition.) As any particular sentiment grows in Stephen over the course of the novel, his response to the influence of ethos will vary greatly. Perhaps the greatest achievement of the narrative's close study of the formation of Stephen's identity is the representation of Ireland's inhibitive effect on an artistic temperament without as a consequence demonizing it.

Style

In addition to central themes shaping the narrative, a number of important stylistic techniques distinguish *A Portrait of the Artist as a Young Man* from Joyce's earlier writings as well as from the work of many contemporaneous authors. The use of *Free Indirect Discourse*, already discussed in the chapter on *Dubliners*, takes on a more sustained and more important function here. Within the seeming objectivity of a third person expositional discourse, it allows for an oscillation between the intimacy necessary for a deeper awareness of the nature of Stephen Dedalus and simultaneously it provides a distance from that subjectivity that facilitates a critical assessment of him. (The ambiguity of the source of the voice of the opening lines in the novel is a good illustration of this.) Both perspectives are crucial to a full and balanced understanding of the various stages of his maturation over the course of the novel.

Because the narrative concentrates so much reader interest on the development of Stephen Dedalus, it is important to have an intimate view of his feelings blended into straightforward accounts of events. At the same time, given the central character's noticeable lack of a sense of humor, sustaining the personal views and responses that Stephen makes over the course of the novel with no alternative perspective to balance his self-absorption would imbue the narrative with a reductive view and a priggish tone. Free indirect discourse allows both the intimacy of Stephen's thoughts and the detachment of a third party to complement and at times to offset one another.

Free indirect discourse also facilitates the narrative's ample use of *Irony*. Stephen's near-humorless self-absorption, mentioned above, would make him intolerable to most readers were there not some leavening features to mitigate his pomposity. Irony provides just such opportunities. It enhances the complexity of the narrative, tempers some of Stephen's more outrageously solipsistic reactions to the world around him, and, most importantly, opens the text to multiple interpretations of his thoughts, actions, and assumptions.

An example from chapter five nicely illustrates this. As the narrative describes Stephen's feelings as he is about to compose an autobiographical poem in the self-consciously precious form of a villanelle: "Towards dawn he awoke. O what sweet music! His soul was all dewy wet" (p. 191). While Stephen's exultant tone celebrates his sense of creative genius, the narrative, as several commentators have noted, suggests that this exuberance may have come in part at least from having just experienced a nocturnal emission.

Irony is not the only stylistic element contribution to Modernist writing that Joyce made. The narrative's division into *Episodic Incidents*, presenting isolated events without a clear transition between what precedes or follows each, stands as one of the most innovative stylistic aspects of *A Portrait of the Artist as a Young Man*. From chapter to chapter and from section to section within each chapter, the discourse presents self-contained episodes that are chronic examples of the maturation of the central character. Rather than offering a linear account of the development of Stephen Dedalus, the novel presents representative moments in his life and gives readers the freedom to link them. This undercuts the concept of the discourse laying down the features of a definitive interpretation and highlights the Modernist commitment to formal independence and contextual indeterminacy.

As an outgrowth of episodic incidents, time and time again the narrative employs *Thematic Inconclusiveness* as a liberating interpretive factor throughout the novel beginning most clearly with the Christmas Dinner scene of chapter 1. (This scene is discussed in detail in the Alternative Readings section below.) At the conclusion of a terrible argument during the dinner, we learn nothing more than that Stephen is "terrorstricken" (p. 34). Readers are left to decide its long-term effect. As in other descriptions of key episodes in Stephen's development, the single word stops short of a full explanation or even a complete account of Stephen's reactions. In doing so, the narrative resists presenting prescriptive interpretations but rather pushes readers to come to their own unified sense of the text by judging the effect on their own.

Additionally, Joyce was meticulously careful about his formal representation of the intellectual development of his main character. To catch Stephen's way of seeing the world, each chapter employs a vocabulary comparable to what Stephen at that age would understand and use. To that end, if one compares the language of the first chapter with that found in the last, the marked changes in diction, tone, and cognitive sophistication become immediately apparent. This subtle shift in tone neatly underscores the developing consciousness of the central character without the least sense of artifice.

Finally, starting in the second chapter, there is also a *Modulating Quality*, one that Hugh Kenner has suggested inverts the rise and fall of Dædalus' son Icarus. From this chapter on, each begins with Stephen in a low emotional state. At the end of each of these chapters, Stephen experiences a moment of exaltation. In this subtle rhythmic movement, Joyce's writing reflects the ebb and flow of feelings that punctuate Stephen's growth and development.

Taking style and themes together, one sees in *A Portrait of the Artist as a Young Man*, an innovative exploration of the struggles of a creative mind seeking to form an identity outside the confines of a parochial society. At the same time, it rejects the simplistic, vitriolic approach to which a writer like D.H. Lawrence too readily yielded in his bildungsroman, *Sons and Lovers*. Instead, while putting the artist's need for an independent consciousness in the foreground, *A Portrait of the Artist as a Young Man* refuses simply to dismiss completely the society from which it emerged.

An Overview of the Novel

A great deal occurs in every section of *A Portrait of the Artist as a Young Man*. However, before beginning an assessment of the key events and significant characters in each of the five chapters, we wish to examine the expectations raised for readers by the work's title and epigraph. Both features have important roles in orienting one's responses to the narrative that follows, but they also introduce a sense of the mutability of language. At first glance, they may seem to offer definitive guidance for understanding what follows. In fact, on closer examination one sees in either an indeterminacy that previews interpretive challenges readers will encounter throughout the text.

The title plays on the effects of paradox—with apparently straightforward words and images quickly giving way, after closer examination, to a considerable amount of ambiguity. The process begins quickly, with the opening phrase of the title, "A Portrait," offering mixed signals about what will follow. The indefinite article—"A"—seems to affirm that this document is only one of an unspecified number of possible delineations of the subject under consideration.

The noun that follows—Portrait—seems to reinforce that way of seeing the work. However, it also introduces a measure of incertitude regarding the work's status as a reproduction or interpretation question. On the one hand it can suggest a precise delineation of the figure being observed. When one goes to a National Portrait Gallery (and every country seems to have one), viewers take for granted that the images before them are faithful reproductions of the renowned figures who served as their subjects. At the same time, anyone familiar with the process of portraiture understands that its particular creative structure ensures that the final product comes out of its originator's understanding of the subject being studied. In this opening gambit, Joyce subtly introduces the play between objectivity and subjectivity that will infuse the narrative that follows.

In contrast, the word Artist, preceded by its definite article, concentrates attention on a single figure and confers upon that individual what seems to endow it with a paradigmatic objectiveness. On the other hand, when followed by the phrase "as a young man," that portion of the title can problematize the concept of when, if at all, that individual under scrutiny achieves a measure of artistic status in the novel. It equally draws attention to a differentiation of this particular artist from all others, underscoring subjectivity of the exposition.

The epigraph to the work has a similar function of ambiguation, though the suppleness of Latin grammar enables its mutability to be represented more compactly. The epigraph carries the distinction of being the only one that appears in any of Joyce's published fiction. Like the title, but with even greater subtlety, it too invites readers to embrace rather than to resent ambiguity. *Et ignotas animum dimittit in artes*—he turned his mind to unknown arts—is a quote that Joyce drew from Ovid's *Metamorphoses*. It records the response of Dædalus, the fabulous artificer, when told by King Minos that Dædalus and his son, Icarus, would not be allowed to leave the Crete. Just as Dædalus invents new ways of coping with Minos' impediment by forging the wax wings to fly from the island, the reader is directly told of the author's aim to infuse the narrative with an innovative content.

Further, one can discern an implicit invitation to imitate Dædalus and to reorient one's own ways of interpretation. Within that of course comes an imbedded warning against the sort of hubris that led Icarus to fly too close to the sun causing the wings to melt and the boy to fall down. (Joyce, ever the careful linguist, knew that the Latin phrase would support either "he turned" or "she turned" as the nominative pronoun of the sentence and thus preclude the possibility of ignoring half his audience.)

Admittedly, our teasing out this theme of ambiguity from the book's front matter before even beginning a discussion of the narrative may at first seem annoying or even contrived. However, highlighting the shifting meaning within the title and the epigraph is not so much a matter of underscoring the quaintness of structural configuration or of exposing Joyce for playing tricks on readers. Rather the point is to show how from even before the narrative begins, Joyce invites readers to incorporate a tolerance of ambiguity into their responses to his writing. He is in short suggesting to them that a range of possible responses are imbedded in the text, and that reading ultimately turns within itself for understanding rather than delves through the text in fruitless search for definitive meaning.

Chapter One

The chapter opens with a childish vignette that immediately challenges conventional expectations for narrative structure and reinforces the imperative for interpretive flexibility that the title and the epigraph have asserted. In the first few lines, one encounters with the fragmentary recollection of a childish story told to the toddler, Stephen Dedalus. "Once upon a time and a very good time it was there was a moocow coming down along the road and the moocow that was coming down along the road met a nicens little boy named baby tuckoo" (p. 5). As the reader begins to take it in, however, the straightforward charm of this unselfconscious rendition immediately becomes clouded by the ambiguity of the source of the account.

Readers with some familiarity with Joyce's form of writing will see that the narrative's deft application of free indirect discourse opens the possibility of one of three different voices reciting these initial lines. The young Stephen seems a likely source, for he has heard the tale of baby tuckoo so often that he can easily rattle off its opening. At the same time, the next line—"His father told him that story"—suggests either that the young boy is providing the source for his own recitation or that we have heard the baby tuckoo story told by someone else, perhaps the narrator, and that the narrator is identifying Stephen as someone who had listened to it. Of course, Stephen's father, **Simon Dedalus,** had told that story countless times, and the opening passage could easily be a direct quotation.

In any case, whatever choice the reader makes as to the source of the novel's opening will inevitably shape the interpretation that follows in a way different from the result derived from either of the other possibilities. The point is not that one answer is correct and the other two wrong. Rather, since any of the three options could logically serve to identify the speaker—as Stephen, Simon, or the narrator—in a few deftly written lines Joyce makes his readers aware of the range of uncertainty that is imbedded in the narrative.

This ambiguity is heightened by a repetition of free indirect discourses albeit with a far more ominous tone in the next few lines. The scene of the narrative abruptly shifts to a disturbing representation of retribution. A conversation, between May Dedalus and Dante Riordan, introduces disruptive themes of sin and punishment into the young boy's previously tranquil world. Though readers do not know why Stephen's mother asks him to apologize or what prompted Dante's minatory statement that "eagles will come and pull out his eyes" (p. 6), the arresting imagery and the stylistic dexterity demands the same degree of attention evoked by the opening.

The typographical assertiveness of two four-line stanzas with two identical lines repeated in each stanza but in reverse order in itself commands attention. The shifting possibilities for attribution only increase the reader's engagement. They can be ascribed to the narrator recounting the event, to the direct discourse of May Dedalus and Dante, or to the young Stephen Dedalus who may be transforming what he is hearing into verse and thus providing for the reader a glimpse into his future as an artist. As with the story of baby tuckoo, the essence of the exchange does not change with the perspective that the reader assigns, but the emphasis on its significance certainly does.

Though meaning is important, the impact on the reader's orientation in these early exchanges takes on equal consequence. The variability evoked by these examples affirms the legitimacy of a range of individual interpretive expectations for the rest of the novel, all based on the specific reader's provisional or temporary resolution of the ambiguity. Thus, from the start, indeterminacy runs through the narrative and paradoxically frees the reader to adopt a range of possible understandings each of equal validity. This application of ambiguity frees readers to produce resolution, on their own terms, for the remainder of the work.

After a glimpse of Stephen's precocity and the occasioned harsh response to it by **Dante Riordan**, the scene shifts to his initial experiences outside the home. Stephen is sent at the age of six to the prestigious Jesuit boarding school Clongowes Wood College, about 25 miles west of Dublin. The narrative details Stephen's predictable awkwardness and homesickness. It also gives a taste of the vicissitudes that mark a child's daily life at a private boarding school.

Although objectively the experiences recounted will seem to be relatively predictable events in any schoolboy community, Stephen's acute sense

Approaching A Portrait of the Artist as a Young Man 67

Figure 3.1 Clongowes Wood College, founded in 1814 by the Society of Jesus, is located west of Dublin in Sallins, County Kildare. (Courtesy of the Irish Tourist Board)

of self gives each a highly dramatic tone. As Stephen tries to settle in at Clongowes Wood, a classmate, **Wells**, embarrasses him with a trick question about whether he kisses his mother. Then, after Stephen refuses to relinquish a prize possession, Wells pushes Stephen into a muddy square ditch filled with stagnant water. Later, when Stephen develops a fever and is sent to the infirmary, an abject Wells piteously asks, "Dedalus, don't spy [inform] on us, sure you won't?" (p. 18).

The narrative presents such interactions in an emotionally charged fashion through the prism of Stephen's mind. In fact, when seen dispassionately, this and other incidents recounted in the chapter make up the normal give and take especially at a boarding school. Overall, quite the contrary to Stephen's self-pitying view of being a weak and vulnerable target for the others, examples show that his intelligence and good humor allow him to gain a measure of respect from the other students.

When the narrative scene shifts again, Stephen is home on holidays and has reached the point of having his first Christmas dinner with the adults of the family rather than of eating with his younger siblings. Though the occasion begins with good cheer, the meal quickly turns into a bitter debate on national versus religious loyalty. Simon Dedalus and **Mr. John Casey** vigorously defend the memory of the now dead political figure, Charles Stewart Parnell, whose adultery had been condemned by the Church and led him to lose control of the Irish Parliamentary Party. Dante Riordan, though no less committed to freeing Ireland from English rule than Dedalus, Casey, or Parnell for that matter, defends the Catholic bishops' position. In the midst of it all Stephen's mother tries ineffectually to stop the quarrelling and preserve a semblance of Christmas cheer. It ends with Dante violently rising from the table storming out of the room and with Simon breaking down in tears.

All this leaves Stephen "terrorstricken." However, in terms of the narrative development, this is more than an unfortunate and ill-timed argument. The harshness of the family disagreement, highlighted by its sharp criticism of Catholicism and its conflicted sense of the meaning of Irish nationalism, offer the first signs to young Stephen of the inherent flaws in the social institutions—family, church, and state—that have heretofore laid down the criteria for defining his identity.

Back at Clongowes, the narrative recounts all of his classmates' interest in and bewilderment over an unspecified but scandalous incident that has recently occurred at the school and that has involved several of the older boys. One of the students discussing the situation, **Athy**, announces with assurance but without elaboration that the harsh punishments meted out to the offenders were because they had been "smugging" (p. 37). The narrative here introduces an infrequently used word that, according to the *Oxford English Dictionary*, may derive from the obsolete verb *smuggle*, meaning to fondle or caress and not from *smug*, a term denoting a self-satisfied attitude. Whatever its origin, Joyce employs its unfamiliarity to engage readers, inviting them to derive its meaning from contextualizing it, and thereby drawing them into the creative process.

Whatever the particulars that led to the disgrace of several of the older boys, the event has profoundly unnerved the Jesuits at the school. Their nervous response has meant to a heightened approach to enforcing discipline through corporal punishments. In consequence, Stephen, who has been excused from schoolwork because his glasses have been broken in a schoolyard accident, is pandied for not participating in class by **Father Dolan**, the prefect of studies. (This was a common punishment in which a student is hit on the hand with a leather strap that contains within in it a hard object.) Father Dolan dismisses the explanation for the boy's not participating in schoolwork and accuses Stephen of breaking his own glasses.

The incident is a shocking revelation for Stephen of his own vulnerability. He is stung as much by the unfairness of Father Dolan's accusations as by the physical pain the consequent punishment produced. At the other boys' urgings Stephen goes to the school's rector, **Father Conmee**, to seek justice. Although this may seem a fairly innocuous gesture to adult readers, the narrative underscores the feeling in Stephen of the momentousness of his gesture. In relatively short order, Father Conmee reassures Stephen that he will speak to Father Dolan so that the injustice will not be repeated, and the chapter ends with Stephen being lauded by his classmates for his courage and determination and Father Dolan derided as a tyrant and bully.

Chapter 2

The chapter, in a pattern replicated in the others that follow it, opens with a shift in tone from the euphoria of the conclusion of the preceding episode to an atmosphere of unhappiness. Stephen is no longer attending Clongowes Wood College because of his father's inability to pay the school's fees. As a result, Stephen is left more or less to fend for himself, under the putative, sporadic care of his **Uncle Charles**. He befriends local boys and lives a great deal in his imagination. A move to Blackrock, a suburb south of Dublin, and then another into the city itself makes Stephen increasingly aware of the family's deteriorating finances. Despite his father's bravado—"There's a crack of the whip left in me yet, Stephen, old chap . . . . We're not dead yet, sonny" (p. 57)—this seems an ominous change of circumstances.

Conditions improve markedly for Stephen when a chance meeting of Simon Dedalus and Father Conmee, now no longer at Clongowes Wood, leads to a scholarship allowing Stephen to attend Belvedere College, a prestigious Jesuit day school located in the city at the head of North Great George Street. Simon's encounter also provides readers with a very different version of the visit to the rector. Stephen's father tells the family, including of course his son, of Father Conmee's recollection of meeting with Stephen and then of teasing Father Dolan over it at dinner. Simon accompanies the story with gestures and mimicry turning the event into something more comic and less momentous than the boy had assumed. Despite what one might fairly assume as a rather momentous revelation for Stephen, the narrative gives the reader scope to interpret the boy's response to this alternative review, since no reaction to this deflating news is recorded.

At Belvedere, with intelligence and a growing measure of individualism, Stephen quickly establishes himself as a class leader and, after a rocky start with another student who considers himself exceptional, **Vincent Heron**, a friendly rivalry develops. Their initial discord dated back to early in Stephen's time at Belvedere. Heron and two other boys had seized on a mild reprimand by a teacher, **Mr. Tate**, as an excuse to give Stephen a beating as punishment for his independent nature. Though at the time recounted in the chapter the boys are friendly, the narrative makes clear that Stephen has not forgotten the incident.

In the midst of the chapter, Stephen accompanies his father to the city of Cork where Simon Dedalus sells the last of the family property there to raise money. In addition to the embarrassment most adolescent children feel when with their parents, Stephen has the added burdened of his father's drunken competitiveness and maudlin nostalgia: "I hope he's [Stephen's] as good a man as his father. . . . Thanks be to God, Johnny', said Mr. Dedalus, 'that we lived so long and did so little harm'." (p. 83). Characteristically, the narrative offers little specific insight into Stephen's reaction to his father's behavior, and instead it leaves readers to come to their own determination as to its impact.

After this stark contrast between a father's irresponsibility and a son's reserve, in the final section of the chapter the narrative shows how Stephen behaves when he has a windfall. He wins an academic prize of thirty guineas. (Conversion rates are notoriously tricky, but it is safe to assume that as of 2021 the amount would be somewhere between $10,000 and $15,000.)

Stephen's behavior perfectly captures the hopelessness of the family's situation. His award is too little to have any lasting effect upon the way the family lives but quite enough to support pointless indulgences. Consequently, imitating his father's spendthrift ways, Stephen squanders it all on extravagant gestures—gifts, dinners, uncompleted home improvements—and, with the prize money nearly gone, the chapter's final scene chronicles Stephen's visit to a prostitute. All of this is described in neutral tones that leave to readers the task of assessing what this behavior says about Stephen's character and how different, if at all, it is from his father's nature.

Chapter 3

The chapter opens with Stephen daydreaming in a Belvedere classroom about beef stew and Dublin whores. Its blunt rendition presented through deft prose descriptions emphasizes the scope of his gross material appetites. In an abrupt interruption of these fantasies, the Rector of the school appears in the classroom to remind the boys of the impending annual retreat that they will attend. With this section as prologue, the remainder of the chapter focuses on selected portions of the retreat and records Stephen's response to the commentary by the priest leading it: an abrupt transformation from a sensualist to a pious young man.

While much of the accounts seem melodramatic to contemporary readers, the organization of the Belvedere retreat in fact follows what was at the time the conventional, liturgical form. On consecutive days, the retreat master, **Father Arnall**, follows the standard structure of such spiritual recollections. In a series of sermons he directs the boys toward specific topics for meditations, focusing their thoughts on death, the Last Judgment, Hell, Purgatory, and Heaven. Although it is not apparent from the narrative, such retreats are designed to move participants from contemplation of their human weaknesses to an awareness of the love God has for them and from there introduces the promise of the eventual consolation of eternal life with Him.

The chapter's discourse presents readers only with selections of the religious exercise, and, in keeping with Stephen's Manichean point of view, they are usually those presentations that are devoted to sin and retribution. Stephen, in his solipsism, appropriates it all to himself—"Every word of it was for him" (p. 101)—and his reactions are dominated by guilt and fear of punishment over all other feelings. Nonetheless, despite their hyperbolic tendencies, the descriptions offer insight into the complexities of Stephen's nature. With egoism as a prime motivator, what might seem as a satire on Catholic ritual in fact reveals yet another aspect of Stephen's self-absorption and of his striving to find a direction for his life.

Near the end of the chapter the rector announces that following the retreat's end all the boys will attend Mass together. To insure all will receive Holy Communion, the Sacrament of Penance is offered at the school. Stephen, however, chooses not to go to confession at Belvedere, but instead goes to a parish church, still called a chapel because the English appropriated the designation of church to their own creed. No explanation is given for this decision, though presumably Stephen wished to avoid having his voice recognized by one of the Jesuits in the confessional box. Though a minor demonstration of pride and perhaps shame, it calls into question the sincerity of his reformation, particularly since the Seal of Confession would bind the priest from ever revealing what Stephen told him.

Chapter 4

This section shows the sharpest contrast in Stephen's behavior, yet at the same time it provides a clear and consistent sense of the evolution of his identity. The chapter begins with accounts of Stephen's fervid spiritual recommitment through a disciplined, even fanatical, regime of self-mortification seemingly grounded on religious doctrine. At the same time, despite his professed ardor, the dull descriptions of Stephen's routine of self-denial give a claustrophobic, mechanistic, rule-bound sense to the form of religious life to which he has committed himself, and the very intensity of his devotion suggests to sensitive readers that it will be short-lived.

A discussion at the episode's midpoint with the Dean of Studies proves to be the turning point in the focus of his belief. During their conversation, the Dean introduces the possibility of a religious vocation, and he urges Stephen to consider entering the Jesuit order. Stephen is flattered by the suggestion, and wrestles with the idea. In the end, however, he rejects the discipline and constrictions of religious life in favor of an equally complete dedication to a secular vocation.

His imaginative maturation is now devoted completely to the pursuit of artistic creativity. One day, while his father is attempting to secure a scholarship for Stephen to University College Dublin, the young man walks aimlessly along Dollymount Strand overlooking Dublin Bay. At one point, he sees a beautiful young girl, whom critics have come to label the Birdgirl, wading knee-deep in the water. Stephen is overcome with the joy of this vision of material beauty and with the realization of the possibility of evoking that kind of exuberance through art. It is one of many descriptions in his writing of moments of sudden insight that Joyce came to label epiphanies, and it exemplifies a number of instances over the course of this novel during which Stephen experiences a sudden illumination. This episode at the end of the chapter reveals that Stephen has discovered an even deeper, more abiding faith in the power of aesthetics, and demonstrates his new and complete commitment to art.

Chapter 5

This final segment pulls together the diverse feelings of rebellion against a spectrum of social conventions and institutions with which Stephen has contended over the course of the novel, and it shows how his struggles have

Figure 3.2 University College. (Courtesy of the Croessmann Collection of James Joyce, Special Collections/Morris Library, Southern Illinois University, Carbondale)

reached the point of his complete rejection of the ethos that surrounded him from birth. The narrative is careful to avoid the melodramatic technique of using a single momentous clash with the institutions that define the Irish society which Stephen inhabits—family, Church, and nation—to sensationalize his break. Rather, like a satellite gradually escaping the gravitational pull of a planet, over the course of the novel Stephen has come to a slow but profound awareness of his need to reject those forces. By chapter five that process is complete, and it serves as a coda to that struggle, recapping the transformation of Stephen's attitudes and clarifying his new perspectives personal, communal, and artistic.

The first instance of delineating his break comes through a recollection of conversations with his close friend Davin (the only character in the novel to call Stephen by the diminutive, Stevie). Stephen clearly feels great affection for his friend, but he can only dismiss the Nationalist ardor that consumes Davin, reminding his classmate of all of the instances of betrayal that have undermined Irish efforts at achieving independence. It is the easiest break for Stephen to make, for, since the Christmas dinner quarrel, the narrative has given no indication of any nationalist inclination in his character.

Before turning to Stephen's dismissal of other Irish institutions, we get a sample of the features of the new identity, that of an artist, that he has adopted. The narrative does this through an exchange in which Stephen pedantically expounds his laboriously constructed aesthetic theory to his

Figure 3.3 National Library, Dublin. (Courtesy of the Irish Tourist Board)

university classmate, **Vincent Lynch**, as they walk around the streets of Dublin. The section is full of the sententiousness and self-importance that has characterized Stephen's attitude at various points throughout the narrative, but, putting that pomposity aside, one can see that it illustrates the intense commitment that he has made to the life of the artist. While Lynch's laconic responses, fueled by a ragging hangover, help to lighten the tediousness of the moment, it is noteworthy that Stephen's commitment to art involves a dedication every bit as intense, and by the way equally as humorless, as any religious fervor that he had earlier experienced.

Following this episode, the narrative recounts a long and much more personal conversation that Stephen has with perhaps his closest university friend, Cranly. Over the course of their discussion, Stephen articulates his disenchantment with Ireland and with his life there frankly and passionately. As a form of counterargument, Cranly brings a mixture of sympathy, cynicism, expediency, and sentimentality to his responses. In the end, although his intentions seem to be the best, Cranly propounds a position antagonistic to artistic freedom, advising Stephen to adopt an approach that would lead to a life of accommodation and hypocrisy.

In a particularly poignant passage, Cranly argues for a course of action that would combine pragmatism with filial love. He urges Stephen to give lip service to Catholic beliefs and rituals, which Stephen's mother urges on him, simply to avoid conflict with the rest of society and to give comfort to May Dedalus. "Whatever else is unsure in this dunghill of a world a mother's love is not" (p. 213). (They are speaking specifically of making one's Easter Duty, a practice no longer enforced by the Church. It is an injunction to all Catholics under pain of committing a mortal sin to receive the sacraments of Confession and the Holy Eucharist at least once during the period from Ash Wednesday to Pentecost Sunday.) While Cranly acts only out of a practical sense of what would meliorate Stephen's life, the latter sees the profound danger of taking this counsel. He vehemently dismisses those suggestions as threats to his artistic soul every bit as profound as ones to his spiritual essence. For him, pretending to accept the authority of the institutions around him would be more damning to his nature than doing so sincerely.

Near the end of the chapter, Joyce introduces a final significant shift in his narrative's form. Stephen has determined to leave Ireland, and the narrative adopts a journal entry layout to record his impressions before departure. There is a measure of the grandiosity in these passages that one would expect from what the chapter has shown of Stephen's temperament, but there are also sincere expressions of commitment that demonstrate Stephen's complete engagement with his art. Further, the staccato presentation of events and ideas over a series of days suggestions the uproar in Stephen's mind as he gathers his resources—material, emotional, and imaginative—for what he expects to be a momentous break form the world that surrounded him as he grew to adulthood.

Alternative Readings—Two Views of the Christmas Dinner Scene in Chapter One

The Last Merry Christmas

Throughout the opening pages of *A Portrait of an Artist as a Young Man* the narrative punctuates a relatively settled inner life of the young Stephen Dedalus with instances of the turmoil that surrounds him. The charmingly sentimental tale of the moocow and baby tuckoo is followed immediately by a violent scene in which Dante Riordan threatens the boy with hyperbolic punishment—"the eagles will come and pull out his eyes"—for a vaguely identified transgression. Then, Stephen's solipsistic world is shaken when he is sent off to Clongowes Wood College. There he must learn to contest his identity against those of other boys: "Rody Kickham was a decent fellow but Nasty Roche was a stink" (p. 6). He must begin to comprehend new hierarchies: "His mother had told him not to speak with the rough boys in the college" (p. 7). And to begin to reconsider how he understands the environment that surrounds him: "All the boys seemed to him very strange" (p. 11).

However, the first real threat to Stephen's complacent view of an orderly, nurturing world comes during his holiday visit home, an event in the narrative called the Christmas Dinner scene. It begins with the usual sentimental descriptions of the ritual celebration. Then, in a relatively short time, old animosities resurface challenging Stephen's assumptions about the world. The tipping point comes when anticlerical remarks by Simon Dedalus and

Mr. Casey are sharply challenged by Dante. The dispute is over the response to the Parnell divorce case that set many Catholics at odds with one another. Dante defends the right of priests to censor an adulterer. Simon Dedalus and Mr. Casey vehemently condemn the Church's interference in political matters. Predictably, the dinner ends in a shambles.

In the process, young Stephen sees that the seemingly unshakeable institutions of Family and Nation are more complex and contain a measure of contradiction heretofore unknown to him. The dispute over nationalism is perplexing to Stephen since he knows that Dante as much as his father and Mr. Casey ardently supports it. The possibility that men for whom he has great respect can so harshly criticize the clergy, for whom he was taught to have great respect as well, is equally unsettling.

More to the point, the Christmas Dinner scene introduces the topic that will dominate the narrative of the novel: the inability of social institutions to offer true nourishment to an independent mind. Of course, a single incident does not cause Stephen to lose his faith in Family, Church, or Nation. However, it does introduce the conception that no institution merits blind allegiance and that some in fact have detrimental effects on individuals.

Masterfully, the narrative does not record Stephen's reaction to this imbroglio beyond noting "his terrorstricken face." Readers know that he is present at the dinner table, and they are already aware of his childish loyalty to each of the institutions criticized and defended during the argument. By not articulating, at least not beyond his initial shock, exactly how Stephen responds, the narrative pulls readers into the interpretive process, forcing each to come to a conclusion that will in turn shape how the reader sees Stephen over the course of the narrative

The Hidden Narratives at Christmas

Stephen Dedalus's first Christmas dinner with adults is an initiation into a world that ends with a "terrorstricken" expression on his face. Ironically, celebrating the birth of the Prince of Peace in the Dedalus household becomes the setting of a bitter disagreement over politics and religion. The heated quarrel disrupts the joyfulness that an occasion such as Christmas should inspire and gives credence to Freud's insight that arguments are of no avail against the passions. Passions run high between Simon Dedalus and John Casey on the one hand and Mrs. Riordan (Dante) on the other. Though in certain passages of this Dinner scene the narrative voice reflects a genuine tenderness toward the young Stephen, it also seems deliberately impartial in presenting two antagonistic attitudes toward nation and church. However readers may judge or side with these irreconcilable positions, the narrative matter-of-factly reflects the emotionally charged attitudes surrounding opposing views in a colonized country seeking Home Rule. Mrs. Dedalus's plea to refrain from a "political discussion on this day of all days of the year" (p. 27) goes unheeded as the anger of the others at the dinner table escalates. For Mrs. Riordan, the authority of the church takes precedence over political independence from an oppressive foreign power: "'God and religion before everything!' Dante cried" (p. 34). But for Simon Dedalus and Mr. Casey, the authoritarian interference of the church's vitriolic opposition to Parnell, because of an adulterous affair, is as oppressive as a colonizing force.

Stephen witnesses this rancorous clash between his father's politics and Dante's defense of an authoritarian church, but the narrative does not directly indicate any emotional response in Stephen nor does it include his thoughts as it does earlier in the episode when he wonders why one of his teachers, Mr. Barrett, calls his pandybat a turkey and even earlier in the chapter when at Clongowes Stephen, thinking of politics, virtually anticipates the argument at Christmas. In ending the Christmas Dinner scene, the narrator observes that Stephen sees his father's eyes fill with tears and may expect the reader to fill in Stephen's doubts by recalling his thoughts at Clongowes as to which political position is correct. The narrator is very subtle here in foreshadowing Stephen's articulation of aesthetics and the growth of his artistic and personal temperament. The Christmas dinner reflects that process.

This foreshadowing occurs again in chapter two with the performance of the Whitsuntide play at Belvedere College. For the play to be performed in the chapel, the removal of the Blessed Sacrament from the tabernacle to a secluded place was mandatory, lest it be desecrated. The act of removing this central mystery and symbol of Catholic faith becomes in itself a symbol of art displacing religion. Including this fact early on in the narrative suggests Stephen's literary aesthetics in the last chapter of the novel where he contemplates an understanding of the artist as "a priest of eternal imagination" who transmutes "the daily bread of experience into the radiant body of everliving life" (p. 195).

Church/religion and state/nation may be in conflict with one another at the Christmas dinner, but for Stephen both together are in conflict with art. The oppressed nation of Ireland oppresses its artists; this nation, too, must be eclipsed by the artist to find freedom to write. "When the soul of a man is born in this country," Stephen explains to his nationalist classmate Davin, "there are nets flung at it to hold it back from flight. You talk to me of nationality, language, religion. I shall try to fly by those nets" (p. 203).

The Christmas dinner is one example of how the narrative provides more than just storyline information; its comments parallel other passages throughout the novel and intimate characteristics of Stephen's emerging identity and perception of literary aesthetics. This scene contains a tacit dimension of Stephen's evolution as artist.

Topics for Further Discussion

1. What do you think is the value of the shifting narrative perspectives in the novel?
2. What are its drawbacks?
3. Is Stephen Dedalus a sympathetic character?

4 Is he a heroic character?
5 Are the social, political, and cultural environments of *A Portrait of the Artist as a Young Man* comprehensible to contemporary readers?
6 Each chapter shows Stephen Dedalus at a different age. Does the narrative present convincing representations of him at each age?
7 Does a reader's opinion of Stephen change over the course of the novel?
8 Do elements in the narrative support the idea that James Joyce is angry with Irish society?
9 Is it possible to tell whether the novel offers an accurate representation of Ireland or of any modern society?
8 Is the end of the novel dissatisfying?
9 Is the novel coherent?
10 Is Stephen the only fully developed character?
11 Is the ending optimistic?

A Glossary of Characters

Father Arnall—the Jesuit priest who first appears in chapter one where he is Stephen's Latin teacher at Clongowes Wood College. In chapter three, he conducts the retreat that Stephen attends at Belvedere College.

John Casey—an Irish nationalist who had been imprisoned by the British and a friend of Simon Dedalus. In chapter one, he sides with Mr. Dedalus in a fierce argument with Dante Riordan over the treatment of Charles Stewart Parnell by the Catholic hierarchy. The Fenian John Kelly, a friend of Joyce's father, served as a model for this character.

Rev. John Conmee, S.J. (1847–1910)—an actual Jesuit priest and the rector of Clongowes Wood College from 1885–1891. In 1893 Father Conmee arranged for Joyce and his brother, Stanislaus, to attend Belvedere College on scholarships. Fictional versions of Father Conmee appear in both *A Portrait of the Artist as a Young Man* and *Ulysses*. In the former, Conmee intercedes for Stephen at Clongowes after the boy has been punished, and later, after the family's financial problems begin and Stephen leaves Clongowes, Conmee helps secure a scholarship for him at another Jesuit school, Belvedere College.

Cranly—Like Stephen, Cranly is a student at University College Dublin, and, in chapter five, Cranly critiques Stephen's views on family and Church, though he shows a highly cynical perspective in his observations. He is based on Joyce's university friend, John Francis Byrne.

Dante—see Dante Riordan.

Davin—a university classmate and close friend of Stephen Dedalus. His nature is antithetical to Stephen's. He is a nationalist, he comes from rural Ireland, and is a devout Catholic. The character is based on Joyce's University College Dublin friend, George Clancy, an ardent Nationalist. Clancy was

Mayor of Limerick during the Irish War of Independence and was murdered by members of the Royal Irish Constabulary Auxiliaries in 1921.

May Dedalus—Stephen's mother and the wife of Simon Dedalus. She is doubtlessly modeled on Joyce's mother, Mary Jane "May" Murray Joyce. Though the narrative does not present Mrs. Dedalus as an assertive personality, her love for Stephen has a strong influence on the boy's development. She is a pious Catholic, and her concern that Stephen make his Easter Duty—a requirement that all Catholics receive the Eucharist at least once a year during the Easter season, that is from Easter Sunday through Pentecost—provokes a deep crisis for both her and Stephen. (She dies before the action of *Ulysses* begins, but Stephen recalls her with tenderness and sorrow at several points in its narrative.)

Simon Dedalus—he appears in both *A Portrait of the Artist as a Young Man* and *Ulysses*. He is modeled on the author's own father, John Joyce, and emerges in the novel as the feckless, acerbic, witty, cynical, alcoholic father of Stephen. Early in *A Portrait of the Artist as a Young Man*, Simon's improvidence disrupts the security of the family, and his continued inability to provide financial or emotional support for the family leaves them materially and psychosocially impoverished. Stephen describes him to his friend Cranly as:

> A medical student, an oarsman, a tenor, an amateur actor, a shouting politician, a small landlord, a small investor, a drinker, a good fellow, a storyteller, somebody's secretary, something in a distillery, a taxgatherer, a bankrupt and at present a praiser of his own past.
>
> (p. 213)

In spite of Mr. Dedalus's failures, his volatile mood swings, his intolerant attitudes toward the Catholic Church, and his fanatical if superficial nationalism, he remains celebrated as an entertainer man with an acerbic sense of humor. His skill as a raconteur and his admirable tenor voice make him a delightful pub companion. His overall failure in life, despite an abundance of talent and blessed circumstances, suggest what could happen to Stephen were he not to break free of Ireland.

Stephen Dedalus—he is the central character of *A Portrait of the Artist as a Young Man* and an important figure in *Ulysses*. Joyce drew on many of the events in his own life to create Stephen's experiences in the novel. Certainly, Stephen's gradual disillusionment with the dominant Irish social institutions and his painstaking efforts to shape himself into an artist parallel many of the same conditions and efforts that informed Joyce's life. However, it would be a mistake for a reader to see Stephen as an autobiographical representation of the novel's author. It is unlikely that the young Joyce was a grim and devoid of humor as is Stephen, and certainly Joyce's capacity for irony was far better developed in his youth than is Stephen's. (This disparity seems to diminish a bit in *Ulysses*, where, particularly in the Proteus chapter, Stephen shows an ability to see himself in a detached and sardonic fashion.) The point is not so much the parallels between Joyce's experiences and Stephen's. Rather, Stephen's life from childhood to young adulthood reflects the tensions and challenges that any talented young Dubliner would encounter during the period of the novel, and as such it becomes a broad statement on the formation of any artistic identity.

Father Dolan—he is the heavy-handed prefect of studies at Clongowes Wood College. When he appears in chapter one, he seems to be acting as dean of discipline as well. Father Dolan unjustly pandies Stephen, striking the boy's hands with a leather strap in chapter one, accusing Stephen of purposely breaking his glasses to avoid studying. It is an important moment not so much for what happens in the pandying but for the way the unjustness of the act calls into question for a young Stephen the nurturing qualities that he had heretofore associated with the Church. His visit to Father Conmee, the rector, may seem to redress this injustice but the awareness of the imperfect perception of a representation of the Church can hardly be erased from Stephen's consciousness.) Joyce modeled the character on Father James Daly who was prefect of studies when Joyce was at Clongowes.

Vincent Heron—he appears in chapter two as both rival and friend of Stephen's at Belvedere College. Both boys are seen as class leaders, and initially Heron attempts to cow Stephen through bullying. Ultimately, Stephen earns Heron's respect, though Stephen while outwardly friendly never forgets his initial harsh treatment. Heron embodies the conventional attitudes of middle-class Catholic Dublin to which Stephen is becoming increasingly resistant.

Vincent Lynch—he is a student at University College Dublin. In chapter five Lynch, nursing a hangover, listens somewhat glumly as a sounding board for Stephen's exposition on aesthetics. Lynch's sardonic responses punctuate Stephen's disquisition disrupting the pedantic tone of his presentation in a clever stylistic gesture that presents the reader from becoming bored by the tedium of Stephen's earnest disquisition. Lynch appears in both *Stephen Hero* and *A Portrait of the Artist as a Young Man*. He is also seen in *Ulysses* where he is now a medical student. Joyce based Lynch on a Dublin friend, Vincent Cosgrave, who was equally feckless and ultimately vindictive toward Joyce.

Charles Steward Parnell—see his entry found at the end of the *Dubliners* chapter.

Dante Riordan—she appears in chapter one. Dante is a nickname, a corruption of Auntie, signifying familiarity and affection. She is based on Dante Hearn Conway, a Cork woman who came to the Joyce household in 1887 as a governess. Neither the real nor the fictional character is a biological relative, but each seems to have lived for a time with the family, possibly helping to care for the children. Dante shows herself to be a strict disciplinarian when first introduced in the narrative, and later, despite her ardent nationalism, during the Christmas Dinner in an argument with Simon Dedalus and Mr. Casey she staunchly defends the behavior of the Catholic clergy toward Charles Stewart Parnell. After a heated exchange, she stalks out of the room and disappears from the narrative. Her biographical model seems to have had a similar disagreement with John Joyce, and she too left the household shortly after the dispute occurred.

Mr. Tate—one of Stephen's teachers at Belvedere College. He first appears in chapter two where, at one point, his friendly teasing about the content of an essay unintentionally leaves Stephen vulnerable to being bullied by Vincent Heron and two other boys. Joyce based the character of Mr. Tate on that of George Dempsey, a man who taught Joyce English at Belvedere.

Uncle Charles—he is Stephen's elderly maternal granduncle. He is present at the Christmas Dinner scene in chapter one, but he says little. He appears again early in chapter two shepherding Stephen around Blackrock.

Charles Wells—he appears in chapter one as a classmate of Stephen's at Clongowes Wood College. He bullies Stephen by first embarrassing him over the question of kissing his mother and then pushes him into a pool behind the dormitory that causes Stephen to become ill. He also appears in *Stephen Hero* as a young seminarian who reminisces with Stephen about their time at Clongowes Wood.

Selected Annotations

Anderson, Chester G., ed. *A Portrait of the Artist as a Young Man: Text, Criticism, and Notes*. New York: Viking, 1968.

Gifford, Don, and Robert J. Seidman. *Joyce Annotated: Notes for **Dubliners** and **A Portrait of The Artist as a Young Man***. 1967; 2nd edition, Berkeley, Los Angeles and London: University of California Press, 1982.

4 Approaching *Ulysses*

Ulysses, Joyce's second published novel, is set in Dublin on a single day, 16 June 1904. From the moment of its publication, *Ulysses* was acclaimed as one of the most notorious novels to appear in the twentieth century. In 1922, there was no other work that could match its frankness. Even now, Joyce's novel stands as a shockingly direct discourse on the most intimate details of human thought and behavior.

The narrative of *Ulysses* contains a great many explicit descriptions of the most personal aspects of an individual's life. The recorded fantasies of the central characters match the most extravagant desires of any human, and descriptions of ordinary, if highly personal, bodily functions—defecation, urination, masturbation, fornication, and menstruation—are represented without euphemism or apology. The novel uses a complex narrative form—stream of consciousness—that builds on styles like free indirect discourse that introduced in Joyce's earlier fiction, and the overall narrative form provides readers with intimate, unfiltered glimpses into characters' natures heretofore absent in literature. Extravagant in its allusive detail, *Ulysses* provides a wide-ranging picture of middle class, urban life at the turn of the last century.

Joyce began work on *Ulysses* in late 1914 or early 1915. By June of 1915, he had drafted the outline of the novel and had written several chapters. World War I disrupted Joyce's writing. Because of his British passport the Austro-Hungarian authorities expelled him and his family from Trieste on 28th June. They journeyed to neutral Zurich where, between 1915 and 1919, much of *Ulysses* was written. Unfortunately, the high cost of living in post-war Zurich proved too much for the family's strained resources.

Seeking some relief, the Joyces briefly returned to Trieste to stay with his brother Stanislaus. Unsurprisingly, Joyce found it difficult to continue work on his novel in Stanislaus' crowded apartment, and, at the invitation of Ezra Pound, the family moved to Paris in 1920 with the plan to remain there only until *Ulysses* was completed. They stayed for the next 20 years, and Joyce not only finished *Ulysses* in Paris but also wrote *Finnegans Wake* there.

Ezra Pound's enthusiasm for Joyce and his novel convinced Margret Anderson to begin a serialization of *Ulysses* in the American journal she had founded with the help of Pound and Jane Heap, the *Little Review*. Fourteen chapters—from Telemachus to the first part of Oxen of the Sun—were

DOI: 10.4324/9781003223290-5

Figure 4.1 Slipcase and front wrapper for the first edition of *Ulysses*. (Philip Lyman, Gotham Book Mart)

published from March 1918 through September–December 1920. The final scheduled issue was suppressed by the United States Post Office on charges of obscenity. (In February of 1921 Anderson and her coeditor Jane Heap were fined $50 each and prohibited from publishing further episodes.)

Pound also was instrumental in getting portions—Nestor, Proteus, Hades, and parts of The Wandering Rocks—published in the English journal *The Egoist*. That journal endured many of the same criticisms that the *Little Review* faced. Nonetheless, the journal's founder, Harriet Shaw Weaver, would have continued serialization of Joyce's novel, but finding an English printer willing to take on the job proved ultimately to be an insurmountable task to a large degree because by English law printers were as liable to prosecution over the contents of works they produced as were publishers and authors.

These censorship problems presaged the difficulties that Joyce would face when he attempted to bring out the full novel. As was the case with *Dubliners* and *A Portrait of the Artist as a Young Man*, English printers refused to take it on, specifically fearing that they would be vulnerable to prosecution for disseminating obscenity. In 1921, when Joyce was on the point of abandoning his project, publishing help came from an unanticipated source. Sylvia Beach, an American expatriate running a Parisian bookshop, Shakespeare & Company, offered to bring out the novel through her bookshop. Beach fount a printer in Dijon, Maurice Darantiere, who not only agreed to print the work but willingly provided Joyce with multiple galley proofs so that he could continue revising and expanding his work. He did so almost to the day of its publication, his fortieth birthday, 2 February 1922, increasing the length of the work by nearly one third. Although early editions of the novel were difficult to procure, *Ulysses* has never gone out of print, and it remains essential reading both in literature courses and among members of the general public fascinated by its powerful writing.

Key Issues

As noted above, Joyce set his novel in Dublin on a single day, 16 June 1904, between 8 a.m. in the morning and about 3 a.m. on the following morning. It contains many of the same characters who appeared in *Dubliners* and *A Portrait of the Artist as a Young Man*, and it introduces a range of other individuals with attitudes, experiences, and problems similar to those who appeared in Joyce's earlier works. *Ulysses* also replicates the main features of the communal environment of the other novels, but the narrative goes into far greater detail in its descriptions of the quotidian rhythms of the characters' lives.

This returned to the examination of the issues and themes that dominated his earlier writings can hardly be surprising. The Dublin from which Joyce emerged when he left Ireland in 1904 remained at the center of his imaginative consciousness for his entire life, a world preserved with a mixture of nostalgia and rancor. Nonetheless, the attitudes that he adopts in *Ulysses* toward these topics bear strikingly different from the feelings represented his earlier works. It sounds a much less optimistic note. While it dismisses the authority and even the legitimacy of social institutions, it presents an ambivalent attitude regarding the redemptive possibilities for the individual nature. Indeed, some readers see it moving from the Modernism of the previous novel to suggests a tendency toward a post-Modernist view of life as a material, arbitrary existence and nothing more. (There is by no means a consensus on this issue, but the varying responses amply illustrate the rich interpretive opportunities of Joyce's writing.)

In any case, *Identity* definitively remains a central narrative concern within the narrative. Unlike **Stephen Dedalus** in *A Portrait of the Artist as a Young Man*, the novel's central figures—Stephen, **Leopold Bloom**, and **Molly Bloom**—have fully formed personalities. However, their worlds are in much greater flux and their degrees of self-awareness remain in each case an issue for readers to resolve.

Stephen seems to have fully embraced his impulse toward a complex detachment from the Irish milieu that he had been moving toward in the previous novel. He has already rejected traditional Irish institutions while growing to maturity, and now he endeavors to sustain his self-created conception as an artist through an aloof engagement with the world around him. Intensely revealing accounts of his relentless personal evaluation show that he does not seem fully confident that he has a sense of what it means to be an artist. Nonetheless, the narrative reiterates his commitment to achieving it, while leaving readers to determine his degree of success.

Bloom is both ambivalent toward his Jewish heritage and at the same time acutely conscious of how it constantly sets him apart in the eyes of other Dubliners. Despite repeated instances of marginalization coming out of the perception of Bloom as Other, he very much wants to see himself accepted and defined by the ethos of Dublin institutions. In consequence, he strives continually though not always successfully, to assert his right to a place there. At the same time, despite his relentless move toward integration into the Irish ethos, at moments of reflection he presents a deeply pessimistic view of the overall purpose of life and of his own ability to achieve happiness.

Early in the narrative Molly's world view may seem far less complex than that of either Stephen or Bloom. However, that comes in large part from secondhand evidence: the sneering one sided perspectives of her character offered by various Dublin men. In fact, in the long final chapter dominated by her consciousness, she displays a variety of attitudes that challenge the reader to create a unified impression of her.

There, Molly shows a nature driven by narcissistic inclinations but simultaneously frequently undermined by insecurity. She combines this inner turmoil with a passive–aggressive relationship with the Irish environment and with her perceived place in it. She has a Spanish mother and has spent over half of her life outside Ireland, yet she identifies herself as an Irish woman, a view also held by most other Dubliners who know her. At the same time, she finds many of the roles imposed upon her as a consequence difficult to accept. Like Emma Bovary, she is a bored housewife seeking release through adultery, but Boylan provides diversion rather than satisfaction, and by the novel's conclusion Molly seems to reject a life with him in favor of conventional domesticity with Bloom.

Although chapter five of *A Portrait of the Artist as a Young Man* suggested that Stephen had resolved all his issues with the concept of *Family*, the trauma of his mother's death has called his resolution into question. He feels profoundly guilty over not doing more to easy her mind during her final days, specifically for refusing an uncle's command to pray at her bedside. He also experiences conflicted ambivalence over the suffering of his siblings, apparent when he meets his sister, Dilly, at a quayside bookstall in chapter eleven, Wandering Rocks. Ultimately, he rejects the possibility of doing anything significant to help her or the others and privileges his artistic ambitions. At the same time he cannot simply ignore the impact of his family on his nature, for throughout the narrative, he is both threatened and overwhelmed by the personality of his father, a man equally noted for his wit and financial failure who stands as a grim model for what Stephen might become should he fail as an artist.

Family relationships also have a profound effect upon Bloom's identity. He deeply grieves over the loss of his father, **Rudolph Bloom**, by suicide and for the death of his young son, **Rudy Bloom,** 11 days after childbirth. He has fond memories of the childhood of his daughter, **Milly Bloom**, now living away from home in Mullingar, and he feels deep concern, as well as a sense of powerlessness, over evidence of her growing sexuality. He is also unsettled by suspicions that Molly and **Blazes Boylan**, an advertising agent and a local empresario are about to cuckold him. These feelings are further complicated by his mildly salacious expostulatory dalliance with **Martha Clifford**. Nonetheless, the narrative makes clear Bloom's sense of self is linked to his devotion to Molly, Milly, the memory of Rudy, and to a conventional family life.

Molly's views, detailed in the final chapter, prove less easy to discern or evaluate. The death of Rudy has touched her as deeply as it has Bloom, and their consequent emotional scars have isolated them both rather than led to mutual consolation. The friction she has felt in her relationship with Milly further attenuated whatever familial ties she had. It is challenging to discern what perception of family Molly retains, and the incipient affair with Blazes Boylan only complicates such an assessment.

Joyce brings another key thematic element from the narrative of *A Portrait of the Artist as a Young Man* into the discourse of *Ulysses*, *Religion*. Although its significance in the narrative comes largely from habitual, social concerns rather than theological positions, it nonetheless plays a defining role in the lives of many characters in *Ulysses*. Representations of religion in the novel do not focus the individual's struggle over belief in God, resistance to Church authority, or conformity to Catholic liturgy. In *Ulysses*, religion functions as a demographic marker rather than as an anchor of faith. Sectarian affiliation sets up specific expectations, both communal and personal, not so much about what one believes theologically but rather about what mores condition one's views of the world. Despite this secularized application, religion remains an important feature in the lives of Joyce's Dubliners.

The Church has social rather than spiritual ramifications for many of the characters in *Ulysses*. Catholicism identifies certain social attitudes and often highlights particular economic classes. The same is true for Protestantism. Equally, Judaism, for the Dubliners in the novel, stands less as a faith than as the category of Other. No matter how much an individual like Leopold Bloom has striven for assimilation, being recognized and then categorized as a Jew puts him automatically outside the bulk of society, and, as the narrative illustrates in multiple instances, it leaves him open to a range of indignities.

As it does with *Religion*, the narrative presents *Nationalism* as a means of social differentiation rather than as a reflection of a genuine commitment to any particular political philosophy. Its various manifestations emerge throughout the novel on the nature of being Irish and on who has the right to claim that designation. In the Hades episode, with a perfunctory visit to the grave of Parnell after Paddy Dignam's funeral, there are clear reminders of the self-satisfied and self-absorbed chauvinism so evident in "Ivy Day in the Committee Room." At the same time, particularly in the Cyclops chapter, readers see evidence of nationalism having degenerated into little more than a pose with scant evidence of the genuine patriotic feeling. Indeed, for most Dubliners nationalism proves to be not so much a philosophic belief as a tool for promoting clannishness and ostracizing fellow citizens like Bloom who seem averse to the embracing the tenets of their tribal mentality.

The determined frankness and unabashed intimacy of the novel's narrative makes *Sexuality* an inevitable topic. Graphic examples of copulation, masturbation, and other sexual activity abound. Sexual fantasies of all varieties fill the minds of a range of characters. Adultery, casual sex, and cherished memories of physical intimacy are stimuli that inform senses of individual characters and shape our understanding of them. These cumulative depictions of sexuality show readers that the ethos of the novel spurns judgment of human behavior and acknowledges a wealth of powerful appetites.

Perhaps the most arresting and least ambiguous issue taken up in the narrative is the depiction of *Anti-Semitism*. There can be no delusion in *Ulysses* as to the breadth and intensity of anti-Semitism. Casual anti-Semitic remarks punctuate the novel. They dog Bloom as he traverses the city over the course of the day, and in the Cyclops chapter gives vent to the deepest hatreds while offering Bloom a fleeting opportunity to defy such virulent slanders. The challenge for readers is to see this abhorrent bigotry as what it is rather than to incline oneself to mitigate its worst expressions with the thought that such views were more permissible at the time of the novel. While that may well be the case, readers who ignore the fundamental corrosiveness that Joyce's narrative reveals will seriously impair their understanding of the novel.

Style

Although *Ulysses* experiments with a range of styles, the most often discussed formal achievement of Joyce's novel is his use of *Stream of Consciousness*, an unvoiced account of personal impressions arranged without concern for presenting observations as complete thoughts or for establishing clear links from one reaction to another. Without prelude, the form plunges readers into the uncensored thoughts of various characters—primarily Stephen and Bloom but on occasion others—offering fragmentary insights into their innermost feelings.

Unlike other writers who give some attention to grammatical coherence (Virginia Woolf is a prime example), Joyce's stream of consciousness unfolds in a fashion that evokes the usual patterns of personal, unspoken reflections: without any effort at contextualization; free of transitions; often without syntactic or grammatical mediation. Joyce's approach provides an intimate look into the mind of a character without the social filters of direct discourse and with more authenticity than third person evocation of an individual's feelings. Its abruptness is a challenge, initially at least, to any reader, but the consistency of the form for each character and the inevitability of a reader's growing sense of the individual's biographical facts make it increasingly accessible.

The narrative also continues to use forms that Joyce had perfected in earlier writings, *Free Indirect Discourse*. For some, stream of consciousness can seem to overshadow it, but it is a form equally important to advancing the narrative. Unlike its use in *Dubliners* or in *A Portrait of the Artist as in Young Man*, in *Ulysses* the narrative employs free indirect discourse in an expanded format that covers a broad range of characters and greatly enhances our sense of each figure in a subtle but effective form.

Joyce showed time and again a willingness to break from stylistic expectations and to trust his readers to follow his experimentation. In a seemingly straightforward fashion, Joyce makes *Episodic Narration* a complex and innovative form, going well beyond earlier efforts. Although linearity seems at the core of a narrative that moves progressively through the day, a closer examination with these episodic features in mind shows incredible flexibility with which Joyce endowed it.

Ulysses does and does not take place from 8 a.m. on the morning of 16th June to around 3 a.m. the next day, for after the first three chapters from eight to 11 a.m. it doubles back and begins again at 8 a.m. Though it does generally proceed methodically from one hour to the next over the course of the day, each chapter is a unique episode without transition or even clear links to the preceding chapter: Stephen appears on Sandymount Strand miles in Proteus away from Deasy's school where he was at the end of Nestor; in Hades Bloom steps into a carriage in front of Paddy Dignam's house sited across the river from the bathhouse he planned to enter at the close of Lotus Eaters; in the Lestrygonians chapter Bloom recalls bits of conversation with Molly that did not appear in the narrative in Calypso. This all concentrates the reader's attention and compels one to participate more closely in the creation of meaning by filling in the blanks.

Even with all these other stylistic innovations, *Chapter Structures* seem to represent the most insistent example of Joyce's approach to narrative experimentation. Despite the often-disorienting stream of consciousness discourses challenging reader's expectations, the relatively straightforward structures of the first six episodes offer familiar grounding for interpretations. That form changes abruptly and almost continuously in the subsequent chapters.

While on one level the discourse of Aeolus appears to move forward through conventional linear, its unexplained and to a degree unacknowledged headings insistently disrupt efforts to enforce a traditional form. Chapters like Scylla and Charybdis and Sirens offer self-contained moments when the narration seems to go in a different direction as the style of one shifts and the narrative reliability of the other falters. The Cyclops episode challenges readers with lengthy interpolations imbedded in the narrative, making them even more arresting and disconcerting than those which appeared in Aeolus. Nausikaa has a radical shift in narrative with the voice of the first half of the chapter seemingly mimicking the tone of a woman's magazine, and then the tone of the second half coarsening into a very different voice that delves into the brutal side of Bloom's consciousness. Oxen of the Sun offers a tour de force of English literary styles from Roman times to the nineteenth century, giving readers a rigorous and often frustrating view of the evolution of a national literature. Circe's dramatic layout heightens its performative qualities, and the questions and answer format of Ithaca underscores the tedium of sustaining late-night conversations. Molly's flowing monologue in Penelope matches layout with personality and provides a capstone for the diverse chapter formulations throughout the novel.

In perhaps the most subtle stylistic feature, given the striking forms of the other innovations, the narrative cultivates that same impulse for interpretive diversity seen in Joyce's earlier fiction through its widespread use of *Incertitude*. In what has become a familiar challenge to readers of the previous works, many moments in the narrative demand the intervention of the reader to supply an explanation or interpretation of the event. Stephen's discussion of belief with **Haines** in the Telemachus chapter, for example, through a wonderful combination of wordplay and ambiguity gives readers no more definitive idea of his views than that Haines discerns. Bloom's apparent masochistic tendencies in Circe may or may not be the result of hallucinations. And perhaps most famously, Molly's yes in the final lines of the Penelope chapter may just as easily mean no. All this is left to readers to resolve, and their determinations often change with each new reading.

An Overview of the Chapters

As noted above, the events chronicled in *Ulysses* cover a single Dublin day. The narrative is organized around 18 chapters, distributed through three sections: Chapters one to three, informally known as the Telemachiad, highlight Stephen's domestic, public, and inner lives. Chapters four to fifteen, commonly called the Wanderings of Ulysses, emphasizing in greater details elements of Bloom's domestic, public, and inner lives while also presenting recurring appearances by Stephen that elaborate on reader's impressions from the first three chapters. And Chapters sixteen to eighteen, dubbed Homecoming, present readers with final aspects of the natures of Stephen, Bloom, and Molly.

Throughout the composition process, Joyce referred to separate chapters by names he took from the *Odyssey*. Although he chose not to include them in the published version, they have become handy designations for readers and are reproduced below with brief explanations of their origins as part of the chapter summaries.

I. Telemachus—refers to the son of Odysseus who opens the *Odyssey* with a resolution to find out what happened to his father who, ten years after the fall of Troy, has still not returned to Ithaca.

The day begins at 8 a.m. in a Martello Tower at Sandycove, just south of Dublin. (The tower is one of a series of coastal fortifications built by the British during the Napoleonic wars to guard against a possible French invasion of Ireland.) The narrative account offers a glimpse into Stephen's chaotic domestic arrangements, but more significantly it foregrounds two attitudes that will dominate his consciousness throughout the novel: guilt over his mother's death and an ambivalence about his artistic identity.

As they prepare for the day, Stephen and **Buck Mulligan** exchange witticisms on art and aesthetics while at the top of the towering looking out

Figure 4.2 Sandycove where the Martello Tower is located. (Courtesy of the Irish Tourist Board)

on Dublin Bay. Mulligan ostentatiously demonstrates his cleverness by using a shaving bowl to a parody of the act of consecration at the Catholic Mass and by a series of patronizing remarks about taking Stephen in hand. The still sleepy Stephen replies somewhat sullenly but with subtler wit. (He uses the term "cracked looking glass of a servant" in a way that earns Mulligan's admiration, but it also shows that Mulligan has missed the point that Stephen has borrowed it from Oscar Wilde.)

As the conversation unfolds, it introduces the competitiveness that punctuates their relationship throughout the narrative. It also makes apparent the public roles they have chosen to play. Stephen clearly wants to be taken seriously as an artist. Mulligan is more concerned with being well-regarded as an entertainer.

After being caught in a particularly insensitive remark, Mulligan defensively brings up the commonness of deaths like that of May Dedalus and offers a clumsy apology as a way of covering his own thoughtlessness. Although Stephen dismisses this by speaking of the offense given to him, his thoughts reveal the ongoing sorrow he feels over his mother's death and the guilt that lingers over his unwillingness to please her by praying at her deathbed.

The pair's deft exchanges are balanced by slapstick when the narrative introduces of their houseguest, Haines, the English friend of Mulligan. Haines' fatuous lack of full comprehension of almost everything that is said serves as an ironic foil for the wit of the two others over breakfast. Afterwards, when trying to engage Stephen on matters of belief, Haines slips into an English type, the uncomprehending colonizer whose view of Ireland proves to be too literal to comprehend the complexities of Stephen's response: "You behold in me ... a horrible example of free thought" (1.625–626). The scene ends at "the Forty-foot Hole," a swimming area near the tower. As Stephen leaves, the last word in the chapter is "Usurper" (1.744), leaving the reader to determine who uttered it—Stephen or the narrator—and to whom it applies—Buck, Haines, or Stephen.

II. <u>Nestor</u>—a man reputed to be the wisest of the Greeks fighting before Troy. Telemachus visits Nestor to seek his guidance while searching for Odysseus.

The episode introduces Stephen's public world. It opens at around 9 a.m. with a view of him as a teacher attempting to conduct an unruly class at a boy's school in Bray. During a history lesson, he exerts minimal control over his class, and expresses unvoiced envy over their smugly comfortable social conditions. Their lack of interest is paralleled by Stephen's own restiveness.

After the class has been dismissed, Stephen remains in the classroom to try to help one of his struggling students, Cyril Sargent. The young boy, who seems helpless and alienated, reminds Stephen of himself at Clongowes Wood, although for the careful reader the differences between the natures of the teacher and student are far greater than any similarities. Sargent lacks Stephen's wit and intelligence, and the loneliness Stephen felt as a young student was a transitory adjustment while Sargent's sense of isolation seems imbued in his nature.

After ending his ineffectual efforts to enlighten Sargent, Stephen goes to the office of his pompous employer, the school's headmaster Garett Deasy. Classes are only in session for a half-day on Thursdays, and Stephen means to collect his salary before leaving. Deasy, however, uses the occasion to hector Stephen on a range of topics all designed to reinforce the old man's smug sense of self-satisfaction.

After paying Stephen, Deasy launches into a pompous, digressive lecture about personal economy, Irish history, and the depravity of the Jews, getting his fact wrong more often than not but ploughing ahead with little concern for accuracy or audience. The tactless headmaster makes clear that he feels Stephen is ill-suited to his teaching post. At the same time, he shows no hesitation in imposing on Stephen to use his influence to get a letter that Deasy has written on the dangers of cattle disease published in one of the Dublin newspapers.

Stephen leaves unvoiced most of his objections to Deasy's appalling views. Nonetheless, although Joyce seemingly allows the old man's final words to go unchallenged, their blunt and unashamed bigotry cannot fail to appall readers or to underscore Deasy's self-satisfied bias. He wrongly claims that Ireland "has the honour of being the only country which never persecuted the Jews," and compounds the offensiveness with the equally false punchline "she never let them in" (2.442).

III. Proteus—is the shape changing god of rivers and oceans who would transform himself into a variety of creatures and objects as a way of avoiding answering questions. After the sack of Troy, Menelaus captured Proteus and, by retaining his grip no matter what shape the god took, Menelaus compelled Proteus to reveal how to placate the gods and so be allowed to return home.

The chapter begins a bit after ten o'clock with Stephen walking along the beach on Sandymount Strand, a spot just below the River Liffey and eight miles north of Deasy's school. (The narrative offers no explanation regarding how Stephen traveled there in such a relatively short time. However, it seems likely that he must have gone by tram.) Stephen is thinking about approaches to aesthetics, about the mechanics of the artistic process, and about what a range of philosophers have said about perception and existence. While these topics call to mind those that Stephen addressed in his discussion of art with Lynch in Chapter 5 of *A Portrait of the Artist as a Young Man*, his tone is much less strident and more inquiring. He now seems to have sufficient confidence to admit what he does not know as well as to elaborate on what he feels he can understand.

This change in tone becomes even more apparent as he thinks of his own artistic ambitions. Mocking his intensity and pretentiousness, Stephen, at least in his own mind, shows an ability to laugh at himself in a way that was impossible in the previous novel. "You bowed to yourself in the mirror, stepping forward to applause earnestly, striking face. Hurray for the Goddamned idiot" (3.138).

Joyce punctuates these ruminations on fame with examples of Stephen's developing talent. As he nears Strasbourg Terrace, his thoughts turn to stopping to visit his Aunt Sally and Uncle Richie Goulding. The description of his approach to the house and his seeming interaction with his uncle unfolds with such skill that it comes as a surprise to readers a few pages later when Stephen reveals that he has walked past his aunt and uncle's home and the account was generated completely from his imagination.

As he continues to walk, Stephen's mind moves easily to evocative recollections of his time in Paris. He gives a lively description of Paris street life, and he offers a moving account of his meeting with the Irish political exile **Kevin Egan**. As he goes further along the beach, Stephen is frightened by the sudden appearance of a dog belonging to two cockle pickers, and them makes a furtive effort to capture a line of poetry that has just come to him by tearing off the bottom of the letter that Deasy has given to him. The fragment has a derivative tone of second-rate verse and underscores for readers the idea that, while he has shown himself more adept at prose narratives, Stephen still has not come to a clear sense of where is artistic talents lie.

IV. Calypso—the nymph who lived on the island of Ogygia where she detained Odysseus for seven years. At the intercession of Athena, Zeus compels Calypso to allow Odysseus to leave the island to return to Ithaca.

The narrative moves backwards to 8 a.m., restarting its discourse from the perspective of Leopold Bloom and giving readers a sense of his domestic life.

92 *Approaching* Ulysses

The Blooms live on the northside of Dublin at No. 7 Eccles St., at nearly the opposite end of the metropolitan area from Stephen's residence in the Martello Tower in Bray. As the chapter begins, Bloom, an ad canvasser for *The Freeman's Journal*, is making breakfast for himself and his wife before he attends the funeral of a friend, **Paddy Dignam**.

Figure 4.3 Leopold Bloom by Paul Joyce. (Courtesy of Paul Joyce)

Figure 4.4 A painting, by Flora H. Mitchell, of 7 Eccles Street, the address of Leopold and Molly Bloom in *Ulysses* (Courtesy of the Croessman Collection of James Joyce, Special Collections/Morris Library, Southern Illinois University)

The episode touches on a number of features in Bloom's nature. Most prominently it reveals his uxoriousness in the way he dotes upon Molly. It shows him serving his wife breakfast in bed, picking up her underclothing, and getting instructions about the books she wishes to him to acquire for her reading. Bloom can be pompous and patronizing when speaking to Molly, but she takes no notice—"O, rocks. Tell us in plain words" (4.343)—and retains control over even the most minor of tasks—telling him to "scald the pot" (4.270) when he goes off to make tea.

At the same time it shows Bloom's obsequiousness toward Molly, from the opening lines the discourse underscores his sensuality: "Mr. Leopold Bloom ate with relish the inner organs of beasts and fowls" (4.1–2). And, over the remainder of the chapter, its discourse offers numerous instances of the sensuousness that dominates his inner thoughts. Throughout the episode his mind returns to Molly's desirability and to moments of their intimacy. At the same time, while waiting to be served at the butcher shop, he cannot resist leering at the maid from next door and fantasizing about her sex life. Bloom is both a man of appetites, yet one who remains cautious about their pursuit.

Bloom's thoughts are by no means completely self-centered. The morning mail, with a letter from his daughter **Milly Bloom** to him and one from Blazes Boylan to Molly, turns his thoughts to the sexuality of both, incipient in Milly and rampant in Molly. Casual remarks in Milly's letter brings him concern about the growing sexual precociousness of his fifteen-year-old daughter. The "bold hand" of Boylan's letter introduces in Bloom's mind suspicions, quickly suppressed, of Boylan's intention to lead Molly to commit adultery. (Throughout the day, Bloom will repeatedly suppress any references to Molly's afternoon meeting with Boylan and its consequences.) Nonetheless, despite a desire to ignore all the signs before him, Bloom, in both instances, also acknowledges the inevitability of his fears being recognized and of his helplessness to intervene. "Will happen, yes. Prevent. Useless: can't move" (4.447–448).

The chapter closes with a scene that has become infamous (to the point of shocking the normally iconoclastic Ezra Pound into reproving Joyce for its graphic nature). Bloom repairs to an outdoor privy located in his back garden. Once there, the narrative gives a graphic account of his defecation that concludes with Bloom tearing off a piece of paper from a story he has been reading to use to wipe himself. The matter-of-fact manner of the passage signals that no human behavior is off-limits and that ordinary personal activities, no matter how intimate, are going to be treated as nothing more than that.

V. Lotus Eaters—are a race living on an island filled with lotus trees whose flowers they happily consume. Its narcotic effect puts the natives in perpetual state of lethargic euphoria. When Odysseus' crew visit the island, his men too become intoxicated by the lotus flowers and lose all desire to return to Ithaca. Ultimately, Odysseus has to use force to compel them to leave the island.

In this episode, which begins around 10 a.m., Bloom walks around central Dublin. He is running various errands to help him to kill time until he must go to Dignam's funeral in Irishtown. In a soporific fashion, it offers insights into Bloom's private life, just as chapter three has presented a sense of Stephen's personal world through his musings on Sandymount Strand.

Bloom first calls at the Westland Row Post Office, situated south of the River Liffey behind Trinity College. There, using the pseudonym **Henry Flower,** he collects a letter from **Martha Clifford**, a young woman with whom he has undertaken a clandestine and increasingly sensational correspondence. It is clear from his reaction to what Martha has written that he takes pleasure from these epistolary exchanges, but it is also unmistakably evident that he will continue to resist Martha's growing efforts to take the relationship further despite her knowing that Bloom is married.

As he leaves the post office, Bloom runs into **C.P. M'Coy,** an acquaintance whose transient employment history roughly parallels Bloom's and who has a wife who, like Molly, is an aspiring singer. Despite these superficial similarities, the narrative highlights differences in the natures of the two men, noting in passing how M'Coy has earned renown as a sponger and a chancer that is very different from the reputation that Bloom enjoys. Typically, Bloom remains cautious about revealing his feelings. Nonetheless, he mixes suspicion and contempt in his unvoiced response to M'Coy's blandishments. He is particularly wary when M'Coy's, who has a reputation for borrowing and then pawning luggage, begins to hint at requesting a similar loan from Bloom.

After M'Coy leaves, Bloom furtively reads Martha's letter, and then slips into the nearby All Hallows Catholic Church as Mass there is coming to an end. He clearly is acting not out of piety but rather because he wants to find a place to sit quietly for a few minutes. As he rests, he uses to occasion to sneer at the concluding church service, dismissing what he sees as a combination of superstitious beliefs and bogus rituals. Nonetheless, from the factual errors embedded in his remarks, he clearly has no understanding of either Catholic theology or Church liturgy.

The final section of the chapter has Bloom visiting a chemist (druggist to Americans) to refill Molly's order for body lotion and, in anticipation of a cleansing visit a Turkish bath, to buy lemon soap for himself. On the way to the baths, he indulges once again the sensual side of his nature. In a passage that can easily be mistaken for a description of the event itself, Bloom thinks, in languorous anticipation, of the pleasure he will feel when he immerses himself in its soothing waters.

VI. Hades—the underworld region inhabited by the dead in Greek mythology. Odysseus visits Hades seeking guidance from Tiresias on how to return to Ithaca.

The chapter unfolds at around eleven o'clock and describes events surrounding the internment of Paddy Dignam, an acquaintance of Bloom, **Simon Dedalus**, **Martin Cunningham**, and other men in that group of mourners. It begins by relating conversations among the men during the trip of the funeral cortege between Dignam's Irishtown house on the south side of the city and Glasnevin cemetery at the north end, and then it describes the reactions of a range of men to Dignam's internment. As is often the case, the funeral service reminds many of the characters of other lost friends and loved ones. In Bloom's case his recollections underscore his love for those lost, but for others, as with Simon Dedalus' grief over his wife, the emotions excited are more accurately characterized as self-serving and melodramatic than as anything else.

The narrative begins in the close confinement of the funeral carriage in which Bloom rides with Martin Cunningham, **Jack Power**, and Simon Dedalus. Exchanges within this near claustrophobic space give the reader a good sense of Bloom's place in the community. Some critics have been quick to emphasize how isolated Bloom appears to be as the men's desultory conversation unfolds. Certainly, elements of condescension and even of anti-Semitism drift into these exchanges. However, it would be an oversimplification to see this as indicating that Bloom is an outsider. It is more accurately described as his having a lower place in the social pecking order than his more loquacious companions.

More broadly, one gets a clearer picture of the dynamics of Dublin social intercourse by observing the others' careless disregard for the reputations of those who are not present and how competitive they seem to be in their attempts to commandeer the conversation. For example, when Bloom points out Stephen Dedalus emerging from the beach after his walk on Sandymount Strand, Simon Dedalus quickly takes the opportunity to disparage Buck Mulligan for being a bad influence on his son.

When Martin Cunningham recognizes Blazes Boylan who is emerging from the Red Bank Restaurant (known for its oysters), most of the men in the carriage offer some sort of greeting. Bloom, whose painful awareness of what will occur later in the day can only have been enhanced by the association with the oyster's aphrodisiac qualities, says nothing, but instead he studiously considers his fingernails. Subsequently, and much to Bloom's further discomfort, the men discuss the upcoming concert tour in which Molly will participate with salacious references to Boylan's abilities as an organizer.

The appearance walking on the street of **Ruben J. Dodd**, a usurer who has lent money to many of the men in the carriage, provokes a torrent of abuse all around. Bloom tries to take brief control of the discourse by telling an amusing anecdote about Dodd's hapless son and a comical suicide attempt. However, he performs so maladroitly that even the mild-mannered Martin Cunningham loses patience and takes over the retelling, delivering the story's punchline with a flourish (which Simon Dedalus seeks to top) and ending with an oblique observation suggesting that the prudent Bloom is the only one present who has not fallen into Dodd's clutches.

Privately, Bloom's musings take a somber turn when he recalls the suicide of his father, **Rudolph**. Apparently not aware of the circumstances surrounding the death of Bloom's father, Jack Power makes a tactless remark about suicide, prompting Martin Cunningham hastily to change the subject. Bloom also thinks of the death, 11 days after birth, of his son **Rudy**, introducing a motif that will recur throughout the narrative and underscore an ongoing sorry in Bloom's life.

During Dignam's internment, just as he did at All Hollows Church, Bloom takes an extremely skeptical view of the liturgy as he watches the

Catholic burial rites. Although he is careful to restrain his public expressions, in his thoughts Bloom makes unmistakably clear his disdain for what he sees as superstitious convictions and hypocritical over-heated expressions of extreme grief. In a dispassionate fashion, he silently reaffirms his own sense that nothing exists after death. In the final moments of the chapter, as the mourners disburse, a gesture of courtesy by Bloom is gracelessly snubbed by **John Henry Menton,** a solicitor who seems to have at one time been interested in Molly.

VII. Aeolus—the god of the winds who attempts to help Odysseus return to Ithaca by harnessing gusts that would have an adverse effect on the voyage home. These efforts come to nothing, however, when members of Odysseus' crew, suspicious that their leader is withholding gifts that should have been shared, open the bag that Aeolus had given Odysseus and allow the winds to escape. When Odysseus asks the god to repeat the gesture, Aeolus, out of pique, refuses.

The episode is set around noon in the shared newspaper headquarters of the *Evening Telegraph* and *The Freeman's Journal*, where Bloom works as an ad canvasser. The office is filled with garrulous men, generally unemployed or under-employed, passing the time while speaking bombastically.

Those not particularly keen to join the performative conversations, like Simon Dedalus and **Ned Lambert** who have come after attending Paddy Dignam's funeral, leave relatively soon for a drink. Those with nothing better to do, like **Lenehan** and **Professor McHugh**, have wandered in during the course of the morning and compete for attention. Lenehan makes a futile effort to get the others to take interest in his tip for the Gold Cup Race and to laugh at a joke resting on a bad pun. McHugh gains some notice when he recalls a speech by John F. Taylor, though his rendition will seem pompous and heavy-handed to many readers.

Some of the individuals who visit the newspaper offices have more pragmatic aims. Bloom, Stephen, and **J.J. O'Molloy**, are seeking one thing or another from **Myles Crawford**, the editor of the *Evening Telegraph*. Bloom wishes help securing an ad from Alexander J. Keyes. Stephen has a request that Deasy's letter on foot and mouth disease be printed. And the impecunious Malloy wants a loan. All use their varying degrees of rhetorical skills to compete for attention with erratic success.

Like the others, Crawford too is eager to hold the center of attention. He recalls the exploits of Ignatius Gallagher in reporting on the infamous Phoenix Park political murders. As he exuberantly expounds on Gallagher's cleverness, he suggests that Stephen too could benefit from a career in journalism. Whatever chagrin Stephen may evince over such an offer goes unnoticed, for although it is only midday, Crawford already is demonstrably the worse for drink.

In the final section, Stephen proposes treating the remaining men to a drink, and they quickly join him. Walking along the pavement on the way to the pub, perhaps as a way to assert his artistic credentials, he recites to

McHugh and Crawford "A Pisgah Sight of Palestine or The Parable of the Plums" about two midwives taking an excursion to Nelson's Pillar. It is probably composed extemporaneously having been inspired by two old women whom he saw while he was walking on Sandymount Strand. Its ambivalent ending reflects the Modernist tendency to eschew closure, but that only produces bewilderment in the auditors.

An abrupt stylistic disruption runs through the chapter in the form of a series of headings in bold type that offer a range of comments on persons, places, and issues referenced in the episode. They appear with some insistency over the main narrative, and no effort is made to acknowledge them, identify their source, or integrate them into the rest of the discourse. (Like many of the novel's stylistic flourishes, critics have offered a number of explanations for the presence of the headings, but none has proven to be definitive.)

VIII. <u>Lestrygonians</u>—they are a race of man-eating giants. With the exception of the ship commanded by Odysseus, all of his fleet is trapped by Antiphates, king of the Lestrygonians. The ships are destroyed, and the crews are eaten.

The episode takes place around 1 p.m., the typical lunch hour in Dublin. Bloom has left *The Freemans Journal* offices, and as the chapter opens he is crossing O'Connell Bridge from the north side of the Liffey. While walking immediately south of the river, he runs into **Josie Breen**, a friend of Molly's, whose husband, **Denis Breen**, has maniacal tendencies and on this day has been the victim of a cruel practical joke. Breen has received an anonymous postcard with U.P.:up written on it, and this has sent him around Dublin searching for legal redress. (The phrase itself is never explained, though a number of critics have exhausted themselves with generating increasingly bizarre explanations.) Bloom and Mrs. Breen discuss the eccentricities of her husband and talk about a mutual acquaintance, **Mina Purefoy**, who is at the Holles Street Maternity Hospital awaiting the birth of her ninth child.

The conversation with Josie Breen makes Bloom think of a number of women in a variety of unhappy family situations, but, ever the man of appetites, his thoughts quickly turn to food. He walks past Trinity College toward Grafton Street searching for a place to eat. Though hungry, after a quick glance at the diners in the Burton restaurant on Duke Street, Bloom rejects the idea of lunching there when he sees that the men are eating like animals.

Bloom goes instead across the street to Davy Byrne's pub, and he orders a gorgonzola cheese sandwich and a glass of burgundy. While eating, he chats with an acquaintance, **Nosey Flynn**, and the bar owner, **Davy Byrne**. After he has gone out the back way to the toilet, Flynn and Byrne converse about Bloom's character and his devotion to his wife Molly. Their exchange shows readers that Bloom, though his temperate habits distinguish him from other Dubliners, has earned a measure of respect from many of the men who know him.

As Bloom leaves the pub he meets a **Blind Stripling**, a piano turner who will reappear later in the narrative, and Bloom helps the young man find the way to South Frederick Street. The episode ends with Bloom getting flustered when he sees Boylan in the distance. He crosses Kildare Street and ducks into the National Museum to avoid an encounter with the man who will later cuckold him.

IX. Scylla and Charybdis—the two names signal the twin threats, a six headed monster and a whirlpool, obstructing Odysseus' route as he sails on his way home to Ithaca. Odysseus does not reveal the danger to the rest of the crew, but, rather than risk the entire ship's destruction by the whirlpool, he knowingly sails away from it close to the outcrop where Scylla resides. As he does, the monster seizes and devours six of his men.

The episode unfolds at around 2 p.m. in the National Library of Ireland. Stephen Dedalus is holding forth, trying to impress a number of Dublin literati gathered in the chief librarian's office—**George Russell (AE), John Eglinton, Thomas Lyster**, and **Richard Best**—with the theory he has constructed about Shakespeare's creative process that Mulligan had previously mentioned in the Telemachus episode. In fact, it is more a demonstration of verbal dexterity than on the presentation of critical insights. Nonetheless, for Stephen, who has not been invited to a literary evening organized by George Moore to fete rising Dublin creative talents, this is an opportunity to demonstrate to some of arbiters of artistic taste that his rightful place should be in that company. The disquisition has echoes of Stephen's presentation of his aesthetic theory to Lynch in chapter five of *A Portrait of the Artist as a Young Man*, though its logic can be even more difficult for readers to follow. As the chapter opens Stephen is already in the midst of his presentation, and often in what follows he is compelled to digress to respond to questions and criticisms from various listeners.

Those efforts are not always successful, for time and again Russell and Eglinton show open hostility to the theme and do not hesitate to interrupt the presentation. Stephen's stream of consciousness shows that he is infuriated by their snide remarks. However, he attempts to respond to their criticisms with dignity that avoids giving offense. Midway through the talk, Buck Mulligan appears, and Stephen must contend with Mulligan's buffoonery as well as with the antagonism of the others.

In fact, the presentation does not so much offer new ideas as paraphrase the received views of others. Stephen's talk draws liberally from a number of well-known contemporary Shakespearean critics—most notably George Brandes, Frank Harris, and Sidney Lee. The resulting conglomeration is not so much a lucid argument as a synopsis of a wide-range knowledge of details relating to Shakespeares life and work.

Near the end of the chapter, Mulligan's bawdy wit intrudes. In an aside to Stephen, he mocks Eglinton with a vulgar poem on masturbation, and then he abruptly shifts his tone to advise Stephen to be more conciliatory and flattering: "Couldn't you do the Yeats touch?" (9.1162–1163). As they leave the library, he expresses the desire to write a play entitled Every Man His Own Wife, or a Honeymoon in the Hand. Stephen and Buck then pass Bloom on the Library steps, and Mulligan makes a whispered anti-Semitic remark continuing the theme of bias that has run through the narrative since the first chapter.

X. Wandering Rocks—a cluster of floating rocks surrounded by violent seas. Odysseus avoided them by sailing past Scylla and Charybdis.

The action of the chapter begins around 3 p.m. While the central characters—Stephen, Bloom, and Molly—make brief appearances, the bulk of the narrative's concern focuses episodically on 19 vignettes touching on the lives of some of the novel's minor characters. The episode jumps around the city and uses interpolations within its discreet segments to indicate the synchronicity of events.

In the opening section, **Father John Conmee** crosses the city on a mission to find a place for one of the sons of the late Paddy Dignam at the O'Brien Institute for Destitute Children. In the process we see a reflection of the harmless patronizing attitude that emerged in the first and second chapters of *A Portrait of the Artist as a Young Man*. Conmee is depicted neither as a paragon of virtue nor a hypocrite. Rather, in a few deft sentences, Joyce suggests the same complexities and contradictions that delineate his central characters.

In the next, **Corny Kelleher** has a casual word with a passing constable suggesting the accuracy of Bloom's speculation that Kelleher is a police informant. Immediately following this, the scene shifts to Eccles Street where a one-legged beggar receives a coin tossed out the window of Number 7 (Bloom's address) by the hand of a woman. At the same time, not far away, Stephen's siblings are gathered in their home in Cabra for a late afternoon meal provided by the Sisters of Charity from their convent on Gardiner Street.

On the other side of the river, Blazes Boylan purchases a basket of fruit to send to Molly while Stephen chats with his former music teacher, **Almidano Artifoni**, near Trinity College. Meanwhile, north of the Liffey **Ned Lambert** shows off one of his inventions, Lenehan and M'Coy stroll the streets gossiping, and Bloom goes into a seedy bookstore on the quays to pick up a mildly pornographic book for Molly.

In a subsequent section, **Dilly Dedalus**, one of Stephen's siblings, meets her father Simon and berates him for his lack of responsibility. Though Simon is defiant, he also is sufficiently embarrassed to give Dilly a few pennies to buy a bun and a glass of milk. After her encounter with their father, Dilly goes to a used book stall where she spends the money on a French grammar and meets Stephen. He feels a measure of gilt when he beholds her thinness and the state of her clothing, he but rejects the idea of trying to help her and the others.

For the remainder of the chapter, we see a host of others—including Martin Cunningham, Tom Kernan, Buck Mulligan and Haines, and even

Patrick Dignam's son Paddy—going about the ordinary tasks of daily life in Dublin. In the final two sections, as a way of reprising the events of the chapter, a viceregal cavalcade crosses the city from Phoenix Park toward Pembroke township bound to the opening of the Mirus Bazaar and passing many of the individuals mentioned in the preceding section.

XI. Sirens—these creatures are half women half monsters whose songs lead seafarers to rocks which would destroy their ships and leave them to be eaten by the sirens. Before Odysseus' ship passes them, he fills the ears of the crew with wax to protect them from the songs, yet his curiosity will not allow him to eschew listening to their singing. He has them tie him to the mast of the ship so that he might hear them without being able to succumb to their blandishments.

The episode takes place at 4 p.m. in the Ormond Hotel restaurant and bar. A sixty-four-line opening introduces phrases from the narrative that follows in much the same way that an opera's overture precedes and previews the music to follow. The narrative then focuses on two barmaids, **Lydia Douce** and **Mina Kennedy**, talking about the latter's holiday and gossiping about men. They initially suggest the Sirens of the title, but in fact though Lydia will later snap her garter for the amusement of Blazes Boylan, it is Simon Dedalus, Bob Cowley, and **Ben Dollard** who perform.

Outside the hotel, Bloom meets Richie Goulding, Stephen's uncle and Simon Dedalus' brother-in-law, and the two men decide to go into the hotel's restaurant for an early dinner. For the remainder of the chapter, their proximity to the bar makes them aware of all that transpires. At the same time, their places in the restaurant visually underscore their respective positions on the edge of the society represented by the men drinking near them.

In the adjacent bar, a number of familiar characters, like Simon Dedalus, drop in. Lydia and Mina flirt with most of the customers in patronizing or dismissive fashion. However, Lydia seems more concerned with the good opinion of Blazes Boylan who has come in to meet briefly with Lenehan, and she is uneasy when Boylan abruptly departs for his liaison with Molly. Paradoxically, and somewhat perversely, Bloom, who has been observing Boylan, begins to frets about the latter being late for his appointment with Molly.

At the close of his meal, perhaps inspired by Simon Dedalus singing "M'appari," from Frederich von Flowtow's opera *Martha*, Bloom becomes sentimental and takes a moment to write a quick note to Martha Clifford. The narrative quickly turns readers back to the carnal side of love. While **Ben Dollard** entertains those gathered in the bar by singing "The Croppy Boy," Lydia suggestively moves her hand up and down on a beerpull while Bloom and **George Lidwell** watch her in fascination. In the closing moments of the chapter, Bloom, now out on the street, offers the last musical performance when he vents the gas that has built up with his dinner for the episode's final, flatulent word: "Pprrpffrrppffff" (11.1293).

XII. Cyclops—a member of a race of one-eyed giants living in Sicily. When Odysseus and his companions land there and begin to explore the island, one of the cyclops, Polyphemus, captures them and eats six of the men. Odysseus and the others are trapped in his cave, but subsequently escape after making Polyphemus drunk and then blinding him.

The episode begins at around 5 p.m. in an area north of the River Liffey and situated around The Four Courts. There, the unnamed narrator, a **dun** or bill collector, meets **Joe Hynes**. Joe, who works for *The Freeman's Journal* and has been paid that day. He invites the man for a drink at **Barney Kiernan's** pub on Little Britain Street, and the chapter unfolds from there. (This and the final chapter, Penelope, are the only two with a first-person narrator.)

In the pub Joe and the dun encounter a bellicose nationalist who goes by the nickname **The Citizen**. He is happy to join with the dun in letting Joe buy them both drinks. The scene has interesting parallels to the one in the newspaper office in Aeolus. The pub is filled with men, as much intoxicated by the sounds of their own voices as by the alcohol that they consume. Conversations proceed sporadically, jumping from topic to topic and involving a shifting number of the men in the pub, and their efforts seem more directed toward performance than the exchange of information. Simultaneously, the dun, though keeping his thoughts to himself, engages in a running commentary of vituperation directed successively at everyone whom he encounters, including Joe Hynes who has been buying him drinks.

Midway through the chapter, Bloom enters the pub looking for Martin Cunningham whom he had arranged to meet there. (Bloom and Cunningham are part of a group planning to visit Dignam's widow to give her financial advice.) Joe offers to buy Bloom a drink, but after some hemming and hawing Bloom takes a cigar instead. (In the meantime, Joe has conveniently ignored the fact that he still owes Bloom a pound.) Bloom proves as willing as any of the others to enter into vigorous discussions with the topics varying from capital punishment, to Irish sports, to conniving businessmen, to the character of hangmen, to corporal punishment in the British navy, to universal love, and finally to nationality. In every instance the speakers make sweeping claims and introduce elaborate examples while never truly resolving anything.

When Bloom briefly leaves the pub, Lenehan circulates the rumor that Bloom has won money betting on a longshot, **Throwaway**, in the Gold Cup Race held that day and speculates that Bloom has now gone to collect his winnings. On his return, the men in the pub expect Bloom to celebrate good fortune, which of course never took place, by buying the house a round of drinks, and the Citizen jeers at him with increasingly overt anti-Semitic slurs for not doing so. (Treating is a complex ritual among these men, and who buys the drinks and who benefits from that generosity provides an interesting subtext for the chapter's narration.) Martin Cunningham, apprehensive of violence, ushers Bloom out, but the latter responds to The Citizen's insults by reminding him that "Your God was a Jew. Christ was a Jew like me" (12.1808–1809). This enrages The Citizen who throws a biscuit tin at the departing carriage from which Bloom has been yelling.

While this discourse has moved forward in a fairly traditional manner, the chapter also features a radical stylistic departure in the interpolations that take up half the chapter. Like the ones in Wandering Rocks, they simply appear without attribution, in the midst of the discourse. Unlike those, however, the ones in Cyclops are generally parodic responses to places where the action occurs, the behavior of individuals, or the topics being discussed. There are descriptions lampooning figures from Irish mythology, a parody of the execution of Robert Emmet, a mocking rendition of the discourse of English parliamentarians, and various other exhibitions of buffoonery. Like the headings in Aeolus, readers are never offered an explanation for their appearance, nor is a connection made between these discursions and the rest of the narrative.

XIII. Nausikaa—the chapter takes its name from that of the young princess of Phaeacia who finds a shipwrecked Odysseus washed up on a beach in her country. She promises him the protection of her father, and eventually she facilitates his return to Ithaca.

The action begins at around 8 p.m. on Sandymount Strand, the same beach that Stephen walked upon ten hours earlier. The narrative describes three young women—**Gerty MacDowell**, **Edy Boardman**, and **Cissy Caffrey**—tending to three young children—Cissy's two younger brothers, Tommy and Jacky, and Edy's baby brother. All the while, Bloom, who has wandered there, presumably to avoid going home to confront Molly after her adultery, watches from a distance.

The first half of the chapter alternates between the dominant form of sentimental narrative and moments of free indirect discourse that present a sampling of Gerty's varied attitudes: her sentimental view of the world, her often petulant and competitive feelings toward her friends, and her idealized sense of the man, whom she does not know as Bloom, who is watching her. The tone of much of this portion of the narrative mimics that found in contemporary women's magazines and romance novels (which Joyce purportedly read in preparation to writing the chapter), occasionally jarringly interrupted by Gerty's harsh comments about her friends and the children.

At the end of her section, there is a shocking change in Gerty's attitude and demeanor. As her friends move off down the beach, Gerty, using her apparent intentness in watching the fireworks from the Mirus Bazaar that is just closing for the day as an excuse to lean backwards, exposes her underwear to Bloom. Even in the oblique language of the narrative, it is clear that Gerty is fully aware that the man watching her is masturbating. Further, as the discourse adopts a flowing tone and accelerated rhythm that mimics sexual climax, the narrative suggests that Gerty too may well have found orgasmic pleasure in the moment.

The second half of the narration follows a stylistic pattern sharply distinguished from the first. The transition for which the fireworks scene has prepared the reader occurs abruptly and without apology, as he congratulates himself on the enjoyment he has just experienced. It focuses on Bloom's perspective of what has occurred and shows a coarse, even brutal, side of his nature that has not been previously evident. Bloom comments in a calculated way on Gerty's sexual aggressiveness and on the preferability of voyeurism to imagination as an erotic stimulus. He also expresses gratitude that, while masturbating, he had not been aware that she is lame.

This second half of the chapter offers a glimpse of Bloom's most personal and unfiltered thoughts, through a steady application of stream of consciousness punctuated by a measure of free indirect discourse. It foregrounds a harsh, calculated approach that Bloom pursued for unapologetic physical gratification. Readers may feel shocked at the unbridled appetite displayed by a man who, with the exception of his brief outburst against the Citizen in the preceding chapter, had been the model of restraint. However, this forceful expression of the need for self-gratification certainly comes from a man deeply wounded by his wife's adultery. If anything, the episode underscores the complexity and multiplicity of Bloom's nature rather than reverses or overturns previous reader assumptions about him.

XIV. Oxen of the Sun—takes its name from the animals belonging to the god Helios. Odysseus and his crew come across the animals when they land on Helios' island. Despite warnings from Odysseus not to harm the beasts, his hungry crew slaughters them for food, and when the ship leaves the island of Helios a thunderbolt from Zeus destroys it, killing all save Odysseus.

The episode begins at around 10 p.m. at the Holles Street Maternity Hospital. Bloom has gone there ostensively to inquire about the condition of Mina Purefoy, but more likely he is still seeking a diversion that will forestall the inevitability of his return home. The chapter continues the pattern of episodic stylistic variations that began with the headings of Aeolus, this time foregrounding Joyce's interest in diverse forms of writing more assertively than any of its predecessors. Its samplings of writing from various eras mimics a survey of forms of English literature, beginning with an amalgamation of Latin and Irish, shifting to Old English, Middle English, and then to forms from the fifteenth through the nineteenth century.

As with his other stylistic innovations, no explanation is given for the sudden appearance of these diverse forms, but two reasons spring to mind: In mimicking the works of his literary predecessors, Joyce enforces the impression in the minds of his readers that he is capable of producing art according to any formula and from any era. Additionally, he makes the broader point of the transformative power of literature on human behavior. The linguistic virtuosity of the narratives camouflages drunkenness of most of the characters, a condition that increases over the course of the chapter with their unrelenting consumption of alcohol. The effects of their drinking do not become apparent until the final section of the chapter when the narrative ceases to imitate other literary forms and lapses into patois. The resulting incomprehensibility of the characters' babbling conversations demonstrates the uplifting effect of art on representations of human behavior.

Once one is able to meet the challenges of the episode's variable forms, its plotline unfolds in a fashion relatively easy to follow. At the hospital, Bloom encounters a group made up primarily of young medical students with a few hangers on—among them Stephen Dedalus, Vincent Lynch, and the not so young Lenehan—who are carousing in a room set aside as a refectory, drinking Bass ale presumably provided by Stephen's money. There are loud discussions on sex, conception, birth control, abortion, and artistic creativity.

As he did in Nestor, Aeolus, and Syclla and Charybdis, Stephen attempts to perform for the others, but, as is often the case in a drunken group, he has vigorous competition as everyone strives to be heard at once. Midway through the episode, Mulligan appears, much as he did when Stephen was at the National Library. He has been to a literary party, to which Stephen had not been invited, at George Moore's house on Ely Place just off St. Stephen's Green. Mulligan is far more sober than the others, with of course the exception of Bloom. As it has in the Telemachus and the Scylla and Charybdis chapters, Mulligan's bawdy wit dominates the flow of the conversation, and puts Stephen in the shadows. However, by this time the drunkenness of the party is such that no one can lead the discussion for any significant length of time.

As it approaches 11 p.m., closing time for Dublin pubs, the groups rush off to the nearest one, Burke's, for a last drink. There, in the absence of literary styles, readers see just how drunk and incoherent most are. The episode ends with the group leaving the pub and Stephen proposing to Lynch that they go to Nighttown, the name Joyce created to designate the notorious red-light district of Dublin.

XV. Circe—an enchantress who transforms Odysseus' crew into swine. Odysseus is protected from her magic by an herb given to him by the god Hermes. (The herb was called *moly* in Greek, a pun that Joyce enjoyed.) This immunity allowed Odysseus ultimately to force Circe to restore his men to their former condition so that they could continue the journey home.

The episode takes place in the red-light district of Dublin, and begins at around midnight. It is by far the longest chapter in the novel and is laid out in dramatic form. The action takes place around Mabbot and Mecklenburg Streets and in Bella Cohen's adjacent whorehouse.

Throughout the episode hallucinations blur and even break up perceptions of reality for both characters and readers. Early in the chapter, as Bloom stands in the street looking for Stephen, his wife Molly appears riding a camel and dressed as if she belonged to a harem. Late in the chapter's narrative Stephen's mother, May Dedalus, appears, seemingly back from the grave in the form of a rotting corpse. She confronts Stephen with the guilt he feels over her death while he capers about Bella Cohen's parlor.

These and other extravagant hallucinations that recur over the course of the chapter can tempt one to psychoanalytic interpretations of their causes, but any easy generalizations about the motivations within the characters that bring forth these images quickly prove reductive. Any number of the hallucinations that the central characters encounter (or project) alternately confirm and contradict specific impressions of Bloom's or Stephen's emotional or psychological state up to this point. They underscore the characters' conflicted sense of their worlds, but at the same time they do not offer unambiguous clarifications of the complexities of their natures.

Stephen has gone from Burke's pub to Nighttown with Lynch, ostensively seeking a particular prostitute, **Georgina Johnson,** but in his alcoholic stupor his motivations are both impulsive and unclear. Bloom, concerned because he is aware of how drunk Stephen has becomes, follows the pair in an effort to keep Stephen out of trouble. In the subsequent narration and in the complementary hallucinations, perspectives generally alternate between Bloom's and Stephen's view of events. They both experience distorted visions—the one because of physical and emotional fatigue and the other because of the presence of alcohol and the absence of solid food—and readers are left to form a unified sense of what transpires.

At various times, Bloom sees phantasms associated with Molly, with Josie Breen, with his mother and his father, with Molly's adultery with Boylan, and with various women Bloom knows. He also experiences panoramic fantasies, such as one where he imagines himself as a nationalist politician with a partisan rise and a precipitous fall like that of Charles Stewart Parnell. And, he engages in remarkably projections of personal insecurities, as when he envisions his graphic sex transformation in a sado-masochistic scene with likewise changed Bella/Bello Cohen.

Stephen's hallucinations are more concentrated and more focused in the traumas they represent. He imagines his father, Simon, in the dress of a Cardinal of the Catholic Church, and a manic Garrett Deasy as a travesty of male authority figures, and with more affective emotion he sees his mother, May, coming from the grave to plead with her son to return to the Catholic faith. Though Stephen has fewer illusions than does Bloom, the intensity of his experiences nonetheless have a powerful impact on him and on readers as well.

Stephen's last image, in fact, leads to the chapter's catharsis. After his vision of his mother, a terrified Stephen runs into the street. Bloom follows and finds the young man in a confrontation with two British soldiers—Privates **Carr** and **Compton**—over a supposed insult to Cissy Caffrey. (She, Edy Boardman, and Gerty MacDowell improbably appear, seemingly have migrated from the beach of Sandymount Strand to the streets of Nighttown. The contrast in their behavior from Eumaeus seems too great for them to be the same characters. At the same time, they emerge in scenes when Bloom is not present and there is no evidence that Stephen has seen them before. Consequently, the most likely explanation is that they too are hallucinations, with the narrative projecting their images on local prostitutes.) Bloom tries ineffectively to defuse the situation, and, at the goading of Private Compton, Private Carr knocks Stephen to the ground.

When constables arrive to investigate the melee, the soldiers flee. Bloom attempts to prevent Stephen's arrest, but his efforts seem only to irritate the policemen. Ultimately, the situation is resolved with the timely intervention of Corny Kelliher who claims to be in Nighttown at the behest to two commercial travelers. Kelliher, in behavior that reminds readers of the suspicion that he is a police informer, uses a mixture of charm and cajoling to change the constables' minds about taking Stephen into custody.

After Kelliher leaves, the chapter ends with Bloom bending over the still supine Stephen. Bloom hears the young man mumbling words from W.B. Yeats' poem "Who Goes with Fergus," and the older man mistakenly believes that Stephen is referring to a sweetheart named Ferguson. Bloom then looks up and has his final vision, an image of his son Rudy dressed in an extravagantly dandyish fashion and in what might have been an extravagantly dandyish fashion we he alive that day.

XVI. Eumaeus—the chapter takes its name from the swineherd, an old family retainer, who first shelters Odysseus, who is disguised as an old beggar, on the latter's return to Ithaca. When Telemachus visits the swineherd, Odysseus reveals his true identity, and the father and son concoct a plot to destroy Penelope's suitors.

The action takes place around 1 a.m. Bloom and Stephen walk from outside Bella Cohen's in Nighttown to a cabman's shelter (the equivalent to an all-night café) located near the Customs House by the River Liffey. Clichéd language and mixed metaphors fill the chapter, typified by the exaggerated pompous vocabulary and contradictory images of opening sentence: "Preparatory to anything else Mr Bloom brushed off the greater bulk of the shavings and handed Stephen the hat and ashplant and *bucked him up generally in orthodox Samaritan fashion . . .* " (italics added; 16.1–3).

Some readers have asserted that this worn-out language reflects Joyce's exhaustion after the composition of Circe. A closer look makes it seem more likely that Joyce once again was demonstrating his ability to create sharp artistic impressions from even the most prosaic constructions. Further, the slippage in meaning created by tired language underscores the diminished perceptions of Bloom and Stephen, both of whom have been worn out by the day's events.

The cabman's shelter where Bloom and Stephen are headed is run by a man who reputedly is **James "Skin the Goat" Fitzharris**. That was the name of the person who drove the carriage used by the assassins to get away after in the Phoenix Park Murders, though there is no clear evidence that the two are one and the same. The indeterminacy of the proprietor's identity and that of others like the sailor **D.B. Murphy** enforces the sense of misperception that runs throughout the chapter. (Early editions of *Ulysses* erroneously printed the name as W.B. Murphy, thereby raising questions about Joyce using the figure to lampoon Yeats. Thanks to the work of Hans Walter Gabler and his editing team the mistake was corrected in the 1984 edition of the novel.)

As they walk toward the cabman's shelter, Bloom and Stephen see in the distance **Gumley**, a friend of Simon Dedalus, dozing next to a fire and ineffectually discharging his duties as a night watchman, a job given to him by the Dublin Corporation. They also run into **John Corley**, a character who appeared in the *Dubliners* story "Two Gallants" and who is now homeless. After a brief and desultory conversation, Stephen gives Corley money to purchase a night's lodgings and suggests, probably facetiously, that, if he needs employment, Corley should apply on the next day to Mr. Deasy's school in Bray.

At the cabman's shelter, they join patrons whose attention is being held by the bombastic sailor D.B. Murphy, a pseudo-Ulyssean figure who has been recently discharged from serving on a merchant ship. As his performance unfolds, Murphy recounts a series of increasingly unbelievable stories relating to his seafaring experiences. In the midst of Murphy's exhibition, a skeptical Bloom offers a steady sotto voce critique of them while they unfold. Stephen on the other hand maintains a glumness and general unresponsiveness to Murphy and everyone else everyone else around him. Despite Bloom's efforts to get him to eat and to engage him in conversation, Stephen does little more than make the barely civil rejoinders characteristic of someone in the process of sobering up, telling Bloom at one point "We can't change the country. Let us change the subject" (16.1171).

After one of the men in the shelter mentions Parnell, Bloom takes up the topic with Stephen. Clumsily, Bloom turns the conversation to women's attractiveness and then shows Stephen a picture of a younger Molly wearing a lowcut dress. His manner makes it unclear whether he is boasting about his wife or playing the pander. Bloom finally gives up on attempts to get Stephen to eat something, he and invites the young man to return with him to number 7 Eccles Street to spend the night. Bloom quickly pays for their coffee. They exit, and while walking toward Bloom's home their conversation turns to music.

XVII. Ithaca—one of the Ionian isles and the kingdom of Odysseus to which he returns at the end of the *Odyssey* after a 20-year absence and in where he eventually triumphs over Penelope's suitors and reclaims his kingdom.

The chapter is arranged as a series of questions and answers. As is the case with other stylistic variations throughout the narrative, the text again offers no explanation for the shift in form. It is, however, useful to keep in mind that the format follows the traditional layouts of catechisms and of the turn of the last century grammar school textbooks, both of which transmitted information by relying upon the rote memorization of prepared questions and answers.

The discourse begins with a brief summary of the route the two men followed to Bloom's house. (Joyce used the location of the house of his university friend, J.F. Byrne—the model for Cranly, a character who appears in *A Portrait of the Artist as a Young Man*—as Bloom's address.) Arriving in Eccles Street with Stephen at about 2 p.m., Bloom realizes that has forgotten his door key, a motif that has run through the narrative and that some readers see as phallic imagery (though they rarely explain why that has any interpretive significance). Rather than waking Molly, Bloom climbs over the house's area railings, goes in through the kitchen in the basement, and then up to the ground floor to unlock the front door to admit Stephen.

While Molly sleeps above, Stephen and Bloom have cocoa in the kitchen. Through the episode's question and answer format, the narrative provides quotidian details of the things like the physical elements that delineate the kitchen, the personal idiosyncrasies that distinguish their social exchanges, and the municipal arrangements that contribute to Bloom's ability to draw water, bring it to a boil, and use it to make cocoa. The conversation unfolds by touching randomly on the diverse interests and opinions of the two men and the recollections of ordinary events in both their lives.

Stephen is now more talkative and congenial than he was in the previous chapter, though at one point, and much to his embarrassment, he makes a thoughtless reference to the medieval myth of Jews kidnapping Christian boys and killing them. Throughout this interlude, Bloom seems less loquacious and more pensive. This can hardly be surprising since he is on the brink of confronting the unpleasant *fait accompli* of the event that he has spent the day trying to ignore. In this frame of mind, while he and Stephen converse, Bloom thinks of Molly and Milly while trying to accommodate his unwillingness to confront painful aspects of their lives.

When they have finished their cocoa, Stephen, with newfound good grace, declines Bloom's offer of a bed for the night, but they make tentative, though likely insincere, plans for future "intellectual dialogues." Bloom takes Stephen into the backyard. They urinate, and then Stephen leaves.

Bloom returns to the house, thinking about his future and tentatively touching on his previously never quite acknowledged feelings of entering the house for the first time since Molly's adultery. He discursively considers what options he has for responding to this breech, including leaving his wife and wandering around the world. In the end, he gets into bed with Molly, kisses her rump, has a brief conversation with her in which he gives a highly selective account of how he spent his day, and then he falls asleep.

XVIII. Penelope—the chapter's title is the name of the faithful wife of Odysseus who waited 20 years for his return from the war with Troy. During the time that Odysseus is away, 108 young men invade his house demanding that Penelope marry one of them. With nothing to defend herself with but her wits, Penelope must use all her skills to fend them off until her husband returns.

The chapter offers the reader the longest and most detailed representation of Bloom's wife. Heretofore, besides a brief appearance under the bedclothes in Calypso and an even briefer exposure (only an arm) in Wandering Rocks, the narrative has offered few firsthand glimpses of Molly. Most of what readers know of her comes from Bloom's uxorious daydreams, the leering inuendo of Blazes Boylan, or the salacious gossip of other Dublin men. That all changes in the final episode.

There, in a rambling monologue made up of eight separate sections with almost no punctuation, Molly reveals a great deal about her feelings, her ambitions, her concerns, her insecurities, and her appetites. In some ways, particularly in her frank admissions of enjoyment of her carnal appetites, Molly's declarations conform to the often-scandalous views of her held by other Dubliners: a selfish and not terribly thoughtful woman concerned chiefly if not exclusively with the satisfaction of her own senses. However, in her solitary reflections, Molly reveals sensitivity, vulnerability, and even a measure of concern for others. While she does not appear inclined to think deeply about many matters, she has a practical intelligence that allows her to cope with her often difficult situation.

Molly begins her monologue by commenting on what she knows or suspects regarding Bloom's relations with various women. She then turns to her adultery with Boylan, and touches on the guilt she feels over it. She compares Boylan with Bloom, and each man emerges as flawed in his own way.

Sexual reverie turns Molly's mind to **Stanley Gardner**, a young British Army officer whom she met a few years earlier in Dublin and with whom she carried on a relationship that seems to have touched her deeply but it remains unclear whether it proceeded as far as physical intimacy. She remarks bitterly that Gardner later died of enteric fever in South Africa during the Boer War, though the narrative does not specify how she came to know this.

Her recollections of Gardner turn Molly's thoughts from the specific to the general: a revelry in her own sensuality and considerations of her sexual attractiveness. It quickly becomes clear that her own sense of self-worth is informed by how it measures up to her keen sense of the power of sexuality. She has a calculated view of what draws men like Boylan and even Bloom to her, and she is continually assessing the possibly diminishing power of her attractiveness. Overall, however, Molly has a heathy enjoyment of her animal nature. Her mind ranges unselfconsciously over the erotic and sensual side to her life as she speaks candidly of her enjoyment of physical pleasure.

That is not to say that Molly is insensitive to the elements of her life that threaten to marginalize her. When her reveries turn to her isolated existence as a girl growing up at British outpost in Gibraltar where her father **Major Brian Tweedy** was stationed, it becomes clear just how isolated she felt. Molly has only vague memories of her mother, **Lunita Laredo**, a woman of Spanish origin whose disappearance early in Molly's life is never explained. She rebelled against the puritanical prohibitions of her Spanish nanny, and yet remained under the influence of the woman's restrictive views of life. Molly recalls **Hester Stanhope** an older woman who befriended her for a time and perhaps served as a mother substitute, and she thinks of the loneliness that she experienced when Hester and her husband left Gibraltar.

Throughout the monologue, Molly is quick to displace frank recollections of unhappiness or insecurity with memories of success with men. To offset the impact of thoughts of her loneliness on Gibraltar, she turns to more amenable and quite specific recollections of the attention paid to her by **Harry Mulvey**, a lieutenant in the Royal Navy, who became her first youthful admirer. He pursued her while she was still a teenager, and their masturbatory encounter under Gibraltar's Moorish wall seems to have been Molly's first sexual experience.

After getting out of bed to urinate and noting with relief that her period is beginning—"anyhow he didn't make me pregnant" (18.1123)—Molly's mind turns to a nagging concern that she has had with possible gynecological problems. She then brusquely turns her thoughts to life with Bloom and Milly and of Bloom's bringing Stephen back to the house. As noted above, this sleight-of-hand gesture of Molly's is typical, for she often prefers diversion and denial to face facts squarely.

She recalls with pleasure the vigor of Boylan's lovemaking, but she also admits that it never fully satisfied her. In fact, her recollections give the lie to the insinuations of her sluttish appetites that Lenehan, Simon Dedalus, and others have suggested. In fact, over the course of the soliloquy, despite her apparent frankness, Molly's degree of sexual experience becomes increasingly difficult to gauge. Contradictions and misconceptions punctuate many of her remarks as do surprising flashes of prudishness, and the imprecision of her language makes judging her worldliness a problem. There is among critics a great deal of disagreement over how many lovers Molly may have had or indeed if she has had intercourse with anyone other than Bloom and Boylan. In the end, that issue seems less important than how much aspects of sex and sexuality define her.

At several points Molly thinks of her dead son Rudy. It quickly becomes clear that she still deeply feels the pain of his loss. Molly cannot understand why he died, she feels guilt over it, and supposes, resentfully, that others blame her for the baby's death. What goes unsaid but seems obvious is a terror of having to face again this tremendous emotional pain were she to become pregnant again and to be confronted with the dreaded possibility of having the child die shortly after being born. The same fear seems to haunt Bloom.

A reader's awareness of that perspective clarifies a passage in Ithaca revealing that the Blooms have not had "complete carnal intercourse, with ejaculation of semen within the natural female organ" (17.2278–2279) since shortly before Rudy's birth. Though some have read the lines to mean that the Bloom's no longer maintain a sexual relationship, it is more precise to say that they take care that relations will not result in pregnancy, as evidence by Molly's recollection, early in her soliloquy, of "and the last time he came on my bottom" (18.77).

Near the end of her monologue, Molly's fatigue becomes apparent. She reacts defensively to anticipated criticism of her sexual behavior while evincing a kind of romanticism toward relationships with men similar to that which Gerty MacDowell presented in the Eumaeus chapter. In the final passage, her thoughts return to a sensuous day spent on Howth Hill, just north of Dublin overlook the Irish Sea, with Bloom, but her final repetition of a series of yeses—"I put my arms around him yes and drew him down to me so he could feel my breasts all perfume yes and his heart was going like mad and yes I said yes I will Yes" (18.1606–1609)—leave ambiguous specifically what it is to which she assents or indeed if she is assenting at all.

Alternative Readings

"Molly's Lulabye"

Except for a brief conversation with Bloom in Calypso and a glimpse of her arm as she throws money out the window to a beggar in Wandering Rocks, until the final chapter every impression of Molly comes secondhand. Bloom's obsessive reveries reveal the powerful sensual, emotional, and psychological hold that she has over him. Casual salacious remarks by Simon Dedalus, **Jack Power**, Lenehan, Nosey Flynn, and others suggest that she is a woman of dubious morals, pampered by her husband and allowed the free reign of her appetites. Each of these observations has an element of truth, but none provides a clear, accurate sense of her nature. It is only in the final chapter, a soliloquy of eight nearly unpunctuated sentences, that Molly speaks of herself, by herself, and for herself, presenting in her rambling, digressive way a more complex, more contradictory, and more misunderstood figure than any of the others conjectured.

The narrative quickly reveals Molly to be a canny woman, albeit one of meager education. She has aspirations as a musical performer, but there is little indication that her singing or piano playing rise much above mediocre, perhaps because her undisciplined nature naturally resisted the practical work necessary to improve her craft. She is a woman intent on self-gratification and evinces little concern for the usual restraints imposed by society. At the same time, an ambivalent recognition of a moral system, putatively Christian but verging on superstition, blunts full enjoyment of anything outside the scope of respectable behavior. The frank reverie and sometimes uneasy second thoughts in which she engages affirms that simple labels will not sum up her nature.

Molly welcomes pleasure in all forms. Her recent adultery naturally puts sexual gratification in the forefront of her mind as she lays awake considering her life. She thinks of, and probably exaggerates, the number of times she and Boylan had intercourse, but surprisingly for someone who seems to have such strong sexual appetites, she also demonstrates an uninformed, sentimental view of male and female relations. She speaks enviously of the pleasure that men get from women, grumbling at the inequality of the satisfaction. She even speculates on the enjoyment she might feel were she a man, though the lustiness of her recollections suggest that she is more than able to ensure the satisfaction of her own appetites. In terms of physical gratification, however, she does not limit herself to sexuality. She recollects with satisfaction the food she has eaten and the drinks she has consumed. She even revels in the comfort of her bed.

At the same time, material pleasure itself does not always provide her with complete satisfaction. She complains that Boylan's behavior toward her is insufficiently respectful and hardly romantic. She criticizes Bloom as being clumsy and selfish in his foreplay. She frets that food leads to weight gain, and that drink can lead to dependence. She even protests that the bed creaks too much. For Molly, no pleasure seems to be unadulterated, and no joy proves to be perpetual.

In fact, Molly is a deeply lonely woman. She thinks of her isolation as a girl at Gibraltar, she resents the puritanical impositions on her behavior by her chaperone, she decries the too brief and too superficial love affair with Mulvey. She bitterly regrets the ultimately disappointing friendship with Hester Stanhope, and she now chafes against what she sees as stifling social atmosphere of Dublin and the confining relations of her marriage. All of these restraints touch her deeply and circumscribe her full enjoyment of life.

Molly's monologue also shows that she can be at times a sad and a resentful woman. The death of her son Rudy, which she and Bloom do not seem to discuss, remains a heavy emotional burden, an ongoing source of guilt, and a nagging concern about sexual behavior. Her bickering relationship with her daughter Milly, while normal for a mother and a teenage girl, leaves her frustrated, wounded, and resentful. And she cannot decide whether she feels contempt, love, loyalty, or indifference toward her husband.

Molly's soliloquy ends *Ulysses* as a tour de force of Joyce's creative abilities. Molly's blunt, unaffected language nonetheless resonates with a range of readers: young and old, male and female, Irish or any other nationality. Her words summarize the complex and contradictory feelings of most human beings and touch us with familiar feelings even if the experiences that provoke them are vastly different. In a brash and breezy fashion Molly both affirms and rebuts the callous gossip that has framed her identity for the bulk of the book. Her often-contradictory observations disrupt any attempt at definitive, linear readings, but at the same time they provide access to a range of alternating interpretive possibilities that continually reward for the careful and open-minded reader, and re-reader. Through her monologue, Molly emerges from Penelope as a character more flawed than previously indicated but also as a figure much fuller that anticipated, well able to hold her own with any other individual in the narrative.

"Penelope's Cadenza as Ulysses' *Last Voice"*

Joyce's fiction may at first appear less musical than his poetry, but the cadence of his prose can, and does, rival the lyricism of *Chamber Music* and *Pomes Penyeach*. These two pieces have repeatedly been adapted to music and so too "The Dead," *Ulysses*, and portions of *Finnegans Wake*. Joyce's musical ear was never too far from the music of his prose and neither was his innate sense of the structure and form of musical composition completely removed from his works, whether poetry or fiction. The Sirens episode of *Ulysses*, chapter 11, is an obvious example. *Ulysses* itself has been referred to by some scholars as a sonata, a frustrated one at that, but, nonetheless, a sonata whose three-fold thematic scheme of exposition, development, and recapitulation finds its coda in the novel's last chapter, a resolution of sorts, and one of the two most concentrated displays of the interior monologue in the whole work, the other being Proteus, chapter three.

Molly's monologue—or as some refer to it, soliloquy—with its interweaving of themes found elsewhere in the novel, is analogous to a cadenza, a virtuosic solo passage appearing in a musical piece or, as in this case, at the end of a literary piece. Molly's is the last performance in the novel. Among other characteristics, a cadenza improvisationally echoes themes modulated by the nuances of the soloist's interpretation. Though not privy to Bloom's exact thoughts during the day of June 16th or, for that matter, the thoughts and opinions others have of her, Molly is not oblivious to his activities or the hearsay of Dubliners. Her judgments and suppositions of Bloom are predicated on 16 years of marriage and the shared experiences of husband and wife; tragically, one of their shared experiences was the death of Rudy, their only son, at 11 days old.

Approaching the Penelope episode as a cadenza with a focus on Molly's adultery and marriage provides interpretative possibilities that reproduce variations on these two major themes in the novel. Certainly, many other themes in *Ulysses* resound in Molly's cadenza, but this reading concentrates solely on Molly's thoughts as they relate to and illuminate these two particular themes of marriage and adultery.

In this last chapter of *Ulysses*, the eight unpunctuated sentences or paragraphs suggest an octave, a complete series of notes reserved exclusively for Molly, the only professional singer and performer in *Ulysses*. Some critics may question the extent of Molly's repertory and vocal training, but she must be good enough to sing at concerts in and outside of Dublin and disciplined enough to recognize the limits of her vocal register (18.1298). Either through some degree of training, undisclosed as it may be, or through a natural talent, Molly cleverly and subtly connects her discernment of the tension and frustration Zerlina faces in the first act of Mozart's *Don Giovanni* to the exigencies of the sexual situation she currently finds herself in. Quoting in Italian lines Zerlina sings (18.1507–1508), Molly betrays her own thoughts that at once express a note of sympathy toward Bloom and an obvious recognition of her own irresistible sexual desires, while in the same breath she blames him for her adultery and even imagines the role he played in orchestrating her afternoon with Boylan (18.1516, 1007–1009). She also laments the fact that she is not a prima donna because of having married Bloom (18.896). These and other disparate reflections on marriage and adultery forge an undulating sexual motif that recurs throughout her monologue. But unlike Zerlina, Molly has given in to her desires.

Molly's account of her sexual enjoyment with Boylan reaches a high pitch that envisions a verbal attack on Bloom: "Ill let him know if thats what he wanted that his wife is fucked yes and damn well fucked too" (18.1510–1511). As spiteful as these words would most likely sound to her husband, they emphasize her suspicion that Bloom had a hand in her adultery and help clarify for readers the narrative indeterminacy of Bloom's own thoughts regarding his lack of pleasure in sexual intercourse with Molly. Earlier in the day in the Lestrygonians episode, chapter 8, he reflects on his experience of having sex after the death of his son, but avoids the noun or pronoun in his thought: "Could never like it again after Rudy" (8.610). Who could never like it—I, she, Molly, we—is not at first evident, but in the light of Molly's musings in the wee hours of the morning an answer is possible. Recognizing that something changed after Rudy's death, Molly, too, thinks that "we were never the same since O Im not going to think myself into the glooms about that any more" (18.1450–1451). Though she does not specifically identify what changed, whatever it was does not seem to have been her desire for sex or the pleasure she derives from it. The missing subject in Bloom's sentence fragment can arguably be the pronoun I. The absence of pleasure in the procreative act perhaps stems from his personal sense of inadequacy, a sentiment tying into a previous notion he entertained in the Hades episode: "Mistake of nature. If it's healthy it's from the mother. If not from the man. Better luck next time" (6.329–330). For Bloom, pregnancy is a risk and luck is a needed ingredient for healthy offspring.

Many hours after the Hades episode, Bloom is in the Ormond Restaurant, and, shortly before he leaves, the thought of his fault for Rudy's death emerges again but this time in conjunction with the possibility of taking the risk of having another child: "Well, my fault perhaps. No son. Rudy. Too late now. Or if not? If not? If still?" (11.1066–1067). Molly's tone toward this shared experience of Rudy'a death and the possibility of another pregnancy differs from Bloom's: "was he not able to make one it wasnt my fault we came together when I was watching the two dogs" (18.1445–1446). Bloom, too, vividly remembers this moment when they conceived Rudy. But Molly bears no guilt for either the pregnancy or the death of Rudy, and, as is her tendency, she shifts any blame away from herself and onto Poldy. She wants to move on and no longer think herself "into the glooms." Molly momentarily considers having another child and realizes the risk (18.166–168).

Molly's cadenza begins and ends with the word *yes*, the female word according to Joyce, that serves as both a transition from Bloom's unnarrated request for breakfast in bed at the beginning of the chapter to her final word at the end of the chapter, a rapturous coda expressing an apparent reaffirmation or at least an ecstatic remembering of her consent to Bloom's marriage proposal. True to the name Joyce gave to the episode, Penelope, Molly weaves and unweaves various threads of the novel to fit her own skein of perception and give color to the texture of her life. In significant ways, she expresses not only her views on marriage and adultery but also elucidates Bloom's. Molly's solo performance gives readers a chance to hear her voice and reconsider impressions they may have of her before reaching this last chapter of *Ulysses*. In ways that resonate with interpretative meaning, Molly's thoughts considered here mark a resolution in the novel's leitmotif of marriage and adultery.

Topics for Further Discussion

1 Is *Ulysses* too long?
2 Is it boring?

3   Do the variety of different styles make it a better novel?
4   Does it hold any real interest for a general audience, or is it only useful to academics seeking to impress their students?
5   Does *Ulysses* have a point?
6   Is Joyce trying to make us feel stupid?
7   Do you need to understand all of the allusions to understand the novel?
8   Do you need to know Irish history to understand *Ulysses*?
9   Is the novel critical of Ireland?
10 Is a knowledge of Catholic belief, liturgy, and customs important?
11 Does the novel attack Catholic belief?
12 How important is *The Odyssey* to understanding the novel?
13 Is the novel anti-Semitic?
14 Does the novel treat women fairly?
15 Does the novel treat men fairly?
16 Does the novel see humans as contemptable?
17 Is stream of consciousness a good way to understand a character's identity?
18 Does the narrative offer a humane view of its characters?
19 Does the novel have a hero or a villain?
20 Is it alright for a reader to skip portions that he or she does not understand?
21 Do you believe that anyone fully understands this novel?

A Glossary of Characters

Almidan Artifoni—a music teacher who in the Wandering Rocks episode encourages Stephen Dedalus to continue to develop his voice for singing.

Ellen (Higgins) Bloom—the deceased mother of Leopold Bloom. Given Bloom's ignorance of Catholic ritual and dogma, it is most probable that she was a Protestant. His feelings toward her of love and guilt emerge in Circe. To some degree they are similar to Stephen's for his mother.

Leopold Bloom—a central character in the novel, also known as Bloom or Poldy. He is a 38-year-old ad canvasser, married to Molly and father of Milly and Rudy (deceased). Much of the narrative records his movements around Dublin for a day as he tries to occupy himself to forget his wife's impending adultery. He runs errands, attends a funeral, does some work ad canvassing, confronts an anti-Semite, tries to help the widow of the man who has died. Late in the evening while visiting a maternity hospital, he encounters a very drunk Stephen Dedalus. In a burst of what seems paternal-like concern, Bloom follows Stephen to the Nighttown area of Dublin, and eventually brings him home for late night cocoa. When Stephen leaves, Bloom goes to bed, seemingly reconciled to his wife's infidelity.

Milly (Millicent) Bloom—the 15-year-old daughter of Leopold and Molly Bloom who appears in the narrative only through her correspondence and the recollections of her parents. She has been sent by her parents to Mullingar, a town west of Dublin in County Westmeath, to work as an assistant in a photographer's studio. (Though to contemporary readers she seems too young to be off on her own, this would not have been an uncommon occurrence at the time the novel is set.) Bloom is concerned about her burgeoning sexuality but simultaneously understands that he can do little to avert the normal course of her development.

Molly Bloom—the 33-year-old wife of Leopold and mother of Milly and Rudy. She was born Marion Tweedy in Gibraltar on 8 September 1870 (the Feast Day of the Nativity of the Blessed Virgin) where her father, Major Brian Tweedy, served in the British Army. (Some critics have claimed that Tweedy was actually a Sergeant Major and appropriated the rank of an officer after he had retired. The evidence for this remains dubious.) She moved to Dublin with her father when she was 16 years old. Her mother, Lunita Laredo, either died or left the family when Molly was a little girl. (The narrative does not offer an explanation for her absence.) Molly has acquired a modest reputation as a singer, but does not seem to enjoy particular notoriety. She spends much of the day preparing for her assignation with Blazes Boylan, quite possibly the first time that she has had sexual intercourse outside of marriage.

Rudolph Bloom—the father of Leopold Bloom. He came to Ireland from Hungarian and changed his name, Virag (the Hungarian word for flower) to Bloom. Although Leopold Bloom was not raised as an observant Jew, Rudolph seems to have revived in own interest in Judaism in his old age. Some time before the action of the novel, Rudolph killed himself in a hotel room in Ennis over his grief for the death of his wife.

Rudy Bloom—the second child of Leopold and Molly Bloom. He was born on 29 December 1894 and named in honor of Bloom's father. Rudy lived for 11 days, and the narrative does not specify the cause of his death. Although they do not speak to one another of it, the grief of his death still haunts his mother and father, possibly to the point of fearing that another pregnancy would lead to another loss and more near unbearable pain.

Edy Boardman—a precocious young girl who appears on Sandymount Strand caring for her brother, baby Boardman, in the Nausikaa chapter with Cissy Caffrey and Gerty MacDowell. She appears briefly with her baby brother in one of Bloom's hallucinations in Circe.

Blazes (Hugh) Boylan—an entrepreneur well known in Dublin as an advertising man and an impresario. (In current slang, he might be considered a chancer.) He is an acquaintance of Bloom's and on the afternoon of 16th June he commits adultery with Bloom's wife, Molly. Though he seems to enjoy a measure of popularity with other Dubliners, his coarseness and animal vitality make him the antithesis of Bloom. Although he has proposed including Molly on a musical tour of Ireland that he is organizing, bits and pieces of information about it that emerge over the course of the narrative make the enterprise seem much more modest than Bloom and Molly have been led to believe. Despite the measure of physical gratification she receives from Boylan, Molly in the novel's final chapter indicates reservations about his nature and admiration for aspects of Bloom's character.

Denis Breen—a mentally unbalanced minor character who appears sporadically in the novel's narrative and is the butt of cruel practical joke, a postcard sent to him with what he considers an insulting phrase. He wanders around the city all day seeking some form of redress, much to the amusement of other Dubliners.

Josie (Josephine) Breen—the long-suffering wife of Denis Breen and a friend of Molly's and possibly and old-flame of Bloom's. In Lestrygonians, Josie confides in Bloom about her husband's erratic behavior.

Davy Byrne—owner of the pub by the same name on Duke Street where Bloom has lunch in Lestrygonians. It is immediately across from the Burton where Bloom chooses not to dine.

Cissy Caffrey—a young girl who appears on Sandymount Strand in Nausikaa in the company of Edy Boardman and Gerty MacDowell. She is there minding her twin brothers Jacky and Tommy. She seems to appear in Circe as a prostitute walking with Privates Carr and Compton, though it is more than likely that she is the product of hallucination.

Pvt. Harry Carr—a drunken British soldier who knocks down Stephen Dedalus on the street in Nighttown after Stephen supposedly insulted King Edward VII. The real-life model for Carr, Henry Carr, was a staff member of the British diplomatic corps in Zurich with whom Joyce was involved in an acrimonious lawsuit over a pair of trousers.

The Citizen—this is the *nom de guerre* of a belligerent, nationalist character who appears in Barney Kiernan's pub in the Cyclops episode. He is presented as a lay about and a blowhard throughout the episode, with an opinion on everything and a violent hatred of the English. He allows Joe Hynes to buy him several rounds of drinks and becomes outraged when Bloom does not do the same, mixing his anti-Semitism with the unfounded suspicion that Bloom successfully wagered on Throwaway in the Gold Cup race, a slander perpetrated by Lenehan. The Citizen's anger over Bloom's reluctance to share his good fortune by buying a round of drinks leads to a confrontation with a surprisingly aggressive Bloom that stops just short of violence. The Citizen is based on a well-known Irish nationalist of the time, Michael Cusak.

Martha Clifford—a woman whom Bloom met after he placed a newspaper ad for a typist. (It was actually a ploy that he used as a way to make contact with young women.) By the time of the novel, Bloom and Martha have begun a steady correspondence that has progressed from professional inquiries to exchanging sexually titillating letters. This epistolary sex-play seems to be all that Bloom wants from the relationship. He resists her desire to meet and signs his letters to her with a pseudonym, Henry Flower, and he suspects that her name may not actually be Martha Clifford.

Bella Cohen—the madam who runs a whorehouse in Nighttown. Stephen and Lynch, followed by Bloom, go there looking for one of the prostitutes, Georgina Johnson. Bella is part of Bloom's sado-masochistic fantasy of becoming transformed into a female prostitute and she as Bello becomes his dominator. Later, Bloom must placate her when she threatens to call the police after Stephen damages a lampshade.

Rev. John Conmee, S.J. (1847–1910)—a character based on a Jesuit priest of the same name whom Joyce knew. He first appears in chapter one of *A Portrait of the Artist as a Young Man* as the rector of Clongowes Wood College when Stephen was a student there. In the Wandering Rocks chapter, Father Conmee, now Prefect of Studies at Belvedere College and Superior of St. Francis Xavier Church, travels across Dublin trying to find a place for one of Paddy Dignam's children, Patrick, at the O'Brien Institute for Destitute Children.

Myles Crawford—the fictional editor of the *Evening Telegraph*, a newspaper that shared offices with *The Freeman's Journal*, who appears in the Aeolus chapter. His drunken bombast punctuates much of the dialogue in the Aeolus chapter where he encourages Stephen to become a journalist.

Martin Cunningham—a character who first appeared in the *Dubliners* short story "Grace." He is Dublin Castle official, that is, someone working with the British civil administration of Ireland, with a generally benevolent disposition. In the Hades episode, he begins organizing donations to help Paddy Dignam's family, and in the Cyclops chapter he tries to prevent a violent altercation between Bloom and The Citizen.

Garrett Deasy—the headmaster of the boys' school in Bray where Stephen teaches. He appears in Nestor as a misogynistic, anti-Semitic, eccentric imperialist with a pompous and often misguided sense of his knowledge of the world. He intimates, perhaps as a threat, that Stephen will not long remain a teacher at his school, yet he has no compunction asking Stephen to use his influence to secure the publication of a letter advocating strong measures to combat cattle disease.

Dilly (Delia) Dedalus—one of Stephen's sisters. She is seen in Wandering Rocks confronting her father, Simon, over his spendthrift ways and unwillingness to do anything to care for his children. She also meets Stephen who sees her desperate situation, malnourished and in a ragged dress. Stephen feels a measure of guilt and concern, but he chooses not to help.

May Dedalus—she first appears in *A Portrait of the Artist as a Young Man* as the long-suffering wife of Simon Dedalus and the mother of Stephen and his siblings. The memory of her death from cancer a year before the action of the novel begins haunts Stephen throughout the narrative. He feels particularly guilty knowing how deeply his agnosticism worried and wounded her. Stephen sees her ghost in the Circe chapter.

Simon Dedalus—he first appears in *A Portrait of the Artist as a Young Man* as the husband of May Dedalus and the feckless father of Stephen and his siblings. Though callously unwilling to do much to care for his now motherless children, he remains popular among his acquaintances because of his wit, sarcastic sense of humor, and fine tenor voice. He embodies what Stephen could become if he gave himself over to being a barroom raconteur rather than an artist.

Stephen Dedalus—he first appears in *A Portrait of the Artist as a Young Man* as the title character and is one of the central figures in *Ulysses*. He lives in Sandycove with Buck Mulligan, and he teaches at Garett Deasy's school in nearby Bray. On 16th June, after an early release from his classes, Stephen spends the rest of his day wandering around Dublin carousing on the salary he has just received from Deasy, getting progressively drunker and spending his money with increasing recklessness. It is clear from his thoughts that he struggles with his artistic ambitions and a desire for recognition. He also continues to feel guilt over the death of his mother and continues to wear black as a sign of mourning although it has been almost a year since her death. When he leaves Bloom's house at the end of the Ithaca chapter, the reader has no clear sense of how he will turn out.

Paddy Dignam—the deceased friend of Bloom, Martin Cunningham, Simon Dedalus, and others who in the Hades chapter attend his funeral and internment at Glasnevin Cemetery on 16th June. Like Simon Dedalus, Dignam is a heavy-drinking, underemployed Dubliner who seems to have done little to provide for his family.

Lydia Douce—a barmaid at the Ormond Hotel who appears in the Sirens episode. She flirts with Simon Dedalus, tolerates Lenehan, and unsuccessfully tries to charm Blazes Boylan. At the end of the chapter, she attracts the attention of Bloom and of George Lydell by provocatively stroking a beer pull while Ben Dollard sings "The Croppy Boy."

The Dun—the nameless narrator of Cyclops. It is with Penelope the only two episodes presented in the first person. He relates the events at Barney Kiernan's pub while letting Joe Hynes buy him a number of drinks. Although he says little during the time he spends in the pub, his stream of consciousness shows a deeply judgmental and highly misanthropic view of almost everyone he encounters.

Kevin Egan—an Irish political agitator living in self-imposed exile while working as a printer in Paris whom Stephen encountered during his brief time there. Joyce modeled Egan on James Casey, an Irish expatriate whom he knew in Paris at the turn of the last century.

John Eglinton (1868–1961)—the pseudonym adopted by William Magee, an essayist and assistant librarian at the National Library of Ireland. He is one of more hostile listeners to Stephen's disquisition on Shakespeare in the Scylla and Charybdis episode.

James "Skin-the-Goat" Fitzharris—purportedly a member of the Invincibles, the gang of political assassins who perpetrated the Phoenix Park murders. He is the proprietor of the cabman's shelter that Bloom and Stephen visit in the Eumaeus chapter.

Henry Flower—a pseudonym used by Bloom in corresponding with Martha Clifford. Virag, the Bloom family's original name, is the Hungarian word for flower.

Nosey Flynn—a character who first appears in the *Dubliners* story, "Grace." He is an acquaintance whom Leopold Bloom runs into in the Lestrygonians episode at Davy Byrne's pub.

Richie Goulding—brother-in-law of Simon Dedalus and uncle of Stephen. While walking along Sandymount Strand, Stephen thinks of visiting his Uncle Richie but, although he paints an evocative picture of the household, does not. Later, in the Sirens chapter, Goulding bumps into Bloom outside the Ormond Hotel, and they go into its restaurant for a meal.

Haines—an Oxford friend of Buck Mulligan staying at the Martello Tower in Sandycove with Buck and Stephen. He first appears in the Telemachus chapter as the stereotypical, blockheaded, patronizing, anti-Semitic, imperialistic Englishman. He evinces an interest in Irish culture, and he appears at various points in the narrative accompanying Mullingan about town. He is based on Samuel Chenevix Trench, an English friend of Oliver St. John Gogarty (the model for Buck Mulligan).

Joe Hynes—first mentioned in the *Dubliners* story, "Ivy Day in the Committee Room" as the author of a maudlin poem about Charles Stewart Parnell. He is a newspaper reporter who appears in Hades to write an account of Dignam's burial. In the Aeolus chapter he ignores Bloom's hint to repay a one-pound loan, and in the Cyclops episode he instead spends his salary treating the dun and the Citizen and displaying his nationalistic fervor.

Georgina Johnson—a prostitute mentioned in the Circe chapter. She once worked at Bella Cohen's brothel. Stephen goes there in search of her only to discover she has left to marry a commercial traveler, Mr. Lambe of London.

Corny (Cornelius) Kelleher—he appears at several points in the novel. In Hades he supervises arrangements for Dignam's funeral. In Wandering Rocks his conversation with a police officer lends some credence to the rumor that he acts as an informant. And, in the Circe chapter he persuades two constables not to arrest Stephen who has been detained for public brawling.

Mina Kennedy—she appears in the Sirens episode, working as a barmaid at the Ormond Hotel. She seems to be both slightly older and slightly more reserved than the other barmaid Lydia Douce.

Tom Kernan—he first appears in the *Dubliners* story, "Grace." He is a tea salesman and, like Bloom, someone who converted to Catholicism in order to marry. He is among the mourners at Paddy Dignam's funeral, and his disparaging remarks there to Bloom make clear his loyalties remain with the Church of Ireland (the Irish version of the Anglican Church).

Barney Kiernan—owner of the pub bearing his name and that is featured in the Cyclops episode. He is not present in the narrative, and he is rumored to be in a mental institution, the House of St. John of God in Stillorgan Park, suffering from delirium tremens.

Ned (Edward J.) Lambert—one of the mourners at Paddy Dignam's funeral in the Hades episode. He is a friend of Simon Dedalus and also briefly appears in the newspaper offices in the Aeolus chapter and again in the Wandering Rocks and the Circe episodes.

Lunita Laredo—Molly Bloom's mother. Details about her background remain obscure, but hints dropped by Molly during her soliloquy in the Penelope episode indicate that Lunita was of Spanish and Jewish ancestry. The novel does not touch on her courtship by Major Brian Tweedy or for that matter confirm their marital status, but it does suggest that she either died or deserted the family when Molly was a young girl.

(T.) Lenehan—a parasite who first appears in the *Dubliners* story, "Two Gallants." He shows up in a number of episodes of *Ulysses* as a hanger-on, lighting cigarettes, telling jokes, giving horseracing tips, and caging drinks. In the Wandering Rocks episode, he gratuitously slanders Molly's reputation and in the Cyclops chapter he stirs up animosity by falsely asserting that Bloom won money betting on Throwaway in the Gold Cup.

George Lydell—a solicitor who appears in the Ormond Hotel in the Sirens episode where he flirts with Lydia Douce.

Vincent Lynch—he appears in both *Stephen Hero* and *A Portrait of the Artist as a Young Man* as a friend of Stephen's. In *Ulysses* he is identified as a former classmate and current medical student who is among the drinkers at Holles Street Maternity Hospital in Oxen of the Sun and who subsequently accepts Stephen's invitation to accompany to Nighttown. At the maternity hospital he makes snide remarks about Stephen's creative output, and in Nighttown he deserts Stephen when the altercation with two drunken British soldiers begins to develop.

Gerty MacDowell—a sentimentally romantic young woman who appears on Sandymount Strand in Nausikaa with her friends Edy Boardman and Cissy Caffrey. The first half of the chapter offers a sense of Gerty perspective of the world written in a prim romance magazine style that presumably appeals to her. Surprisingly, given the narrative that preceded it, during a fireworks display when she notices Bloom watching her, she adopts an unexpectedly aggressive posture, revealing her undergarments to him while he masturbates.

C.P. (Charley) M'Coy—an acquaintance of Bloom who first appears in the Lotus Eaters chapter, again briefly in the Wandering Rocks episode, and finally in several hallucinations in Circe. Like Bloom, he has a wife with singing aspirations but, unlike Bloom, M'Coy is more often than not down on his luck and has a reputation for unreliability. (He reputedly borrowed luggage from Jack Power, "to enable Mrs. M'Coy to fulfill imaginary engagements in the country," and pawned it.)

John Henry Menton—a Dublin solicitor who attends Paddy Dignam's funeral and at the conclusion of the Hades episode snubs Bloom's polite efforts to make him aware of a dinge in his hat.

Buck (Malachi) Mulligan—the first character to appear in the novel and one who continues to pop at select moments in the Syclla and Charybdis, the Wandering Rocks, the Oxen of the Son, and the Circe episodes. He is based on Joyce's friend Oliver St. John Gogarty, and, like Gogarty, he is a medical student. Mulligan shares the Martello Tower with Stephen, as Gogarty did briefly with Joyce. Buck is smart, witty, and creative, but he is more than willing to pander to popular tastes, contenting himself with inventing amusing anecdotes rather than pursuing art seriously. He behaves as both a friend and a rival to Stephen, and he represents the kind of person whom Stephen could become were he less committed to being an artist.

D.B. Murphy—a sailor who appears in the cabman's shelter in the Eumaeus episode bragging about his extensive world travels working as a seaman over the last seven years. Some of his astonishing tales lead Bloom to suspect him of exaggerating his experiences. He appears to be a pseudo-Ulysses in no hurry to go home to his wife in Cork.

Jack Power—who first appears in the *Dubliners* story, "Grace." He is one of the mourners at Paddy Dignam's funeral in the Hades chapter. Later, in the Wandering Rocks and in the Cyclops episodes, he is seen accompanying Martin Cunningham around the city trying to raise money to help Dignam's family.

Mina (Wihelmina) Purefoy—a friend of Leopold and Molly Bloom mentioned at several points in the narrative. She is a patient in the Holles Street Maternity Hospital awaiting the birth of her ninth child. In the Oxen of the Sun chapter, Bloom goes to the hospital to inquire after her, and while he is there Mina Purefoy's child, named Mortimer Edward, is born.

The Blind Stripling—the young piano tuner whom Bloom encounters as the latter leaves Davy Byrne's pub. The Blind Stripling reappears briefly in the Wandering Rocks and the Sirens chapters and as a hallucination in the

Circle episode. Bloom guides the young man north to Molesworth Street and then east to Kildare Street.

Throwaway—the thoroughbred, ridden by W. Lane, who wins the Ascot Gold Cup race on 16th June. While frequently mentioned as a possibly successful long shot, none of the bettors have placed money on him. However, the rumor that Bloom has backed the horse and won causes a measure of ill will among some of those men who put their money on other horses.

Major Brian Tweedy—the father of Molly Bloom. Though mentioned often in the narrative, he has died before the action of the book begins. Before retiring and moving with Molly to Dublin, Tweedy served in the British Army stationed in Gibraltar. Where he seems to have met Molly's mother, Lunita Laredo. However, it is unclear if Tweedy ever married her, and for some critics it remains debatable that he was a Major and not a Sergeant Major, fraudulently assuming the officer's title after he had retired from service.

Virag—The original family name of Leopold Bloom and the Hungarian word for flower. See Rudolph Bloom.

Selected Annotations

Gifford, Don with Robert J. Seidman. *Ulysses Annotated: Notes for James Joyce's Ulysses*. Second edition revised and enlarged. Berkeley: University of California Press, 1988.

Thornton, Weldon. *Allusions in Ulysses: An Annotated List*. Chapel Hill: University of North Carolina Press, 1968.

5 Approaching *Finnegans Wake*

It may not be precisely clear when Joyce discovered that he could do virtually anything with language, but the composition of *Finnegans Wake*, his final and most innovative work, makes that claim indisputable. In early serialized segments of the *Wake*, Joyce was transparent in his intention to expand the boundaries of language beyond what he had already begun to do in the latter chapters of *Ulysses*. Although many readers feel intimidated by the complexity of the work, few still question the scope of its achievement.

Finnegans Wake is at once both structurally simple and linguistically complex. It is written in a radically new narrative style that sought to duplicate the simultaneity and multiplicity of human thought. Its syntax and sentence structure conform essentially to ordinary English writing, but its grammatical mutability and its lexicon of puns, neologisms, and borrowings from foreign languages create an enriched but highly complex text that presents countless challenges for readers seeking to come to some understanding of it.

Joyce experienced early resistance to the project from some of his closest and oldest supporters. Both Ezra Pound and Stanislaus Joyce implored him to give it up as a pointless exercise that wasted his talents. After having read an excerpt from *Work in Progress* published in the *transatlantic review* in April 1924, Stanislaus wrote to his brother in August calling the passage "drivelling rigmarole" and questioning whether it was "written with the deliberate intention of pulling the reader's leg or not" (*Letters III*.102). Joyce did not waver from his commitment to the work, but he certainly felt the need to justify what he was doing. In a November 1926 letter to his benefactor, Harriet Shaw Weaver, Joyce explains his need to break with conventional stylistic structures, asserting that a "great part of every human experience is passed in a state which cannot be rendered sensible by the use of wide-awake language, cut and dry grammar and goahead plot" (*Letters III*.146). He went further, three years later, when he engineered the publication of *Our Exagmination Round His Factification for Incamination of Work in Progress*, a collection of twelve essays and two letters of protest published in 1929 with the aim of aiding readers in grasping what Joyce was accomplishing in his new work. While some of the essays proved as challenging as the work itself, they nonetheless, as its first printed criticism, presaged the variety of

DOI: 10.4324/9781003223290-6

approaches and panoply of responses that *Finnegans Wake* could inspire. The title of this collection was taken from *Finnegans Wake* 497.2–3.

Having some reference points early on proved useful to those with an ongoing interest in Joyce's writings. Before *Finnegans Wake* was published on 4 May 1939, serialized portions of nearly the entire work, appearing under the title *Work in Progress* between 1924 and 1938, were published in a variety of journals and literary magazines. Each fragment laid out distinct linguistic and narrative challenges, but even the most conscientious students of the work who managed to read everything that appeared still found it a daunting task to see a unified narrative in this collection of writing.

Although *Our Exagmination Round His Factification for Incamination of Work in Progress* implicitly invited others to take up the task of illuminating what they had read to this point by rejecting conventional critical approaches, most early responses relied on traditional practices and questions. By the late 1920s, an interpretative approach to these challenges coalesced around a perspective that many hoped to provide clarity to a discourse often informed by ambiguity: they endeavored to see narrative as a dream. This idea was later elaborated on by Edmund Wilson in his 1939 review of *Finnegnas Wake*, "The Dream of H. C. Earwicker," and then again by Joseph Campbell and Henry Morton Robinson in their 1944 publication of *A Skeleton Key to* **Finnegans Wake**, the first full-length study of the novel.

This prevailing approach to reading *Finnegans Wake* as a dream became firmly established in the scholarship surrounding the work during the first three or four decades after its publications. However, by the rise of deconstructive criticism and the challenge it made to conventional epistemology prompted some scholars—Bernard Benstock, Patrick Parrinder, John Bishop, and Derek Attridge being among the more prominent—to question this assumption and see it as one approach among others. Today, methods for reading *Finnegans Wake* are as diverse and complicated as any of the sections of the work itself that baffled so many readers when it first began to be serialized. What follows is not an effort to promote a particular hermeneutic approach but rather an effort to lay out the basic features of the narrative in the hope of making it more accessible to readers who will then feel free to understand its discourse in whatever manner suits them.

The Evolution of *Finnegans Wake* and Published Excerpts

Over the course of his career as an author, Joyce's writing became less and less linear. He composed episodes of both *Dubliners* and *A Portrait of an Artist as a Young Man* in an order that roughly corresponded to their arrangement in the final form of the works. *Ulysses* appears to begin with that same linear perspective, but in fact the time sequence is deceptive; the time of chapter one parallels that of chapter four, chapter two that of five, and chapter three that of six. As page proofs arrived from the French printer, Maurice Darantiere, Joyce's revisions expanded exponentially and any semblance of conventional progression disappeared. (Michael Groden's book, **Ulysses** *in Progress*, gives a wonderful account of this process.) By the time Joyce approached his final work, traditional, linear structures of composition had long since become for him a thing of the past. Time and space in *Finnegans Wake* took on new dimensions.

In March of 1923, 13 months after the publication of *Ulysses*, Joyce started his note taking as preliminary steps to writing the *Wake*. Between this date and October of the same year, he was sketching drafts of passages that were eventually revised to become sections of various chapters by the time the *Wake* was published in 1939. (In *The "Wake" in Transit*, David Hayman provides a full discussion of the importance of Joyce's notetaking in the compositional history of *Finnegans Wake*.) These early pieces include King Roderick O'Conor (*FW* 380–382), Tristan and Isolde (*FW* 383–399), St. Patrick and the Druid (*FW* 611–612), St. Kevin (*FW* 604–606), Mamalujo (*FW* 383–399, incorporated into Tristan and Isolde), and Here Comes Everybody (*FW* 30–34). What began in bits and pieces was designed to be part of a large and humorous work with universal meaning.

In April 1924, the first excerpt from "From Work in Progress" was published in *transatlantic review*, and over the next 13 years fragments, some pirated, appeared in the following journals: *The Criterion* (July 1925, *FW* 104.1–125.23); *Contact Collection of Contemporary Writers* (1925, *FW* 30.1–34.29); *Navire d'Argent* (October 1925, *FW* 196.1–216.5); *This Quarter* (Autumn–Winter 1925–1926, *FW* 169.1–195.6); *transition* (April 1927, *FW* 3.1–29.36). (Between September 1925 and September 1926, these five fragments were pirated by Samuel Roth and published in *Two Worlds Monthly*.) Seventeen fragments appeared in *transition*, a Paris journal, from April 1927 through April–May 1938.

Most of *Finnegans Wake* was published in fragments by 1938 either in journals or separately in booklet form. The following are titles and brief summaries of the individually published extracts, which Joyce, as was his habit, revised before *Finnegans Wake* was finally published in 1939.

Anna Livia Plurabelle, the title given to Book I, chapter 8 (*FW* 196–216), was first published in *transition* in 1927 and then as a booklet by the small New York publisher Crosby Gaige in 1928 and again in 1930 by Faber and Faber in England. One of the most widely recognized chapters in *Finnegans Wake* and arguably the most lyrical, *Anna Livia Plurabelle* narrates the gossip two washerwomen share about Earwicker's behavior and Anna Livia's complicity.

Tales Told of Shem and Shaun, published in 1929 by Black Sun Press in Paris, consists of "The Mookse and the Gripes" (*FW* 152–159), "The Muddest Thick That Was Ever Heard Dump" (*FW* 282–304), and "The Ondt and the Gracehoper" (*FW* 414–419). In 1930, *Imagist Anthology*, a London publication, republished segments of these episodes, titled "From 'Tales Told of Shem and Shaun'; Three Fragments from Work in Progress." Found in Book I, chapter 6, "The Mookse and the Gripes" passage is an allusion to Aesop's fable, "The Fox and the Grapes," and depicts the continuing conflict of opposites prevalent throughout the *Wake* and especially between Shaun (the

Mookse) and Shem (the Gripes). "The Muddest Thick That Was Ever Heard Dump," found in the Lessons Chapter of Book II, chapter 2, humorously narrates how Shaun (Kev) is ill-prepared for Euclidean and non-Euclidean geometry and how the shrewd Shem (Dolph) enlightens him on both geometry and sex. "The Ondt and the Gracehoper," found in Book III, chapter 2, was first published in the March 1928 issue of *transition* and then as a separate piece by Black Sun Press in 1929. Modelled on Jean de La Fontaine's "Fable of the Ant and the Grasshopper," the episode tells the moral lesson one can derive from the carefree-artist Gracehoper (Shem/James Joyce) and the chary-bourgeois Ondt (Shaun/Stanislaus Joyce). Both have a mixture of qualities, good and bad.

Haveth Childers Everywhere, first published in Paris in 1930, by Henry Babou and Jack Kahane, by the Fountain Press in New York in the same year, and again in 1931 by Faber and Faber in England, is a segment of Book III, chapter 3 (*FW* 532–554), that narrates HCE's self-defense against charges accusing him of wrongdoing followed by his litany of achievements.

The Mime of Mick Nick and the Maggies, the title given to Book II, chapter one (*FW* 219–259), was published by the Servire Press, The Hague, in 1934. The edition contains illustrations by Lucia Joyce. As the title indicates, the chapter takes the form of a play in which the Shem (Nick/Glugg), Shaun (Mick/Chuff), and Issy (the Maggies) are the principal characters. As Joyce explained, that the episode is a dramatized version of the children's game "Angels and Devils, or colours."

Storiella as She is Syung refers to the first and last parts of the Lessons chapter, Book II, chapter 2 (*FW* 260–275, 304–308); this fragment was published in the July 1935 issue of *transition* and then as a booklet in 1937 by Corvinus Press, London. Joyce's daughter, Lucia, contributed an illuminated letter on the volume's first page. In the first of the two passages, the Earwicker family arrives home and the children begin their lessons with grammar and history. The second tells of the night letter the children write to their parents.

Referencing Passages in *Finnegnas Wake*

The 17 chapters in the *Wake* are divided into four Books. Book I contains eight chapters; Books II and III contain four chapters each, and Book IV is comprised of only one chapter. With very few exceptions (an abridged copy for instance), all editions of *Finnegans Wake* have identical pagination with the same number of lines on a given page. The general practice is to cite the page(s) and line number(s); for example, 182.31–36 refers to lines 31 through 36 on page 182, and 185.27–186.1–18 refers to page 185 starting with line 27 to line 18 on page 186. Sometimes book numbers, chapter numbers, and page numbers are used; for example, *FW* II.1:219–221 refers to book two, chapter one, pages 219 to 221. To cite the marginalia and/or footnotes of Book II, chapter 2 (Bk II.2), one normally uses the following designations: 281.R2 refers to the second set of notes in the right margin on page 281, and 295.L1 refers to the first set of notes in the left margin on page 295; 293.F2 refers to footnote 2 on page 293. Though it all seems confusing when presented like this, usage quickly brings out the logic of this approach, and the density of the narrative of *Finnegans Wake* gives such an approach a precision that soon proves to be most welcome as one seeks to find one's way through the text.

Organizational Approaches to *Finnegans Wake*

Despite the nonlinearity of the *Wake*, Joyce organized the work according to clear structural boundaries with the 17 chapters gathered into four Books. Below are the designations given to the individual sections by Campbell and Robinson in their *A Skeleton Key to* **Finnegans Wake**:

Book I—THE BOOK OF THE PARENTS
1   Finnegan's Fall
2   HCE—His Agnomen and Reputation
3   HCE—His Trial and Incarceration
4   HCE—His Demise and Resurrection
5   The Manifesto of ALP
6   Riddles—The Personages of the Manifesto
7   Shem the Penman
8   The Washers at the Ford
Book II—THE BOOK OF THE SONS
1   The Children's Hour
2   The Study Period—Triv and Quad
3   Tavernry in Feast
4   Bride Ship and Gulls
Book III—THE BOOK OF THE PEOPLE
1   Shaun before the People
2   Jaun before St. Bride's
3   Yawn under Inquest
4   HCE and ALP—Their Bed of Trial
Book IV—RECORSO [SIC]

As these titles and the episode summaries that appear later show, each major division is devoted to broad topics and general references to characters, and the chapters within each develop variations on those central themes and individuals. For alternative titles given to the breakdown of the book and chapter designations, readers may consult the following works, all of which are cited in our bibliography: William York Tindall's *A Reader's Guide to James Joyce*, Bernard Benstock's *Joyce-Again's Wake*, Adaline Glasheen's *Third Census of* **Finnegans Wake**, and Edmund Lloyd Epstein's *A Guide through* **Finnegans Wake**.

By adopting a narrative structure based on and parodying the form Giambettista Vico gave to the three ages of history (that of the gods, heroes, and humans) followed by a brief *ricorso* or return to repeat the cycle again, the *Wake* depicts the cyclical nature of life and the Aristotelian notion that the universal is contained in the particular.

Perhaps because he still had the somewhat chaotic revision process of *Ulysses* fresh in his mind, when Joyce began writing *Finnegans Wake* he followed a piecemeal method of composition. Joyce explained his approach in a conversation that he had with the sculptor August Suter, recorded by Frank Budgen in *James Joyce and the Making of Ulysses*. When speaking to Suter, he said: "I feel like an engineer boring through a mountain from two sides. If my calculations are correct we shall meet in the middle. If not . . ." (p. 320). The metaphor took hold for him, so in a November 1924 letter to Harriet Shaw Weaver he explained the process in much the same fashion: "I think that at last I have solved one—the first—of the problems presented by my book. In other words one of the partitions between two of the tunneling parties seems to have given way" (*Letters III*.110). As the *Wake* was evolving, Joyce was perhaps the only one who could perceive its inherent unity. However, through his perseverance, the work's linguistic, thematic and orthographic features achieved the coherence that he had always intended. With this master plan guiding him, Joyce consistently reworked, revised and reorganized portions of *Finnegans Wake* throughout various stages of reimagination between 1924 and 1938.

A Particular Note on the Sigla

During the composition of the *Wake*, Joyce used sigla (signs) to identify in shorthand the identity of the work's main characters. He explained these symbols in a March 1924 letter to Harriett Shaw Weaver (*Letters I*.213):

- ᚷ (Earwicker, HCE by moving letter round)
- Δ   Anna Livia
- C   Shem-Cain
- /\   Shaun
- S   Snake
- P   S. Patrick
- T   Tristan
- ⊥   Isolde
- X   Mamalujo
- ☐   This stands for the title but I do not wish to say it yet until the book has written more of itself.

While they seem initially to have been intended as a compositional aid, over the course of his writing, Joyce came to include some of these sigla at various points in the completed form of the *Wake*. In one instance, he grouped seven of them together (see *FW* 299.F4), while changing ⊣ (Isolde) to (Issy).

Throughout their application, Joyce used each siglum consistently but at times would slightly vary its position by rotating it one way or another. By doing so, he would shed light on different aspects of a character or theme or motif. At first the sigla seemed intended as little more than abbreviated designations used to identify characters, but in time they became more intricate and began to connote traits unique to the characters. The more he progressed in composing the *Wake*, the greater role the sigla played; like that of everything else related to the project, the purpose and significance of the sigla changed over time. As the characters in *Finnegans Wake* evolved and took on a more and more distinct personality, the denotations that adhered to the signs representing them expanded.

In one of the many letters about the composition of *Finnegans Wake* written to Harriet Shaw Weaver (31 May 1927), Joyce demystifies the sign for Earwicker: "⊞ means HCE interred in the landscape" (*Letters* I.254); this siglum first appears in the opening chapter of the *Wake* (*FW* 6.32). One of the footnotes in the Night Lessons chapter (*FW* II.2:260–308) shows the flexibility and expansiveness of Joyce's use of these signs. Appearing together with subtle variations, the sigla here represent HCE, ALP, Issy, the Four Old Men, the title of the book, Shaun, and Shem); the note reads: "The Doodles family ⊓, △, ⊣, ×, □, ∧, ⊏, Hoodle doodle, fam.?" (*FW* 299.F4). (A detailed structural and thematic analysis of Joyce's use of the sigla can be found in Roland McHugh's *The Sigla of* **Finnegans Wake**, cited in our bibliography.)

What's in a Name: Wrestling with the Title

For the 17 years during which he was composing *Finnegans Wake*, Joyce used the title *Work in Progress* to refer to the project before it was published. Joyce got the idea for it when in 1924 the British novelist, critic, and editor of the *transatlantic review*, Ford Madox Ford, published an early fragment from the novel in a supplement in his journal entitled *Work in Progress*. The phrase suited Joyce's aims perfectly, allowing him to hide his efforts in plain sight, and he consequently applied it assiduously during the 17 years he spent writing and publishing segments of the *Wake*.

Exactly when he settled on calling his new work *Finnegans Wake* remains uncertain, but from the beginning of his efforts Joyce teased those around him by keeping the title a secret from everyone—that is, everyone except his wife. At the same time, he did not mean to conceal his efforts, and he kept interest alive in what he was doing by teasing his friends about it and encouraging them to guess what it was.

In May 1927, for example, Joyce wrote to Harriet Shaw Weaver, and included a teasing invitation to identify the actual title. "I shall use some of your suggestions about □, [Joyce's siglum for the title of the book] . . . The title is very simple and as commonplace as can be" (*Letters* I.252). Joyce offered a wager to anyone who could accurately name the title of his new work. He was surprised, if not shocked, when in 1938 his friend Eugene Jolas, a cofounder of the experimental literary magazine *transition*, came up with the right title and won the wager of 1000 French francs. (See *Letters* III.427, and Richard Ellmann's in *James Joyce*, 708). The *Wake* critics Danis Rose and

John O'Hanlon suggest that *Finn's Hotel* was Joyce's original title, the name of the place where Nora was working as a chambermaid when Joyce first met her in 1904. Rose and O'Hanlon argue that evidence for this intention exists in the passage: "—. i ..' .. o .. l" (*FW* 514.18). However, there seems to be little else to support such a claim, and it has not received wide acceptance.

Whatever possible intentions he might have had, the source of the phrase by which the book became known seems clear. Joyce fashioned the work's final title from a pun that he had in mind as derived from the Irish ballad, "Finigan's Wake." The song's main character, a hod carrier with the love for the drink, falls from a ladder and is presumed dead. At his wake he revives when raucous mourners accidently splash whiskey on his face. (The word *whiskey* comes from the Irish term *usquebaugh*, meaning water of life. It appears in the novel's opening chapter, 24.14, and in variant forms throughout the work.) In those simple stanzas, Joyce found the themes that occupied him for 628 pages.

Joyce reiterated his narrative's connections to the song throughout the novel. References to this comedic ballad are found on the first page of the *Wake* and resurface again and again throughout the work. The ballad also introduces a secularized versions of one of the major themes of *Finnegans Wake*, that of a fall and rebirth. Tim Finegan (one of the variations in spelling Finigan) is an archetypal figure of one who falls and, as his name implies, rises-*egan*. Additionally, the work's title makes allusion to the legendary Irish warrior Finn MacCool. He is the giant who lies asleep beneath Dublin and whose corpus lays down geographic boundaries across of the city. Finn's head gives shape to the Ben of Howth in the north, his feet delineate the two

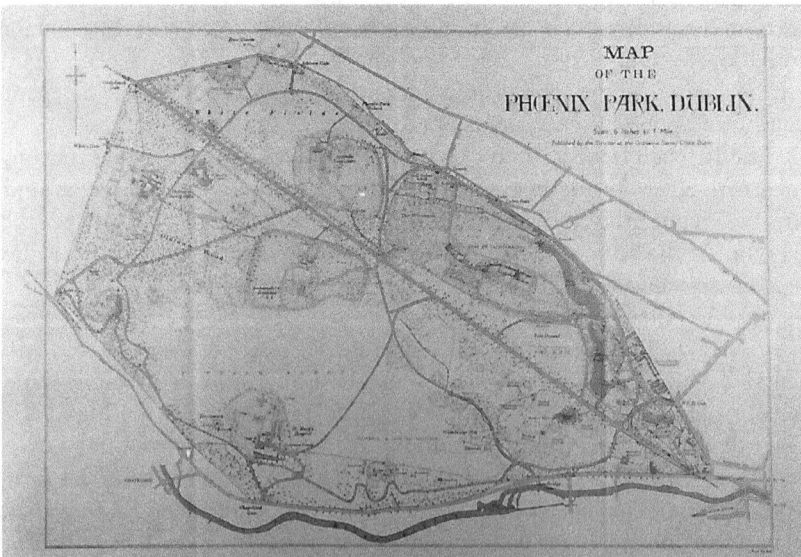

Figure 5.1 Map of Phoenix Park, Dublin

mounds in Phoenix Park to the west, and his body encompasses all that lies between them. When taken together, this ballad and the mythological associations that adhere to it signal the humorous tones and regenerative themes that run through the work.

As a final gesture of independence, the self-conscious absence of an apostrophe at the end of the first work in the title *Finnegans Wake* signals to the reader the work's ambiguous relationship with convention and while using the inherent mutability of the lack of punctuation as an invisible marker of the work's multiplicity of meaning. Similarly, the word *wake* can either be a noun or a verb. As a noun, the word is modified by the proper noun *Finnegans*, either in the singular or plural possessive case without an apostrophe, as in German. As a verb, the word connotes multiple Finnegans waking. As a way of sustaining this sense of variability, the book evokes its title time and again with a range of variation. One sees this, for example, on its last page when **Anna Livia Plurabelle**, in a mixture of exhaustion and triumph utters: "Finn, again! Take" (628.14).

Themes and Motifs

The recurring lapsarian theme forms one of the major motifs in *Finnegnas Wake*, and it also anticipates the complementary subject of renewal that injects a tone of optimism throughout the most anarchic narrative moments. Finnegan's fall—which in short order emerges as an archetypal image of all falls—is introduced on the book's second page followed immediately by the assertion of his inevitable resurrection: "Phall if you but will, rise you must" (4.15–16). As narrative reiterates throughout, Anna Livy Plurabelle, embodying the life-giving waters of the River Liffey, time and again asserts the inescapability of this renewal.

Through the multiple guises and mutations of characters and events, historical repetition on both the individual and collective levels occurs as a motif. On the individual level, **Humphry Chimpden Earwicker**'s ambiguous crime in the park, itself another kind of fall, animates the narrative and foreshadows his eventual fall (replacement) as *pater familias*. On the historical level, the Willingdone Museyroom, housing historical artifacts, is symbolic of the cyclical nature of all battles fought, lost, and won. As a repository of the detritus of Western civilization, the Museyroom is another form of the midden heap that appears in I.5 where the hen plucks out a mysterious letter containing uncertain meanings.

Included in the narrative's exploration of transformation of character identities is an examination of the theme of the conjunction and polarity of opposites, a concept that Joyce first discovered from his readings of Giordano Bruno and then exploited to underline the emphasis he wished to bring out in his account. **Shem** and **Shaun** are the prime manifestation of these forces. The paradoxes that emerge during unrelenting sibling rivalry comes out of the opposite personalities of two warring brothers, who at the same

Figure 5.2 Wellington Monument, Phoenix Park. (Courtesy of the Irish Tourist Board)

time share a common nature derived from their parents and their environment (168.13–14).

One of the most dramatic moments of polarity between Shem and Shaun occurs in I.7 where Shaun berates his artist brother and yet at the same time expounds an extraordinary theory of literature through the use of the theological term *transaccidentation*. Associated with the mystery of the Eucharist, this term describes Shem's bodily transmutation into the words of the text where his spirit perpetually resides. (Though significantly advanced here, Joyce's Eucharistic analogy reaches back to his teens when he was writing poetry.)

This motif of contraries that they embody reappears in variant forms elsewhere in the *Wake*'s narrative. For example, contrasting values of stasis and change, prudence and daring, orthodoxy and innovation are successively manifest in the exchanges between Mutt, the native, and Jute, the invader (15–18), the fable of the Ondt/Shaun and the Gracehoper/Shem (414–419), and the encounter between St. Patrick and **the Archdruid** (611–612). These and other instances underscore the mutability of one's world and the impermanence of human achievements.

It is not simply the nature of character that engaged Joyce's attention over the course of composing *Finnegans Wake*. He had a profound interest in delineating the variations of the way we perceive the world around us and how we endow those perceptions with meaning. Consequently, the variability of language becomes an issue to which the text repeatedly returns.

The mystery of how to engage understanding that seems to be lying just beyond the limits of human comprehension fascinated Joyce's characters who often expressed their views through the deceptively simple language of riddles, first introduced, as noted above, in the slipperiness of the meaning of the work's title. This affinity for puzzles and puzzling reaches its apex in Shem's "first riddle of the universe" (170.4). These riddles, discussed in detail below, serve as an encapsulated form of the exploration of the simultaneous acquisition and ambiguation of knowledge that runs through the whole work. Further, like the structural convolutions of *Ulysses*, this process has heuristic qualities for readers searching for guidance. Within the framework of having fun, suggested by the last words of the song "Finigen's Wake"—"Lots of fun at Finigan's Wake"—the use of riddles in Joyce's *Wake* requires the application of patient ingenuity to engage and eventually come to an accommodation with complexities of being before rising like the Tim Finigan of the ballad to the laughter and fun awaiting them in its chaosmos.

As an almost inevitable feature of any extended examination of human interactions, the theme of frustrated love and lovemaking exercises an insistent demand on a reader's attention throughout the discourse. Joyce introduces the twin concepts early on through the narrative's reference to Sir Tristram (thereby calling to mind the doomed love of Tristan and Isolde) in the *Wake*'s second paragraph. Allusions to this medieval romance recur throughout the work with ample opportunity for the narrative to introduce a range of representations—tragic, comic, and otherwise—of the unfortunate couple.

Though Tristan and Isolde may stand as ironic prototypes, they are by no means the sole manifestations of this theme. The final chapter of the penultimate part (III.4), presents an extended burlesque of manifestations of love and intimacy. There one finds a chronicle of the hapless efforts of **HCE** and **ALP**'s to renew their attempts at lovemaking on their return to bed after checking on their children. However, rather than simply sneering at human ridiculousness, the section underscores the complexity and frustration that impinge on any attempts at physical intimacy when the couple in questions is surrounded by domestic responsibilities.

William York Tindall, in *A Reader's Guide to* **Finnegans Wake**, cited in the bibliography of our book, has noted that this bedroom scene of incomplete lovemaking is the third in a series of frustrated efforts at coitus chronicled in Joyce's writing. The first instance that he identifies occurs in the scene at the Gresham Hotel that takes place near the end of the *Dubliners* short story, "The Dead." Over the course of travelling from his aunt's house to the hotel, Gabriel Conroy's thoughts had been dominated by the idea with intercourse with his wife. However, once in the hotel room the mood shifts radically as he his finds himself confronted with her recollections of a young boy who loved her decades ago. The second example cited by Tindall occurs at the end of the Ithaca episode in *Ulysses*. There, Bloom's intimacy with Molly seems more a gesture of affection than an act of foreplay, for it never progresses beyond kissing the "plump mellow yellow smellow melons of her rump" (*U* 17.2241). Whether these instances embody dysfunctional sexuality or not is of course debatable. They perhaps are more reflective of the complexities of intimacy and the occasional awkwardness of long married couples than on anything else. Nonetheless, it is useful to keep in mind that representations of the stress placed upon family intimacy by the fluctuating features and demands of city life comprises an important theme not only in *Finnegans Wake* but throughout Joyce's works.

Overview of the Chapters in *Finnegans Wake*

A definitive summary of *Finnegans Wake*, even if possible, would go well beyond the space available for it in this volume. However, despite the material limitations that we face, we still feel it possible to give an overview that draws a reader's awareness to the key elements that hold together Joyce's final work of fiction. Although we are all too aware of the need for brevity, we hope that our summary attunes readers to the most dynamic features of the text. As part of that process, we acknowledge the salient features that contribute to its uniqueness.

Finnegans Wake is charged with diverse renditions of shared experiences. It unfolds with a simultaneous multiplicity that comes closer to individual thought than to the conventions of reading. Its linguistic complexities and verbal nuances can be as baffling as they are enlightening. The cadence of passages can take on a force that often appears to run counter to expected rhythms of composition. The recondite contextual determinants and mutable pronunciation of neologisms often disrupt the fundamental sense of narrative unity that a reader struggles to achieve. The subtly of allusions and the use of foreign words can make one restive and resentful.

Despite all this, we retain our belief in the satisfying experience that a careful engagement with *Finnegans Wake* can provide. New methods of reading and interpreting will grow out of conscientious application so that the most vexing words and circuitous passages will eventually lead to an enhanced enjoyment of both the auditory and the visual richness of the text. The following passage from Book III.3 provides useful advice on dealing with Joyce's ludic challenges: "What can't be coded can be decorded if an ear aye sieze what no eye ere grieved for" (482.34–36). What follows attempts to offer a basic clarification of the narrative line from the perspectives we have adopted and through the methods that have worked the best for us. We hope it suits you as well.

Finnegans Wake: Book I.1–8, The Book of the Parents (I.1:3–29)

The chapter chronicles Finnegan's fall, and in its opening sentence *Finnegans Wake* announces a major theme that provides the foundation of much of the narrative that follows: renewal and cyclical return. In elaborating on the paradoxical contiguous discontinuity of the *Wake*'s organization, Joyce explained to his friend and patron, Harriet Shaw Weaver, that his novel "really has no beginning or end. . . . It ends in the middle of a sentence and begins in the middle of the same sentence" (*Letters* I.246). The theme of renewal, as noted earlier, reflects Joyce's adaptation of Giambettista Vico's three recurring ages in history, even as he reinterpreted the concept to suit his own ends. For Joyce, the transitions from one age to another come about through the collision of earth-shaking forces. To mark momentousness of the end of one age and the beginning of another, Joyce evokes literal versions of thunderclaps, ten 100-letter words with the last totaling 101, that punctuate the breath of the narration.

In keeping with this cataclysmic mindset, Joyce uses this first chapter to introduce some of the *Wake*'s most momentous events and to signal the ongoing themes that the discourse will explore over the course of the narrative: Finnegan's fall and HCE's crime in the park touch on individual experience and at the same time evoke the post-Edenic state that conditions the Judeo-Christian perception of the world. From there, the narrative turns to examples of the fluidity and indeterminacy of time that collapse the reader's sense of the linear unity of unfolding events. Adding to our disorientation, scattering allusions to the possibility of renewal are ambiguously counterbalanced by instances of frustrated or doomed love. (Tristan and Iseult's unhappy end, for example, becomes attenuated over the course of the narrative.)

On the social level, macro- and microcosmic associations underscore both unity and disruption. Upheavals within families—especially the fraternal discord that marks the relations between Shem and Shaun—mirror conflicts between nations memorialized by the artifacts in the Willingdone Museyroom where the first reference to the *Wake*'s recurring motif of the letter appears when the guide points out the "gnarlybird" (10.32) digging in the midden heap. The seeming anarchy of these first few pages then blends into the polarity and conjunction of opposites. Personalities are amalgamated with landscape as the initial letters of Howth Castle and Environs evoke the presence of the central figure, HCE. And, the unreliability of perception, metamorphosis and interchangeability of identities (encounter between Mutt/Shem and Jute/Shaun), and the pervasive mutations of words and sounds affirm for readers the narrative's very different approach to representation.

The tale of **the prankquean** and her ill-treatment by the Earl of Howth (Jarl van Hoother) touches on themes of hospitality, legitimacy, and community that have run through Joyce's writing. When the prankquean is refused entrance to his castle by the Earl of Howth, she offers him a riddle that he cannot solve so she kidnaps one of his children. She repeats the process three times, and ends by taking the earl's daughter. The second thunderclap (23.6–7) that occurs at the end of that story provides not so much an explanation as an abrupt transition.

As with so many abrupt shifts in the discourse, it foreshadows a new life and a new beginning. The narrative returns to the now waking Finnegan, addressed in the text as Mr. Finnimore without providing a clear sense of the transition from one state to another. Only metamorphosis seems consistent as when, revived by whiskey (24.14), the resurrected Finnegan/Finnimore now finds himself in Edenborough where HCE "will be ultimendly respunchable for the hubbub caused" there (29.35–36).

I.2:30–47

Before going further, we must offer an important caveat. Though the language is at times obscure and the action more often than not proves to be chaotic, the humor in the opening pages of this chapter (and throughout the *Wake* itself) should not be overlooked as a unifying feature that binds the narrative together. Finnegan seems now to have been replaced by HCE, and the narrative, in its own fashion, begins to tell us about him—his agnomen and reputation. Through the misrule that its humor promotes, the discourse manages both to flesh out HCE's background by offering readers glimpses into pivotal events even as the bathos of the scenes implicitly also warns of the misinformation inherent in the accounts.

What we come to know regarding his heritage and the services he performed from which his name (his agnomen, a nickname) may be derived, for example, shows the provisionality of any recovered account of the past. One story claims that in the peacefulness before the fall, HCE was ploughing for roots in his garden and catching earwigs when a royal hunting party stopped to inquire as to the cause of the potholes on the road. Seeing his vassal Harold or Humphrey Chimpden (HCE) holding a pole used to find earwigs, the genial king William the Conk dubbed him earwigger. A different story claims that the populace turned the initials into the nickname Here Comes Everybody. Yet another recollection has his last initial designate the surname Earwicker, the name that has come to be associated with the crime in the park.

With the introduction of that event, the narrative offers a thumbnail account on the range of speculations on the specific nature of this crime in the park as we receive a summary of how versions of the story spread throughout the community. When he meets "a cad with a pipe" (35.11), Earwicker denies any wrongdoing. However, the cad is not mollified and later tells his wife of the meeting. She in turn offers her version of the news to other friends and neighbors. Rumors of what might have happened continue to spread to be, even by people asleep. While he is having a restless slumber, Treacle Tom's mutterings about it are overheard by Hosty (a Shem the Penman figure), who is consequently inspired to compose and then to proclaim "The Ballad of Persse O'Reilly" (44.24–47.32). Humorously beginning by comparing HCE to Humpty Dumpty, the ballad offers its own thinly veiled version of what Hosty imagines. The *Wake*'s third thunderclap acts as the ballad's antiphon.

I.3:48–74

This chapter—the trial and incarceration of HCE—presents the failed attempt at uncovering Earwicker's crime in the park, first referred to in the Willingdone Museyroom segment of chapter one. Different accounts are shrouded "in a freakfog" (48.2) and exact details of his alleged crime are not clearly discernable. Whatever bits and pieces the narrative offers do not point the reader toward any definitive conclusion. The event remains shrouded in mystery, and even the identities of those connected to what occurred in the park are indiscernible and at best speculative.

Viewing the crime from a distance may not be any more reliable than hearing sound from a distance, in other words, in recollecting rumors of the past inevitable distortion intervenes. Even Earwicker cannot be relied upon. He offers his own televised account of the incident—hoping that "[t]elevision" will kill "telephony" for "the eyes demand their turn" (52.18–19)—but he meets with little success for he presents no factual evidence in support of what he says. One thing seems certain, however, HCE has endured a round of tribunals and, depending on where the trials took place, he was sentenced or acquitted (57.30–36). As opinions about him are solicited from people on the street, Earwicker flees to safety in England where by chance he faces an assailant with a revolver.

By rolling "away the reel world" (64.25), the narrative intersperses a short cinematic account of a scandal analogous to Earwicker's. The shift is brief, and the discourse again switches back to accounts of the inquiries. The first focuses on the arrival of a letter from "A Laughable Party" (ALP) to "Hyde and Cheek, Edenberry" (HCE) and another on a coffin (66.10–27, 30–32). Abruptly, concern turns to a discussion of the coffin removed from a hardware store. Then, a reporter from Austria, Herr Betreffender, observes an unwelcome visitor from the Midwest casting abusive names at Earwicker and throwing stones at his pub before leaving. When the siege against Earwicker and his pub is over, the chapter ends with HCE falling asleep.

I.4:75–103

This is the demise and resurrection of HCE As Earwicker dreams of burial places and mortuary items, the coffin turns up. Then, allusions to various battles, including some from the American Revolution and its Civil War, suggest a dissolution of the existing order of society as well as the possibility of the beginning of a new one. One avatar of this age of renewal is the emergence of the tour guide from the Willingdone Museyroom, identified as mistress Kathe in the first chapter and here called the widow Kate Strong. She guides readers back to Phoenix Park and offers her account of the way things once were. The narrative gives a different account of the encounter between HCE and the Cad. This time the two are seen in the guise of an attacker (the Cad) and the adversary (HCE). Like the Jute and the Mutt encounter in chapter one, this incident presages the central struggle between Shem and Shaun that will dominate much of the second book.

The lengthy and identity-confusing trial of Festy King (HCE) follows, but, even with the remarkable evidence given by a certain W.P., little is achieved. Even the identity of Festy King becomes less certain. Some see him as a Shem figure, others as a Shaun figure, and still others as evolving from one to the other. If the figures of Shem and Shaun switch, one becoming the other, then the witness testifying against the accused logically becomes the accused himself. After the four justices—Untius, Muncius, Punchus, and Pylax—lay their wigs down, the fourth thunderclap sounds during the trial and by its end the mysterious letter reappears and the four judges begin to confuse matters even more. Finally, the King flees like a fox pursued by dogs, with various accounts of what happened to him appear; one is that he died and another that he become a stowaway on a Dutch ship (96.26–100.36).

As a prelude to the next chapter, with imagery of tree and stone and water (all associated with Anna Livia), the narrative turns to her arrival and to her mamafesta and various names (101.2–3).

I.5:104–125

Joyce wrote the opening sentence of the Manifesto chapter in the cadence of the familiar Christian prayer, the Our Father. Thematically, it takes a complex secular role in its invocation to multiple attributes of Anna Livia. Formally, it provides a salutary example of how the rhythm infused in its symphonic-like arrangement employs words and sentences to evoke allusions that function on the specific and the general level to reinforce the narrative's concerns.

A long list of humorous names associated at one time or another with ALP's "untitled mamafesta memorializing the Most-highest" (104.5–107.7) follows. This extended tabulation leads then into the passage focusing attention on the letter's author or authors. Various suggestions put ALP alone as the author or speculate that it is the work of ALP and Shem together, but whoever is the source, the discourse concurs on the difficulty of interpreting it. The narrative (perhaps briefly commandeered by the voice of Shaun) poses the question for the reader: "who in hallhagel wrote the durn thing anyhow?" (107.36–108.1).

Using the right hermeneutic to help in the understanding of the letter becomes a concern, and for the careful reader it evokes a microcosmic exercise that parallels the macrocosmic task of apprehending the *Wake*. Various epistemologies are referenced: textual criticism, historical parallels, and Freudian analysis all receive attention, though none appear completely suited to provide the necessary insight into what the structure of the letter seeks to convey. Nonetheless, it becomes clear that, whatever the compositional specifics of the letter may be, patience and adaptability are needed to derive any sense from the document. Everything must be considered, and even the envelope must not to be overlooked.

Two specifics relating to the situation seem clear: the hen, **Belinda of the Dorans**, unearthed the letter while scratching on the midden heap and the letter came "from Boston (Mass.)" (111.9–10). Having been in the dump for such a long period of time, it has partly deteriorated. The difficulty in interpreting the letter is emblematic of interpreting the *Wake* itself, and, like the Tunc page in the *Book of Kells*, it specifically commented on in this chapter and a prototype of the *Wake* itself, the letter as well as *Finnegnas Wake* "is a perfect signature of its own" (115.7–8). While concentrating on the intricacies of the Tunc page, the narrative parodies the style of Sir Edward Sullivan's introduction to *The Book of Kells*.

The chapter ends with the appearance of the **Four Old Men**—old Jeromesolem, old Huffsnuff, old Andycox, and old Olecasandrum. They ask questions, but no insight recurs beyond the idea "here keen again and begin again to make soundsense and sensesound kin again" (121.14–16). This chapter also contains the *Wake*'s fifth thunderclap, marking a new age.

I.6:126–168

Twelve questions and answers make up the defining feature of this chapter. Except for the last one, posed by Shaun, all are asked by his brother Shem. The questions and answers touch on various topics: the Earwicker family, characters in the narrative, Ireland, and its cities. This structure reinforces a reader's sense of the polarity of the twins and of their oscillating relationship, a central theme that animates the discourse of the *Wake*.

The first and longest question centers on the all-encompassing Earwicker and his complex nature and inimitable feats. Among many other particulars—landscape and vegetation, for example—he is an honorary captain of a fire brigade and friendly with police. Shaun answers Finn MacCool, the legendary hero of Celtic mythology, and in doing so he highlights the link between HCE and his avatar. The second question refers to ALP, the mother of the twins. "Does your mutter know your mike?" (139.15) Shaun's answer

(139.16–28) reveals that he looks upon his father and mother with great pride and describes them in conditional statements; for example: "if he's plane she's purty" (126.22–23).

Shem's third question moves from the familial to the civil. He asks Shaun to decide on a motto for Earwicker's pub. In his response, Shaun plays off Dublin's motto: *Obedientia Civium Urbis Felicitas* (The Obedience of the Citizens Produces a Happy Life). The fourth maintains an interest in the public area by asking for the name of Ireland's capital. He notes that it is a two-syllable word with six letters that can lay claim to four unique features: the largest public park in the world (Phoenix Park), the world's most expensive brewery (Guinness Brewery), the world's most expansive street (O'Connell Street), and the world's most horse-loving population with the most tea-drinking people. The clear answer is Dublin, but Shaun responds by naming the capitals of Ireland's four provinces: (a) Delfas (Belfast), (b) Dorhqk (Cork), (c) Nublid (Dublin), and (d) Dalway (Galway).

Next, Shem turns to a series of domestic inquiries, highlighting supporting figurers in the narrative. Question five asks to name the person who does the lowly day-to-day work at Earwicker's pub. The answer is old Joe. The sixth refers to the Earwickers' housekeeper, the querulous Kate. The answer contains a litany of complaints and statements wishing others misfortune. (Some readers speculate that Kate answers this question while others conclude that Shaun is being sardonic.) The seventh refers to the twelve citizens or customers in Earwicker's pub. The answer suggests that these twelve patrons are asleep and dreaming: they are "The Morphios!" (142.29).

The eighth question takes an uncomfortably personal turn. Shem asks Shaun about their sister **Issy** and her multiple personalities, the maggies or 28 leap-year girls. Shaun answers by identifying their characteristics from being competitive in love to being cunning and annoying. This introduces a theme of competition and incest that will periodically raise issues disrupting family relations from here to the end of the narrative.

The final series turn to issues of hermeneutics grounded in personal experiences. Question nine teases apart the possibilities of what a fatigued dreamer may perceive. The answer: "A collideorscape!" (143.28). The tenth inquiry asks broadly about the nature and meaning of love. Its answer, the second longest in the chapter, takes on a highly personal tone. It seems to be given by Issy herself or, if not directly by her, by Shaun who speaks in Issy's self-reflective voice. Admiring herself in the mirror, Issy vividly imagines a sexual encounter with a Spanish football (soccer) player, but then she dismisses that idea and shifts her thoughts to improving herself by reading novels published in the "New Free Woman" (145.29). But her thoughts are not only about herself; they extend to her 28 school friends, whom she identifies by name, and together they make up the 29 leap-year girls. Her musings culminate in thoughts of marriage.

The eleventh question asks whether Shaun (addressed here as Jones) would come to the aid of his exiled brother in desperate straits with eye troubles and drinking problems. The answer, the longest in the chapter, starts with a resounding No. However, that is only the beginning of a digressive, obfuscating reply. Taking on a pompously erudite role, Shaun as Professor Jones launches into an elaborate monologue on the superiority of space, the dimension associate with Shaun, over inferior time, the dimension associated with Shem. (In an August 1927 letter to Harriet Shaw Weaver, Joyce explains that Shaun's diatribe against time parodies Wyndham Lewis's criticism of Joyce in *Time and Western Man*.)

The first of two examples Shaun gives in support of his saying "No" is an account of the Mookse (Shaun) and the Gripes (Shem), a fable suggestive of Aesop's "The Fox and the Grapes." It evokes the theological controversy, the *filioque* dispute, which caused the separation between the Latin Church of the West, identified as the Mookse, and the Greek Church of the East, the Gripes. In his response, Shaun takes on the tone of infallibility. As the fable comes to an end, Nuvoletta (Issy) in the form of a passing cloud momentarily appears and sheds "the lovliest of all tears" (159.13). After Professor Jones provides a second example of Burrus (Shaun) and Caseous (Shem), an allusion to the assassination of Julius Caesar by Brutus and Cassius, Shaun emphatically reiterates his original answer "No."

The twelfth and final question (*Sacer esto?*) and its answer (*Semus sumus!*) are the shortest of all (168.13–14). *Sacer* in Latin can be either sacred (holy, consecrated) or accursed (detestable, destructive). In the reversal of roles, Shaun becomes the inquisitor and Shem the respondent. The question and answer anticipate central concerns of the next chapter where Shaun casts invectives against Shem, but the answer here seems to be both an indictment of one brother by the other and an admission of their coexistence: *we are Shem (the same)*.

I.7: 169–195

Chapter seven is referred to as Shem the Penman. It concentrates on a portrait of Shem the artist, on the nature of art, and indirectly on Shaun and on his response to his brother's aesthetic life. With the exception of the last two pages, Shaun serves as the chapter's narrator, and much of the text seems to reflect the rivalry between the improvident Joyce and his practical brother Stanislaus: "Shem is as short for Shemus as Jem is joky for Jacob" (169.01).

It begins with a repudiation of Shem's lineage and a barbed description his physical makeup in graphic, unflattering terms. Shaun goes on to assault his brother's nature by offering a derisive caricature of his imaginative efforts. He notes that as a young child, Master Shemmy posed the first riddle of the universe: "When is a man not a man?" (170.5). After a series of responses only tangentially related to the question, it becomes clear that Shem's siblings will be unable to come up with the right answer and win "the prize of a bittersweet crab," (170.7), Shem "took the cake" (170.22), and provides the solution: "when he is a . . . Sham" (170.23–24).

Shaun ridicules Shem's self-imposed exile in a line that Joyce uses as a self-parody (*Letters* I.165–167): "He even ran away with hunself and became a farsoonerite, saying he would far sooner muddle through the hash of lentils in Europe than meddle with Irrland's split little pea" (171.4–6). The culinary metaphors lead to an extended disquisition on diet. Unlike Shaun's gustatory sophistication, Shem's tastes in eating and drinking are unrefined and somewhat disgusting, and Shaun seemingly takes great delight in elaborating upon them.

Shaun continues to talk about Shem's lowness and solipsism. His self-absorption causes him to retire to his infested Haunted Inkbottle of a house outside of the turmoil going on around it. There he resides on the dole away from the world and "self exiled in upon his ego" (184.6–7).

Turning directly to the artistic process, Shaun mocks his brother's practices of making "synthetic ink and sensitive paper for his own end out of his wit's waste" (185.7–8). He describes in vivid scatological terms, first in Latin and then in English, Shem's method of producing ink "through the bowels of his misery" (185.33). He accuses his brother of being "transaccidentated through the slow fires of consciousness" (186.3–4) into his own art.

The imagery repays some closer consideration in terms of its modulating view of art. The use of "transaccidentated" evokes the theological term *transaccidentation*. This in turn suggests an analogy between the Eucharistic mystery that transforms bread and wine into the Body and Blood of Christ and the mystery of art that uses the mundane artifacts of paper, pen, and ink to create profoundly moving imagery. The analogy, however, goes even further. The unabashed blasphemy of the appropriation implies that Shem's spiritual substance is transmuted into ink and words through which he becomes present in his art.

The last pages of this chapter take on an eschatological turn with a suggestion of the displacement of the Old Testament with the New. Shaun as JUSTIUS accuses Shem in the form of MERCIUS of sins of commission and omission and urges him to confess and receive a thorough purging. MERCIUS, who has the last word, defends himself and his art with a messianic gesture—"He lifts the lifewand and the dumb speak" (195.5)—and the sound of a wild goose: "Quoiquoiquoiquoiquoiquoiquoiq!" (195.6).

I.8:196–216

This chapter focuses on the nature of Anna Livia as seen by the relentless scrutiny of the Washers at the Ford. In a letter to Harriet Shaw Weaver, Joyce explained that it "is a chattering dialogue across the river by two washerwomen who as night falls become a tree and a stone. The river is named Anna Liffey" (*Letters* I.213). The typographical image of the first three lines forms a delta (Δ), ALP's siglum, and complements the single letter O that opens the chapter. Together they represent some of the major motifs of the work, the circularity of human experience, completion and perfection, and renewal. As the embodiment of the River Liffey, Anna Livia ends and begins the *Wake*. Reinforcing this motif of fluidity, names of rivers appear throughout the chapter.

Though the chapter begins with an exclamation to tell all about Anna Livia, the gossip of the washerwomen first targets Earwicker. As they do their work the washerwomen speculate about Earwicker's encounter in the park. They make disparaging appraisals of the dirty condition of his shirt. They offer critical dismissals of his personality traits. And, they gratuitously introduce derisive references to his habit of stuttering.

When they tire of pillorying HCE, the chattering females turn their dialogue to ALP. The two women question whether her marriage was actually performed at the Franciscan Church Adam and Eve's. (A reference to this church occurs in the very first line of the *Wake* as the Liffey flows by it.) One of the washer women suspects that she is as bad as her husband and speculates that ALP is involved in his fall. When their talk turns to the letter found by the hen, the conversation reveals the difficulties and hardship of Anna Livia's living conditions.

The interest the washerwomen have covers the uncertain number and names of Anna Livia's children, the way she may have been in her younger days, the plan she framed to get even with those who mock HCE, the ritual she went through in getting ready to deliver Christmas presents to her children, and the course she followed in distributing the presents. What Anna Livia wore is also of interest to the women. The chatter between the two continues until they can no longer hear each other. Keeping with the *Wake*'s motif of metamorphosis, they turn into tree and stone and their chattering turns into the flow of the river. Night falls and Book I of the *Wake* ends as the narrative turns to tales of Shem and Shaun.

(It is interesting, as side notes, that in 1929 Joyce made a recording of the last few pages of this chapter [213.11–216.5] at the Orthological Institute in London. Also, with the Italian writer Nino Frank, Joyce translated this chapter into Italian.)

Finnegans Wake: Book II.1–4, The Book of Sons

II.1:219–259

The Children's' Hour, as the chapter is known, was published as *The Mime of Mick, Nick and the Maggies* in June of 1934, by the Servire Press, the Hague. The first chapter of Book II is a dramatized version based on the children's game that Joyce identified as "Angels and Devils, or colours." In a letter to Harriet Shaw Weaver, Joyce explained that the Angels are girls "grouped behind the Angel, Shawn, and the Devil has to come over three times and ask for a colour. If the colour he asks for has been chosen by any girl she has to run and he tries to catch her" (*Letters* I.295). In the same letter, Joyce also mentioned that he integrated throughout the mime the rhythms of English singing games and that the devil is twice baffled. The first time he vindictively considers blackmailing his mother and father, and the second he retreats into the kind of sentimental poetry Joyce wrote at nine years old.

The devil, Joyce continued, has a painful toothache, throws a fit, and the girls sing a hymn around Shaun.

The drama unfolds at dusk and it is performed at the "Feenichts Playhouse" (219.2). The name conveys rebirth (as in the symbol of the Phoenix) and makes reference to its location near Phoenix Park. At the same time, it proclaims its availability by announcing that there is no entrance fee (fee nix or no charge). The narrative claims that the drama will be broadcast over the seven seas in seven different languages: "certelleneteutoslavzendlatinsoundscript" (219.17). In *A Guide through* **Finnegans Wake** (cited in our bibliography), Edmund Lloyd Epstein points out that the combination of words contains "all the major branches of the Indo-European language family: Celtic, Hellenic, German, Slavic, Iranian, Romance, and Sanskrit" (p. 105). The playbill identifies Shem, the Devil, as Glugg, the Maggies as the Floras (that is, Issy's multiple personalities appearing as angels and rainbow girls), Issy as Izod, and Shaun as an angel portrays Chuff. Other characters include Ann (ALP), Hump (HCE), Customers as citizens at the pub, Saunderson as a spoiled bartender, and Kate as a charwoman. The time of the mime is the pressing moment.

The action of the play depicts Chuff (variously identified as Mick and Shaun) as an angel with a flashing sword and Glugg (known as both Nick and Shem) as the devil with a sword made of clay. When the Maggies appear, Glugg is not able to catch Issy or identify the color of any of the pairs of underwear that the girls are wearing. Though Issy offers a clue (heliotrope) to the color of hers, Glugg guesses wrong three times.

At a seeming stalemate, the Maggies praise Chuff and sing and dance around him, while Issy breaks down in tears when Glugg flees into exile to become a writer. On his return, Glugg fails for a second time to answer the riddle, and he runs off again. Likewise, the 29 girls again dance around Chuff, their shining star. Finally, a remorseful Glugg returns to repent, but his confession reveals more about his parents than himself.

Before the children go in for the night to do their school lessons, Issy gives Glugg more clues about her underwear, but he fails to answer the riddle for the third time. Glugg's three chances to answer the riddle may remind readers of the three riddles the prankquean poses to Jarl van Hoother in the opening chapter of the *Wake*.

The sixth thunderclap is heard, and the game comes to an end; the curtain drops to the sound of applause. With a solemn and prayerful tone, the narrative explains that the doors are closed, the children guarded so they "may read in the book of the opening of the mind to light and err not in the darkness" (258.31–32).

II.2:260–308

This chapter is generally referred to as the Lessons Chapter or the Night Lessons. In a July 1939 letter to his friend Frank Budgen, Joyce described this episode as "a reproduction of a schoolboy's (and schoolgirl's) old classbook complete with marginalia by the twins, who change sides at half time, footnotes by the girl (who doesn't), a Euclid diagram, funny drawings etc" (*Letters I*.406). Joyce also mentions in the same letter that this chapter is seen as "the most difficult" while he proclaims The Manifesto of ALP, I.5 (104–125), as the "easiest" to read. (Students of *Finnegans Wake* might readily attest that "easiest" is at best a relative term.

Like the headings one finds in the Aeolus episode of *Ulysses*, the footnotes and marginalia that run throughout this episode insistently assert their own meanings, maintaining a very loose connection, if any, to the body of the narrative. For example, the first marginalium—UNDE ET UBI (260.R1), "whence and where"—has an uncertain relation to the chapter's opening line that indicates a question of place. Others follow the same pattern.

For the body of the text, along with lessons on grammar, writing, geometry, and history, the chapter includes other topics ranging from the theological and religious to the political and the sexual. The liberal arts (the trivium and quadrivium) are introduced by names of representative figures in their respective fields. However, as the end of the chapter suggests, the actual interest of the notes of Shem, Shaun, and Issy have made seems to lie not so much with the topics of their studies but with the sexuality of their parents. In *A Reader's Guide to* **Finnegans Wake** (cited in the bibliography of our book), William York Tindall suggests that the children's "real concern is with their parents. Through history they arrive at HCE, and through geometry at ALP, who, working at home, created these little homeworkers" (171–172).

In the opening pages of the chapter, the narrative refers to the presence of HCE and ALP by inculcating their initials found in various seemingly innocuous phrases. One example—"Easy, calm your haste! Approach to lead our passage" (262.1–2)—indicates that they are arriving with their children at their inn and residence in Chapelizod next to Phoenix Park. Inside the pub, the patrons are drinking and the publican, Earwicker, content to be making money. While Issy sits and knits on a sofa, the lessons begin with "rhythmatick" (268.8) and continue with grammar (a topic of special interest to Issy because of her concern for letter writing) and history. Through a reference to the close of vespers (the formal recitation of evening prayers in Christian Churches), the narrative indicates the lateness of the hour. This short section culminates in a passage taken directly from the French writer Edgar Quinet that speaks of the perduring nature of flowers outlasting civilizations. In *Structure and Motif in* **Finnegans Wake** (cited in our bibliography), Clive Hart explains that recurring references to this passage and the letter are two of the major motifs throughout the *Wake*.

As the study of geometry begins, it quickly becomes clear that Shaun's method of counting on his fingers will provide little help with this topic. Sure enough, he proves ill-prepared to answer the first Euclidean question Dolph (Shem) poses. After some crafty and unconventional help from Shem, Kev (Shaun) proceeds through an unexpected non-Euclidean methods to map the anatomical curvilinearity of Anna Livia's bottom side. The lessons advance Shaun's sex education when Shem provides a visual aid by drawing and explaining two intersecting circles in which two triangles are sketched. Shaun is amazed to learn about his "eternal geomater" (296.31–297.1) and will continue to be once he follows Shem's advice to carefully lift ALP's apron and learn firsthand her sexual anatomy. As the lessons near their end, Shem, echoing Alexander Pope's memorable line from "An Essay on Criticism," cautions the space-oriented Shaun: "Sink deep or touch not the Cartesian spring!" (301.24–25).

The last few pages of the chapter focus on essay topics and the children's NIGHTLETTER to their parents. In it, they blithely remind their parents that like all old folks past and present they too will die. Perhaps to blunt the shock of their statement, the children wish "them all very merry Incarnations in this land of the livvey and plenty" (308.19–20), and they close by signing their names: jake (Shem), jack (Shaun), and little sousoucie (Issy). (Parts of this chapter—its opening and ending: *FW* 260.1–275.2 and 304.5–308.32)—were published as *Storiella as She Is Syung*.)

II.3:309–382

Opening with a radio broadcast, this chapter, the Tavernry in Feast—the second longest in the *Wake*—takes place in Earwicker's pub. It serves as the setting for the series of vignettes that divide the episode: the story of the Norwegian captain and the tailor Kersse's efforts to fit him with a suit; the account of Buckley's shooting the Russian General while that officer was defecating (Butt and Taff's humorous rendition of a tale from the Crimean War); Earwicker's self-defense and the judgment of the four old men; and the final scene of Earwicker alone in the pub consuming the dregs of drinks left behind.

The *Wake's* seventh and eighth thunderclaps occur in this chapter. One takes place soon after the story of the tailor and the Norwegian captain begins. The other occurs toward the end of that story as the wedding celebration of the captain and tailor's daughter is coming to a close.

The first vignette, one of the more difficult passages of *Finnegans Wake*, is the story of the Norwegian captain, a hunchback and avatar of HCE, who arranges to have a suit made by the tailor Kersse. The tailor agrees to produce the suit, and the captain goes out to sea. On his return, the captain berates the tailor for not having made a suit that fits him. The captain leaves a second time, and on his return he again curses the tailor for a suit whose fit is worse than was the first; his own father would not recognize him in it. Kersse shoots back that no tailor anywhere could piece together a suit for such a humpback. To end the discord between the two, the ship's husband offers a humorous and practical solution; he proposes a marriage between the captain and the tailor's daughter. The marriage takes place and the celebration begins. One of the archetypal images of *Finnegans Wake* is marriage; it is an important theme throughout Joyce's works. Here in the *Wake*, the story of the captain's marriage is but a variation of the marriage between HCE and ALP.

Kate, who first appeared in I.1 as the Museyroom guide, introduces the story of Buckley and the Russian general, which according to Richard

Ellmann, Joyce got this story from his father. The original version takes place during the Crimean War. There, the Irish soldier Buckley was serving on the frontlines, when he saw a Russian general across the field. Buckley raised his rifle, got the general in his sights but refrained from shooting when the soldier started to admire the general's epaulettes. After a moment or two of hesitation, Buckley again raised his rifle only to see the general getting ready to defecate. Again, Buckley refrained from shooting when he saw that the general was in such a defenseless position. However, when he saw the Russian using a wad of turf "to finish the operation . . . Buckley lost all respect for him and fired." (Details of the original story and the role Samuel Beckett played are recounted in Ellmann's biography, *James Joyce*, p. 398.)

In this episode, Taff (Shem) and Butt (Shaun) present a convoluted, televised version of the tale with Butt taking the role of the Irish soldier. In this instance, he takes the general's act of wiping himself as a personal affront, and behaves accordingly: "At that instullt to Igorladns! Prronto! I gave one dobblenotch and I ups with my crozzier. Mirrdo!" (353.18–20)

The broadcast appears to trigger in HCE the need to voice his opinions about universal guilt, for he is ever attentive to allegations against him. As the pub closes for the night, the narrative interweaves the singing of ballads with the guilty judgment being passed on HCE, now associated with the shameless hunchback Richard III. HCE is faced with possible ways to suffer and die, one of which includes being a sacrificial offering to be eaten and drunk (377.36–378.1–5). Alluding to theophagy, the ancient Greek religious practice of ritually eating the god Dionysus (Bacchus), the narrative presents HCE as Buccas (*FW* 378.3), the god of drink, to be consumed. Alone in his pub drinking the dregs left by others, he appears as the last king of Ireland and slumps on his throne as the ship *Nansy Hans* goes out to sea.

II.4:383–399

This chapter—Bride Ship and Gulls—is one of the shortest in *Finnegans Wake*. This last episode in Book II contains two revised versions of Joyce's earliest sketches, both done in 1923, for this novel. The first is a stylized account of the Tristan and Isolde love story. The second, known as Mamalujo, an acronym for the four evangelists Matthew, Mark, Luke, and John, focuses on the Four Old Men—who in fact are separate reflections of HCE: Matt Gregory, Marcus Lyons, Luke Tarpey, and Johnny MacDougall.

The Tristan and Isolde story begins the chapter with a song, sung by "seaswans." It mockingly recounts the humiliation of the elderly Muster Mark by the younger Tristy. Joyce used Joseph Bédier's version of the Tristan and Isolde myth as the framework for his version, and he transformed the four jealous barons of Bédier's account into the four old men who spy on Tristan and Isolde.

Taking turns, the Four Old Men offer their views of history that stray from the facts. Another characteristic shared by them relates to the confusion of the sexes, their own and others. They take vicarious pleasure watching

150 *Approaching* Finnegans Wake

Tristan and Isolde kiss and, by the end of the chapter, the excitement they derive from their voyeurism carries over into their love song to Iseult la belle that includes the preposterous assertion one of them makes of having had sex with her. The donkey's heehaws that immediately follow mock the singers.

(The physicist and Nobel Laureate Murray Gell-Mann adapted the word *quarks* from this chapter's opening line—"*Three quarks for Muster Mark!*"—to identify subatomic particles.)

Finnegans Wake: Book III.1–4, The Book of the People

III.1:403–428

Originally composed as one chapter, Book III.1–2 was referred to collectively by Joyce as Shaun the Post. Joyce explained the label by noting that he is presenting Shaun as "a postman traveling backwards in the night through the events already narrated. It is written in the form of a *via crucis* of 14 stations but in reality it is only a barrel rolling down the river Liffey" (*Letters* I.214). Shaun is the central character in all four chapters of Book III. These four chapters are often referred to as the four watches of Shaun and designated by the following sigla: Λa (the first watch), Λb (the second watch), Λc (the third watch), and Λd (the fourth watch). (For an insightful discussion of these sigla in relation to the structure of the *Wake*, see Roland McHugh's *The Sigla of* **Finnegans Wake**, cited in our bibliography.)

Chapter one of this book, Shaun before the People, opens with bells tolling at midnight. Though only 11 strokes are found in the narrative, or, perhaps, only 11 are actually heard by the speaker "dropping asleep some part in noland" (403.18), the last stroke is clearly 12, the midnight hour.

Recognizing the beamish Shaun standing before him, the current narrator (the Four Old Men's donkey) introduces a vivid description of Shaun's nature and more specifically of what and how he eats. However, most of the chapter involves a lengthy 14-point interrogation of Shaun conducted by the general public that becomes increasingly probing as the inquiries build on one another.

The first question asks who gave him the permit to be a letter-carrier; instead of answering the question, he grumbles about the exhausting nature of the work. The second question is an extension of the first, and Shaun continues his complaints. Not a question per se, the third refers to who will be the bearer of the letter, to which Shaun replies that he has the ability to do so. The fourth requests that Shaun tell where he works; he responds by saying that he mostly walks. The fifth points out that Shaun has painted the town green; he replies by saying it was a "freudful mistake" (411.35–36), a phrase suggesting a joyful mistake and discernibly alluding to one of the major motifs in *Finnegans Wake*, the *felix culpa*.

The sixth question begins by lauding Shaun's singing, and then with a shift in tone the inquisitor asks what Shaun is really attempting to accomplish.

An infuriated, Shaun shouts back and insists that the inquisitor confine his insinuations. The seventh question focuses on the Swiftian allusions in his letter (413.27–29), to which Shaun exclaims, "Hooraymost!" (413.32), that is *Oremus* (Latin for *Let us pray*).

Shaun responds to the eighth comment, what happened to your money, by apologizing, and then he relates the fable of the Ondt and the Gracehoper. In telling this story of the practical-minded Ondt (Shaun) and the prodigal Gracehoper (Shem), Shaun delineates the characteristic differences between the *sans souci* Gracehoper and the disgruntled Ondt. The fable is also a defense of the *Wake* against Joyce's detractors, particularly Wyndham Lewis. (See his comments to this effect in Ellman's *Selected Letters* 329–332.) At the start of the fable, the ninth thunderclap occurs.

Question nine asks whether Shaun the Post can actually read the letter he is carrying; he is capable of judging its contents without having to read it. The tenth question asserts that he does not write as well as his "cerebrated brother" (421.19), to which he responds by labelling Shem notorious.

The eleventh question is really a petition asking Shaun to unravel the letter and to recount another fable. The indignant Shaun skips the fable and berates Shem, whom he accuses of changing what Shaun writes. Question twelve directly asks Shaun why he despises his brother. Blessing himself devotionally, Shaun replies by criticizing Shem's language skills and his creative and literary powers. Ending with a reference to the Norse god of thunder, Thor, Shaun concludes his answer. The thunderclap that immediately follows these remarks is the last in *Finnegans Wake* and contains 101 letters, one more than each of the previous ones.

Question thirteen asks whether Shaun can match Shem's use of language. His answer takes the offensive, unambiguously accusing his brother of copying what he writes. The fourteenth and final comment urges Shaun to compose with the kind of words used by Shem. Shaun haughtily replies that he could, but he would not trouble himself.

The final moments of the chapter play upon the bathetic elements of sentiment. Shaun is momentarily grief stricken and teary-eyed when he thinks of his mother. Then, he loses his balance and collapses into a barrel that rolls into the river.

III.2:429–473

Joyce offered a brief and cryptic outline of this chapter (Juan before St. Bride's): "[A]fter a long absurd and rather incestuous Lenten lecture to Izzy, his sister, [Shaun] takes leave of her 'with a half a glance of Irish frisky from under the shag of his parallel brows'. These are the words the reader will see but not those he will hear" (*Letters* I.216).

As the episode opens, Shaun the Post reappears as Jaunty Jaun. He spots 29 school girls from "Benent Saint Berched's national nightschool" (430.02) dipping their feet in the river. The Don Juan figure and lady killer Jaun (Shaun) doffs his hat at them, and they in turn like honey bees swarm toward him. After greeting his dearest sister, he sermonizes the young girls mostly on what never to do. Specifically, he implores them never to pose in the nude, to avoid reading lewd writers and the philosophy of Bishop Berkeley, and to be attentive to their digestive and menstrual health. Jaun would even burn any book that endangers their innocence. As he becomes more and more enthusiastic and sexually excited, his warnings turn into threats, betraying sadomasochistic impulses. When he again turns to the topic of sex, he focuses on Issy and advises self-control: "the pleasures of love lasts but a fleeting but the pledges of life outlust a lifetime" (444.24–25). Jaun takes this opportunity to disparage Shem and warn Issy about him.

Before ending his sermon, Juan encourages widespread social engagement: "We'll circumsivicize all Dublin country" (446.35). As in the previous chapter, Shaun's penchant for food reappears here. Unhappy that Shaun is to depart, Issy promises that she will wait for his return. Jaun becomes Juan in Issy's eyes and he consoles her by leaving his darling proxy, Dave the Dancekerl, behind. As soon as Dave (Shem) arrives, Shaun urges his sister and brother to embrace each other thoroughly. In imitation of the Maronite liturgy (*Letters* I.263–264), the girls bewail Jaun's departure, but his first attempt at soaring away ends in smoke and an injury (469.5–28). Spurning any help, the resolute Jaun makes "a brandnew start for himself" (471.10–11) and this time succeeds as Haun flowing down the river and out of sight. The aural similarity between Haun and dawn combined with the narrative reference to the crowing of the cock at the end of the chapter seems to indicate that Shaun, like the morning sun, will soon rise again.

III.3:474–554

Book III.3, Yawn under Inquest, is the longest chapter in *Finnegans Wake*. Shaun has now become the wailing Yawn. He is distressed and sprawled out over a mound, and is discovered by the Four Old Men. "Those four claymen clomb together to hold their sworn starchamber quiry on him" (475.18–19).

Before asking him questions on a wide range of topics, they spread their fishing nets over him. Then, one of the Four asks Yawn to identify his background and explain the history of Ireland. Another surmises that Shem is the real author of the letter and not Kevin (Shaun/Yawn) and suspects that Kevin is a counterfeit, an idea that some readers may apply to the language of *Finnegans Wake*: "Are we speachin d'anglas landadge or are you sprakin sea Djoytsch? (485.12–13).

Yawn does not mind answering the questions the Four ask. In fact, as he sees the situation, it would be as unethical for him not to as it would be nonsensical for them not to ask. Yawn sings a brief parody of "*Three quarks for Muster Mark!*" (the song that opens II.4) and, in the voice of ALP, answers the inquisitors' questions about HCE. Evoking the *Wake*'s motif of rebirth, Yawn presents a vision of HCE's death and eventual resurrection.

The dialogue that follows centers on Irish history and ends in what appears to be a disconnected telephone conversation. Advised to take the witness stand, Yawn is asked whether he is acquainted with a certain Toucher Thom and whether he knows a man in his early fifties; he is mad, he answers. Yawn is questioned about his family and HCE's past activities, which include the rumors of his behavior in the park.

The multiple voices Yawn speaks in continue in the versions he gives of Earwicker's fall. This dialogue here between the Four Old Men and Yawn is punctuated with fish imagery and includes an abbreviated parody of Hosty's "Ballad of Persse O'Reilly" that ends chapter 2 of Book I. After commenting on Shem and Shaun, Yawn is reminded that he forgot Issy and her multiple personalities and penchant for looking at her own reflection in a mirror. The inquest takes on new life when the Four Old Men become young again. They call Sackerson, Kate (Kitty the Beads), and Issy to testify. Then, they decide that they want to hear directly from HCE.

Insisting that he is clean-living and well known in the world, Earwicker begins his defense on an upbeat note and even dismisses charges that have not yet been leveled against him. He denies any malfeasance with any youthful girl and declares that anyone who even thinks that way should be arrested. He contends that he would have no reason to do wrong. After bearing his entire past, he insists any punishment would be unjust and something he would protest.

In the very last section of this chapter HCE speaks with pride of his founding Dublin and of the many good things he has done for the city. He explains the Dublin coat of arms and its motto, which contains HCE's initials. Though Earwicker is firm with his wife, he worships her. By feeding ALP spices, HCE endeavors to sanitize a river polluted by sewage. After ending his litany of municipal, commercial, and institutional accomplishments for her, he explains that he taught her the alphabet and brew beer for her. In short, he attends to her needs, and the chapter ends with approval by the Four Old Men.

III.4:555–590

This chapter, HCE and ALP—Their Bed of Trial, takes place in the household of the Porter family (a mirror version of the Earwickers) during the predawn hours. Disturbed by the cries of Jerry (Shem), the now awakened Mr. and Mrs. Porter go upstairs to check on him and on their other two children. Earwicker, who is wearing no sleeping garment to covering his genitals and lower half of his body, turns from the view of his twin sons only to fully expose himself to Issy. She reflects with amazement on what she saw. After returning to bed, Earwicker and Anna Livia attempt sexual intercourse before falling asleep once again, but like Bloom and Molly before them they do not fully complete the act.

The chapter also presents a dumb show in which the Four Old Men are the four bedposts (and four evangelists) viewing HCE and ALP from four different perspectives with four different opinions on what they have seen. Matt's position, which begins at 559.20, is one of harmony, describing parental concern for their children. Mark, beginning at 564.1, takes the position of discord, recalling the episode in the park and assessing the parents' current behavior. Luke's assumes the "Third position of concord" (582.29–30), though in fact it commemorates the parents' interrupted sexual encounter. And John's "Fourth position of solution" (590.22–23) marks the end of the three Viconian cycles and initiates a *ricorso* that anticipates the final book and chapter of *Finnegans Wake*. The dawn of a new day is arriving.

Finnegans Wake: Book IV, RECORSO

IV: 593–628

Book IV contains only one chapter. It begins with a repetition of the Sanskrit word for morning twilight, *Sandhyas*, and anticipates the renewal of a new day and a new Viconian age: "it is our hour or risings" (598.13). The 29 rainbow girls—Issy in the voices of her multiple personalities—sing a song of praise with the arrival of St. Kevin (Shaun), the Hydrophilos, who, in a baptismal act of cleansing and rebirth, dips himself into the waters of a small lake.

This quickly leads into a shift of the thematic interest from renewal and rebirth to questions of perception and truth. A terse exchange between Muta and Juva (evoking the popular characters from the comic's sections of newspapers, Mutt and Jeff) provides variations of the *Wake*'s recurring motif of conflict. It also sets the scene for the more extended representation of the struggle between the Archdruid Balkelly and St. Patrick. The dispute between Paddrock and Balkelly, though ostensively theological, in fact focuses in Einstein-like fashion on different approaches to the understanding of space and time.

The symbols of the rainbow and the shamrock illustrate the main point of each argument. The analogy St. Patrick employs between the shamrock and the Holy Trinity (the divinity of the three persons in one God) becomes a theological explication of one of the most important mysteries of the Christian faith. The rainbow (the regginbrow on the opening page of the *Wake*) evokes the Old Testament story of Noah and the Flood (Gen 9:13–14). Both images reflect two of major themes running throughout *Finnegans Wake*: rebirth and re-creation.

Following the encounter between St. Patrick and the Archdruid, the narrative turns to Anna Livia Plurabelle, the *Wake*'s final voice reaffirming new life while at the same time asserting a determination to move on. "My leaves have drifted from me. All. But one clings still. I'll bear it on me. To remind me of. Lff" (628.6–7). With imagery of a new day dawning, the theme of renewal identified with Anna Livia recurs. She is the River Liffey flowing into the sea to return again with the tide as her words circle back to Howth Castle and Environs: "A way a lone a last a loved a long the" (628.15–16).

A Glossary of Characters

Readers face a formidable task in getting their bearings when first reading the *Finnegans Wake*. The characters themselves play multiple roles with a range of names, and they constantly emerge from the narrative in different forms, including the archetypal, historical, literary, mythological, and geographical. The multidimensionality of the text demands of the reader a disciplined willingness to juggle at once multiple interpretive possibilities and pursue scholarly resources. No one feature of a character exclusively identifies that individual.

In the glossary that follows, we have focused on the central characters and on the various identities and manifestations that they assume. The most thorough tally of the characters who interact in *Finnegans Wake* can be found in Adaline Glasheen's *A Third Census of **Finnegans Wake***. Its full particulars are cited in our bibliography.

Anna Livia Plurabelle (ALP, Ann, Anne, and other variants including the siglum Δ) is the *Wake*'s matriarchal figure, **Earwicker**'s wife, and mother of their three children, the twins **Shem** and **Shaun** and the daughter **Issy**. ALP appears as both the personification of the River Liffey, as the archetypal biblical Eve, as the embodiment of female fluidity, and as the symbol of life and renewal: "Anna was, Livia is, Plurabelle's to be" (215.24). Her initials can appear in any order as well as in words and phrases. As the all-embracing woman figure, her presence, in various guises, recurs found throughout *Finnegans Wake* and, in the form of the River Liffey, she cyclically begins and ends this work again and again. She is the affirmation of life and rebirth. The Anna Livia Plurabelle chapter (Bk I.8:196–216) opens with four lines in the shape of her siglum, but more significantly it contains some of the most lyrical passage in the whole of the *Wake* matched only by her monologue in the novel's closing lines

The Archdruid (Balkelly, The Druid) is St. Patrick's opponent in Book IV (611.4–613.16). In that short, humorous vignette, he is the personification of the philosopher and Anglican Bishop of Cloyne, George Berkeley, who contends that reality is based on perception. With a perspective grounded in the idealism of Bishop Berkeley, the Archdruid opposes St. Patrick and argues a theory of colors. In an August 1939 letter to Frank Budgen, three months after *Finnegans Wake* was published, Joyce explained that the exchange between the Archdruid and St. Patrick "is also the defence and indictment of the book itself, B's theory of colours and Patrick's practical solution of the problem" (*Letters* I.406).

The **Ass** is the "fourpart tinckler's dunkey" (405.6–7) accompanies the **Four Old Men**). Narrating part of the opening of Book III, chapter 1, the donkey clearly recognizes Shaun, who is standing before him. At the end of Book II, chapter 4, the ass with his notable heehaws mocks the Four Old Men after they sing their love song to Iseult la belle. The personification of an ass is a literary motif that reaches back to Biblical times. Balaam's talking ass in

Numbers 22:15–35 is an example. Shakespeare's Bottom in *A Midsummer Night's Dream* may be one of the most recognizable of all portrayals.

Belinda of the Dorans (Biddy Doran, an avatar of ALP) is the hen, who first appears as the "gnarlybird" (10.32, 34) rummaging through a battlefield in the opening chapter of the *Wake*, and then again emerges in Book I, chapter 5, where she is called Belinda of the Dorans (111.5), to unearth a letter from the midden heap (110.22–31). The content of the letter, seemingly written by ALP, is never clearly revealed but it ostensibly relates to HCE's sin in the park that forms a major motif throughout the *Wake*.

The Four appear in the guises of the Four Old Men, the Four Waves, Mamalujo (a portmanteau word for the four evangelists Matthew, Mark, Luke, and John referred to as Matt Gregory, Marcus Lyons, Luke Tarpey, and Johnny MacDougall), and the four bedposts in HCE and ALP's bedroom, who view the two from four different angles. They are also Ireland's four provinces: Ulster (Matt Gregory), Munster (Marcus Lyons), Leinster (Luke Tarpey), and Connacht (Johnny MacDougall). As the Four Masters, they are the compilers of *The Annals of the Four Masters* whose names appear as "Peregrine and Michael and Farfassa and Peregrine" (398.15). Along with their Ass, they are a prominent part of the narrative in Book II, chapter 4, where they spy on Tristan and Isolde, and in Book III, chapter 3, where they hold an extended inquest of Yawn (Shaun). The *Wake*'s voyeuristic theme is especially apparent through them in II.4 and III.4. They also embody the quaternary symbol, a major motif throughout the work. Appearing under the title "From Work in Progress," chapter 4 of Book II (383–399) was the first published segment of *Finnegans Wake*.

Humphrey Chimpden Earwicker (HCE, Haveth Childers Everywhere, Here Comes Everybody, and Howth Castle and Environs) is the central character of the *Wake* and, to those who subscribe to the theory that *Finnegans Wake* is a dream, he is the dreamer in whose dream the narrative of the *Wake* takes place. As Finn MacCool, his mythical avatar, he is identified with the sleeping giant beneath Dublin. If Anna Livia is the principle of life and renewal, Earwicker is the principle of the dimensions of time and space. His initials, like his wife's, can appear in any order in words and phrases. Their variations are associated with multiple meanings and geographical settings such as the theme of universality (Here Comes Everybody) and the motif of the personification of landscape (Howth Castle and Environs). Earwicker's avatars are numerous and, among others, appear as a pub owner, the aging King Mark and his doppelgänger Muster Mark, King Roderick O"Conor, Humpty Dumpty, and of course Tim Finnegan himself whose name and story form the humorous basis of the *Wake*. Earwicker, too, has a fall. Although the precise nature of his alleged crime in the park, one of the central motifs in the *Wake*, is unknown, it remains a source of continual interest.

Earwicker's name, an anglicized version of the French *perceoreille* (earwig or ear-worm) is directly associated with the title figure in "The Ballad of Persse O'Reilly" (44–47). Earwicker's relationship with his daughter, Issy, a younger version of ALP, reflects the theme of incest. The connection between Earwicker's name, the ballad of Persse O'Reilly, and the French version of the word exploit the interpretive possibilities of the pun insect/incest.

Issy (Iseult and its variations: Isolde, Isabel, Isabella, Isabelle, and Izzy) is HCE and ALP's youngest child and sister of the twins Shem and Shaun. At the end of the Mookse and the Gripes (152–159), she appears as Nuvoletta, an Italian word for little cloud, but is unsuccessful in her effort to resolve their problem. Issy is short for the Irish name Iseult, the princess tragically in love with Tristan. The name of this princess forms the basis of the word Chapelizod, chapel of Iseult, a Dublin suburb adjacent to Phoenix Park. Issy is the archetypal image of the young woman who is at once sensually alluring and discerningly innocent in her relations with her father and two brothers. In handling their incestuous impulses, she demonstrates a self-determined control in her attitude toward them. At the same time, Issy is the ingenuous siren figure who exposes male attitudes toward women, both young and old. In a letter to the artist and Zurich friend Frank Budgen, Joyce divulges that Issy writes the footnotes in the Lessons chapter (*Letters I*.406).

the prankquean is Joyce's variation on Grace O'Malley, the sixteenth-century Irish pirate-queen, who was refused entry to Howth Castle on her return home from a visit with Queen Elizabeth I. She expected to meet with the earl of Howth on Christmas day and receive lodging for the night, but the earl, who was dining, did not welcome her. In retaliation for the insult and lack of hospitality, Grace O'Malley abducted the earl's young son whom she held hostage until the earl agreed to keep the castle doors open at dinner. In *Finnegans Wake*, the prankquean is refused entry to Jarl van Hoother's castle; she retaliates by kidnapping one of his three children each of the times that he fails to answer one of her riddles (21.18–19, 22.5–6, 29.30).

Shaun (Shaun the Post) is one of HCE and ALP's sons (Shem's twin and Issy's brother). In contrast to his impractical artist-brother Shem, Shaun is the pragmatic rationalist set on being socially and financially successful. Though their personality traits set them apart and evoke the well-known motif of the warring brothers, their differences are not always noticeable and they share similarities as the marginalia of the Lessons Chapter (II.2) indicate. Among other examples, Shaun's personality type is betrayed by allusions to the Ondt (414.16–419.10), the Archdruid (611.4–613.16), St. Kevin (604.27–606.12), Mick (219–259), and Butt (337.32–355.09).

Shem (Shem the Penman), one of HCE and ALP's sons (Shaun's twin and Issy's brother). He embodies the failed artist in contradistinction to the ambitious pragmatist Shaun. Their opposition or rivalry forms one of the central motifs of the *Wake*. In chapter 7 (169–195), Shaun gives an unflattering depiction of Shem, who as MERCIUS counters what Shaun as JUSTIUS levels against him. In the midst of its disparaging comments, the depiction ironically provides a profound view on the mystery of literary creation. Often presented in opposition to his twin, Shem as the artist figure is portrayed as the Gracehoper in "The Ondt and the Gracehoper" (414.22–419.8) and as

Nick in "The Mime of Mick, Nick, and the Maggies" (219–259). Shem the Penman is loosely identified with Hosty, author of "The Ballad of Persse O'Reilly" (44–47) that satirizes HCE as a Humpty Dumpty figure.

Alternative Reading of Shem's "first riddle of the universe . . . when is a man not a man?" (*FW* 170.4–5)

"when is a man not a man"

Identity is the hallmark of conventional Irish fiction, and indeed fiction the world over. From *The Wild Colonial Girl* to *The Real Charlotte*, characters have striven to define themselves according to the mores of communal institutions, and their triumphs or defeats were measured by the successes of their efforts to integrate themselves into the society that surrounded them. Modernist characters could no longer trust the guidelines of institutions, and instead turned within themselves for assistance on shaping their identities. Postmodern characters no longer believed even in the efficacy of their own instincts and instead faced an arbitrary world with nothing to guide them but their appetites.

From *Dubliners* to *Finnegans Wake*, Joyce's narratives announced the advent of modernist and then post-Modernist perspectives. The arc from the unnamed boy of "The Sisters" to Shem the Penman follows the disassociation from the metaphysical qualities that had served as universal markers for behavior—good, duty, honesty, love, courage—to physical appetites—hunger, fatigue, sexual desire, self-preservation—as motivators for behavior. Much of *Finnegans Wake* offers concrete demonstrations of this newly recognized condition, but seeing the world as transactional and immediate requires a reorientation for interpreting literature. Shem's first riddle of the universe provides a detailed reorientation for postmodern readers.

The question that Shem presents—"when is a man not a man"—gets to the heart of the problem of identity when there are no longer legitimate, consistent abstract standards upon which to base a sense of self. He challenges "his little brothron and sweestureens," (170.3–4) to offer a solution, using the enticement of "a bittersweet crab" (170.6) as the prize for the correct answer. In fact, what Shem presents is not a contest but a moment of instruction, and as his siblings rattle off possible explanations, they come to see the inadequacy of their perspectives.

In a series of answers bordering on the eschatological, the answers underscore a sense of the disruption or even end of world order as conventionally conceived. They detail a wide range of catastrophic experiences: from broad material changes like the crash of thunder ("when heavens are quakers") to the erasure of individuality through death or even old age ("when the angel of death kicks the bucket of life" or ("when you are old") to the disorientation through a lack of belief ("when he is a gnawstick"), drink ("when wine's at witsends"), or love ("when lovely wooman stoops to conk him"), and a range of others (170.9–21). As the narrative peremptorily tells us: "All were wrong" (170.21–22). The "correct solution" as given by Shem—"when he is a . . . Sham" (170.22–24)—announces the end of the Enlightenment and the beginning of a nonlinear sense of the world.

At first reading, it might be easy to see Shem as the aberration, the figure aggressively out of step with the rest of society. He is, as the narrative tells us "a low sham" whose "lowness creeped out first via foodstuffs" (170.25–26). As the paragraph unfolds, details of his alienation mount. He not only turns his back on national cuisine—"Rosbif of Old Zealand" (171.1–2)—he leaves Ireland, denies his heritage, and falls into drink. In fact, Shem is following the example of his predecessor, Stephen Dedalus, who leaves Ireland at the end of *A Portrait of the Artist as a Young Man*. The striking difference, however, is that Stephen retains the ambition to "forge in the smithy of my soul the uncreated consciousness of my race." Whereas Shem sees all forging as a manner of counterfeiting, an effort to present not a simulacrum of the real but a testimony to the falseness of all artifacts. His writing, produced at "The house of O'Shea or O'Shame, *Quivapieno*, known as the Haunted Inkbottle, no number Brimstone Walk, Asia in Ireland" (182.30–31), signals the change in composition that has taken place.

In the opening of chapter seven, part one, of *Finnegans Wake*, Joyce uses the character that represents the artist to encapsulate the new epistemology of his writing. Interpretation's long tradition of referentiality and self-assurance has come to an end. Joyce's final novel embodies the ultimately frustrating experience of anyone seeking to impose closure and order upon a system has forsaken metaphysics and embraced situational behavior. The first riddle of the universe produces not resolution but the triumph of uncertainty. Joyce presents this without rancor or triumphalism but merely as a recognition of how life can be seen when only the material is acknowledged.

"Shem's riddle"

When Shem confronts his brother and sister with "the first riddle of the universe . . . when is a man not a man?" (*FW* 170.4–5), they incorrectly guess, so he supplies the solution: "when he is a . . . Sham" (*FW* 170. 23–24). The one question Shem asks in the previous chapter—*Sacer esto?* (*FW* 168.13) and its answer *Semus sumus!* (*FW* 168.14)—shed light on this riddle. The Latin *sacer* has two meanings, and, like Shem and Shaun, they are opposites. *Sacer* can mean sacred, that which is consecrated and holy, or it can mean accursed, that which is detestable and condemned. In this context, the question asks, *Are you damned?* (*Sacer esto?*). Shaun's answer, which seems to be the voice of Shem, emphatically asserts, *We are the same!* (*Semus sumus!*). Whether or not the voice is Shem's and the words Shaun's, a coincidence of opposites, a major motif associated with them, occurs and with it a composite Shem/Shaun. Shaun represents the upper half of the body and Shem the lower; the composite at this point would make the whole. In his study, *A Guide through* **Finnegans Wake**, Edmund Lloyd Epstein argues, "This answer shows Shem's characteristic modesty about his physical envelope, but it also suggests that

Shem knows he is only half a man, an admission that Shaun refuses to make about himself" (p. 85).

What purpose, then, does this first riddle of the universe play in the *Wake*? It serves as a matrix that intertwines three fundamental motifs. One is the recurring motif of Giordano Bruno's coincidence of contraries or the conjunction of opposites. This union of opposites is reflected in other ways in the text; disjointed words—as in the question *Sacer esto?*—can converge and offer conflicting meanings. The second is the motif of the cyclical nature of life, associated with Giambettista Vico's three-fold cycle of history (the period of the gods, of heroes, and of humans) followed by a *ricorso* or return to repeat the history anew. The last sentence of the *Wake* flows into and becomes the first, returning the reader to the beginning. The third motif, a profound insight into the immortality of the literary artist, relates to the act of literary creation or, for that matter, to any artistic creation. In the artist's work, in this case the artist's words, a transformation from one form of existence into another takes place; the mortal artist achieves an immortal presence.

The answer to this first riddle conveys at once something forged into a composite and something fake (a sham) that gives the appearance of being whole, but is not because ultimately each must be whole in him or herself. The idea of something forged may remind Joyce readers of the penultimate diary entry at the end of *A Portrait of the Artist as a Young Man* where Stephen Dedalus writes, "Welcome, O Life! I go to encounter for the millionth time the reality of experience and to forge in the smithy of my soul the uncreated conscience of my race." The artificer, the artist, like the mythological Daedalus and the *Wake*'s Shem, is one who forges reality into art, and as the forger, Shem is Sham. Forging, as a form of transmutation, leads to a profound understanding of the act of literary creation that *FW* I.7 expounds.

In one way or another, riddles in *Finnegans Wake* focus on the question of identity, and Shem's on that of the artist. Much of *FW* I.7 can be read as an extension of the answer to the riddle: When is a man not a man? The answer in Shaun's eyes is when he is less than a man and accursed and damned and condemned "to the cross of [his] own cruelfiction!" (*FW* 192.18–19). This imagery evokes the crucifixion of Jesus Christ, who died to redeem the world. According to St. Mark's Gospel (15:34), Jesus utters the opening words of Psalm 22, a psalm that contains the line: "But I am a worm, and no man: the reproach of men, and the outcast of the people" (v6). Unwittingly, in his description of Shem, Shaun answers the riddle and continues to do so when he describes Shem as an alchemist whose flesh is transaccidentated into the ink and words that become his literary art (*FW* 185.35, 186. 3–4). A theological term first used by Duns Scotus, according to the *Oxford English Dictionary*, transaccidentation refers to the change in the bread and wine during the consecration of the Eucharist. Transaccidentation depicts Shem's physical transmutation or forging into ink and words where his spiritual substance perpetually remains and becomes present to readers.

A variation of this riddle appears in Book IV, the *Wake*'s last chapter: "The first and last rittlerattle of the anniverse; when is a nam nought a nam whenas it is a" (*FW* 607.10–12). Though unlike the direct answer given in Book I.7, the answer in Book IV is left blank, but implied. The reverse of man is nam and when completely reversed or dissolved it is nought, or it is no longer. The lines that immediately follow indicate that a celebration is dawning; the younger generation is awaking to supersede the old at Finnegan's Wake:

> Heroes' Highway where our fleshers leave their bonings and every bob and joan to fill the bumper fair. It is their segnall for old Champelysied to seek the shades of his retirement and for young Chappielassies to tear a round and tease their partners lovesoftfun at Finnegan's Wake.
> (607.12–16)

The flesh of the old become shades as the young dance on into the light of the coming new day the chapter celebrates.

Questions

1. What is your opinion as to whether *Finnegans Wake* is the dream of H.C. Earwicker or whether it is written in dream language?
2. Can you understand the *Finnegans Wake* better if you read it aloud?
3. Do you think *Finnegans Wake* should be read in a group?
4. Do you find *Finnegans Wake* humorous?
5. What literary and/or aesthetic lessons can you derive from *Finnegans Wake*.
6. Is *Finegans Wake* too difficult to read?
7. Is the narrative technique too confusing?
8. Is *Finnegans Wake* more poetry than prose?
9. Since Joyce published so much of *Finnegans Wake* serially, would it be better to read only portions of the work?
10. Should it be read from beginning to end or should readers tackle it in whatever order they choose?
11. Do fully developed characters exist in the book or is it made up of types and stereotypes?
12. Can it be read like any other novel?
13. If not, is there a useful method for reading it?
14. Is it useful to have read Joyce's other fiction before beginning *Finnegans Wake*?
15. Is it better to read *Finnegans Wake* before reading any other work by Joyce?
16. Does it have a plot?
17. Is a plot necessary?
18. Is this an example of a postmodern novel?

Selected Annotation

McHugh, Roland. *Annotations to **Finnegans Wake***. Revised edn. Baltimore and London: Johns Hopkins University Press, 1991.

6   Approaching the Minor Works

Labelling anything Joyce wrote as minor seems heretical, but changing the phrase to lesser-known writings would not convey the extraordinary literary quality Joyce achieved in the works synonymous with his name: *Dubliners, A Portrait of the Artist as a Young Man, Ulysses,* and *Finnegans Wake.* These titles distinguish themselves to such a degree from his other writings that the latter by definition are cast into the category of minor works. Certainly, they bear the marks of Joyce's genius and creativity, but they do not possess the same intensity or energy of those works for which he is best known. Nonetheless, a careful scrutiny of the minor writings—a partial draft of a proposed novel, poetry, a play, critical essays, letters, early imaginative sketches, and a whimsical journal—can afford useful insights into understanding the literary Joyce. These diverse examples of his creative efforts throw into relief the genius of his novels and short stories. They offer insights into the issues and themes that most concerned him and provide perspective on how these ideas evolved over the process of composition. Finally, if they reveal a level of creative ability that falls short of what he achieves in his fiction, the disparity can enhance the understanding of his artistic stature by offering insights into his emergent creative strengths and youthful weaknesses.

Key Issues

In some instances—most notably the novel fragment, the critical writings, and to some lesser degree the letters—the same general attitudes that informed the narratives of his published fiction occupy his attention, even if they are expressed with less subtlety and skill. In other forms—poetry, a bio-fictional journal, and his only extant play—Joyce focuses his attention more intently on specific and immediate concerns. Taken together, they delineate how particular ideas developed and, in some instances, changed significantly over the course of his writing. To dismiss much of this work as apprentice pieces would be inaccurate, but to categorize them as being artistically less accomplished than his more renowned work remains a valid judgment.

The formation and representation of _Identity_, particularly that of the artist, stands out as consistent, a concern in the writings considered here as it does in all of Joyce's published fiction. However, the emphasis placed on that

DOI: 10.4324/9781003223290-7

characteristic varies from work to work. In the play *Exiles*, and the bio-fiction *Giacomo Joyce*, for example, the writing gives attention to the nature of particular characters, and the same issues raised in the fiction already considered, particularly the Irish ethos that shaped Joyce's own development, receive a great deal of attention. In the poetry, the brevity of a figure's appearance prevents more than particularized judgments. And in the critical writings, the absence of a particular individual makes references to identity much more general; the collective identity of Ireland and the Irish, for example, is not absent from in his critical pieces. Finally, in the *Letters* one has glimpses—and at times vivid glimpses—of Joyce's identity, but in much the same fashion as one would from overhearing random conversations. If identity reveals itself through one's personality, Joyce's letters to his family (especially his brother Stanislaus), publishers, and friends reveal an identity reflective of his dedication to his literary ambitions. The usefulness of such fragmentary expositions seen in his letters would depend upon how much emphasis a reader gives to the psychological profile of the author.

Thematic examinations of issues related to <u>Family</u> are even more varied. Though family issues are present throughout Joyce's writings and reach a high point in *Finnegans Wake*, the most intense assessment of familial relations in his minor works is *Exiles*, which looks at nontraditional constructions of family and explores the tensions created between putative marital bonds and a range of sexual situations. Blunter and more emphatic comments on the family relations pepper portions of the *Letters*, but they have episodic qualities lacking the continuity of the exchanges in the play. In either form, however, comments on the conflicting and even contradictory impulses relating to family echo those found in Joyce's fiction. In contrast, there are several quite evocative passages in the poetry that offer more selective, immediate commentaries. They are addressed to his father, to his partner (and later wife) Nora, and to their children. Far from presenting a radical representation of an unconventional lifestyle Joyce may have felt that he lived, they convey consistently traditional feelings.

Joyce's minor works offer similar though less intense views on both <u>Nationalism</u> and <u>Religion</u>. In the *Letters*, critical writings, and poems, his feelings are stated emphatically, taken as givens, and present a *de facto* sense that they require little elaboration, though that of course does not prevent him from contradicting himself over the course of these expressions. In *Exiles*, the feelings for both topics are compressed and hence more intense, but they too, unlike the examinations in his major fiction, are presented in a fashion that brooks no debate and is further blighted by melodramatic expression. In none of these forms does he develop the complex and creative exposition of ideas that appear in his fiction, nor does he give the options for alternative ways of seeing the issues that he allows in his fiction. In consequence, the observations come across as offhanded and unquestionable.

Of all the themes and issues carried over from the fiction, <u>Sexuality</u> receives the most comprehensive and most interesting treatment. In the *Letters* and the poems, physical aspects of desire and gratification are mentioned in great detail (in some cases perhaps too specifically for oversensitive readers). Nonetheless, these expressions are by no means gratuitous in terms of the basis that they provide for understanding his creative perspective elsewhere. In *Giacomo Joyce*, the intertwined issues of sexuality and desire are explored in ways that give useful insight into passages in the published fiction, albeit with less creative polish. While little is said on the topics that have not been represented imaginatively in the published fiction, the very bluntness of these views can usefully enhance a reader's understanding not only of Joyce's fiction but also of the adeptness with which Joyce controlled his creative imagination.

Stylistic Innovations

The formal experimentation that characterizes Joyce's major fiction is almost completely absent in the other writings. Though Ezra Pound included one of the poems from *Chamber Music*, "I Hear an Army," in his anthology of Imagist verse, there is little in it to suggest a real break from traditional modes of poetry. The *Letters*, critical writings, *Exiles*, and his novel fragment *Stephen Hero* are equally conventional. What may seem innovative in *Giacomo Joyce*'s journal-like format in fact is more often than not little more than vagueness. In short, Joyce simply did not have the same inclination for experimental forms or innovative constructions in other genres that he felt for his fiction.

An Overview of the Minor Writing

Although much of Joyce's work outside his major fiction has received little attention, justifiably so in the opinion of some, an outline of that work can usefully supplement a reader's conception of his artistic range. Joyce composed works in every major genre—poetry, drama, and memoir—in addition to his fiction. In this section, we propose a detailed but not exhaustive survey to give a sense of that scope.

"A Portrait of the Artist"

This is a prose sketch, not quite an essay and not really fiction, that Joyce completed on 7 January 1904. He wrote it in a form that combines fictional narrative and philosophical speculation. It examines the evolution of the artistic consciousness of an unnamed young man. It touches on themes and even incidents upon which Joyce would elaborate in *Stephen Hero* and *A Portrait of the Artist as a Young Man*. Perhaps most notably, it touches on aesthetic values that the young Joyce was formulating to guide his subsequent work. It was commissioned by the short-lived Irish journal *Dana*, but the editors rejected it when they read what Joyce submitted. One of the editors W. K. Magee commented: "I can't print what I don't understand."

Stephen Hero

Background and Summary

In one sense, *Stephen Hero* is an earlier version of *A Portrait of the Artist as a Young Man* and part of a compositional continuum that began with "A Portrait of the Artist," discussed above. Joyce began writing it on his twenty-second birthday, 2 February 1904, shortly after he learned that the editors of the journal *Dana* had rejected his essay, "A Portrait of the Artist." By April 1904, Joyce had completed the first 11 chapters of the planned novel, and he continued writing until June or July of 1905 when he ceased working on it. At that point, by his own estimation, he had completed half the book.

During the time he spent composing *Stephen Hero*, Joyce was also writing short stories for the *Dubliners* collection, and the contrasting forms of the two projects are quite striking. Although only a fragment of the original manuscript of *Stephen Hero* remains, there is a sufficient amount of manuscript to provide a clear sense of its form and direction. The narrative follows the early life of Stephen Daedalus in what seems to be a chronological parallel to Joyce's own life, and it adopts a conventional construction that would have been quite familiar to Edwardian and Victorian readers but markedly different from that adopted in *Dubliners*.

There is an apocryphal story of Joyce attempting to burn the *Stephen Hero* manuscript only to have it saved from the fire by his sister Eileen. While that has not been verified, it is known that Joyce gave the extant manuscript to Sylvia Beach who sold it to the Harvard College Library in 1935 (with no signs that any of its pages had been near a fire). In 1944, with permission from Harvard, Theodore Spencer published the fragment under the title *Stephen Hero*. He did this despite a 1939 letter written by Paul Léon on behalf of Joyce expressing uneasiness over the possibility of the publication, and his own assurances to Joyce that he would not pursue plans to publish the fragment.

While, as noted, the entire manuscript is not available, the portion of the fragment that survives is of sufficient length to underscore how different this early effort was both from the short story collection being written in tandem to it and from the subsequent novel that became *A Portrait of the Artist as a Young Man*. Although the themes crucial to the narrative of the latter work are similarly explored, indeed as already noted in this study Joyce was remarkably consistent in his choice of themes to explore. However, the structure of *Stephen Hero* follows that of a conventional nineteenth-century novel. It moves linearly and predictably, without the stylistic innovations that move *A Portrait of the Artist as a Young Man* from the domain of traditional fiction and into the world of the Modernist movement. The manuscript itself has been extensively studied since it was first published, and the noted textual critic Hans Walter Gabler has offered a compelling case for a slight adjustment of the chapter numbers assigned by Theodore Spencer. Here we follow Gabler's revised form.

The truncated fragment opens in mid-chapter describing the life of **Stephen Daedalus** (as Joyce spelled it in *Stephen Hero*) in an English composition class at the University College Dublin. The next segment, chapter sixteen, elaborates on Stephen's creative development while at the university, detailing some of the writing he did to hone his artistic skills. It also touches on his often uneasy relations with other students who are baffled by his taste and behavior.

In chapter seventeen, the narrative goes on to describe Stephen's home life and his exchanges with **Madden** (who will become Davin in *A Portrait of the Artist as a Young Man*) and his budding interest in **Emma Clery,** a young woman who will be identified in *A Portrait of the Artist as a Young Man* only by her initials E____ C____. The next chapter, eighteen, has Stephen meeting **Charles Wells**, an old classmate from Clongowes Wood who is now studying for the priesthood. The chapter also discusses Stephen's essay "Drama and Life" that attempts to articulate his aesthetic views to the university community. It reflects his twin motives of asserting his aesthetic independence while gaining the legitimacy of public acceptance.

Chapter nineteen gives an account of the presentation of Stephen's paper and of the audience's responses to it, both laudatory and hostile. Later, the narrative describes Stephen's developing friendship with **Cranly** and his growing alienation from Catholicism. Their discussion of Catholicism and of its docile acceptance by their university classmates continues into chapter twenty.

Chapter twenty-one offers a meandering description of his desultory courtship of Emma Clery. It underscores Stephen's inability to change to accommodate the views of others, and it underscores how threatening those views can seem to more conventionally minded people. The harsh and chaotic homelife of the Daedalus family and Stephen's alienation from his father dominate chapter twenty-two. Chapter twenty-three underscores Stephen's growing intellectual restlessness while chapter twenty-four examines his paradoxical but not contradictory ongoing intellectual attraction to the Catholic Church, despite his resistance to its authority. The chapter ends with Stephen describing his aesthetic theory to Cranly in much the same way that he would describe it to Lynch in *A Portrait of the Artist as a Young Man*. The final chapter, twenty-five in the new numbering, relates the final weeks before the end of the college's spring term.

A Glossary of Characters

Emma Clery—a conventional young Dublin woman in whom Stephen has a romantic interest but who is shocked and offended by the bluntness of his sexual propositions.

Stephen Daedalus—the central character of the unfinished novel. With the slight spelling variant in the surname, it is easy to see an analogue to the central character of *A Portrait of the Artist as a Young Man*. However, while similarities are undeniable, the former Stephen represents a stage in the evolution of the artistic consciousness rather than a reiteration.

Madden—a university friend of Stephen's who serves as a foil for Stephen's views on Irish nationalism. In *A Portrait of the Artist as a Young Man*, a similar character appears with the name Davin.

Charles Wells—a former classmate, and antagonist, from Clongowes Wood College who is now studying to become a priest seemingly out of pragmatism rather than piety. He will have a role in the first chapter of *A Portrait of the Artist as a Young Man*, as a tormentor of Stephen at Clongowes Wood, but does not return after that brief appearance.

Poetry

Chamber Music

This is a collection of 36 lyrical poems that Joyce composed between 1901 and 1904. Elkin Mathews published the volume in 1907 on the recommendation of the literary critic and poet Arthur Symons. It is Joyce's first book-length publication and his first work to be the basis of musical adaptation. Its verse reflects the range of attitudes engaging the mind of an emerging poet. Joyce himself, in a 1907 letter to his brother Stanislaus, called it "a young man's book" (*Letters II*.219), and in *Finnegans Wake* three decades later, he seems to refer to it as "the first rattle of his juniverse" (*FW* 231.1–2). Nonetheless, the collection touches on many of the themes that would recur in later writings: friendship, love, betrayal, loneliness, the role of the poet, and the function of art. At the same time, the views that Joyce expressed on these topics generally emerge in a circumscribed fashion that gives them less impact than the more expansive observations that appeared in his fiction. The order of the poems, however, is an early example of Joyce's attentiveness to the structural components of his art, especially the progression of time. In *Chamber Music*, the movement of time from morning to evening with noon at the center and the progression of seasons from spring to winter reflect the changing mood of the poems and the reality of love's seduction and dissolution.

As with the work of many developing poets, there are unmistakable derivative elements in the verses. One can see similarities in many of the *Chamber Music* poems to Elizabethan lyrics, and they reflect Joyce's desire that the poems be set to music. (There are a number of conflicting explanations for the choice of title of the book. One of the most popular, and one of the coarsest, comes from Joyce's first biographer Herbert Gorman who claims the inspiration came from the sound of a woman using a chamber pot to urinate. Joyce himself, in an earlier letter to his brother, wrote that he disliked the title because "it is too complacent" and preferred one that "to a certain extent repudiated the book, without altogether disparaging it" [*Letters II*, 182].) The style, diction, and imagery of the verses are shaped by musicality. They

Figure 6.1 Title page for Joyce's first book. (Courtesy of C.W. Post Library of Long Island)

also go beyond Elizabethan tradition to draw on Irish tradition, Symbolism, and even popular Victorian verse for their forms and tones. Through it all, the poems' central voice evokes, in the words of Herbert Hoarth, "a gravemannered gentleman of a pre-industrial world, a courtier." Arthur Symons, a well-respected critic who had done much to promote French Symbolist poetry, gave the collection a generally favorable, if guarded review in the 22 June 1907 issue of *Nation*, but neither this book nor subsequent poetry has ever received the same level of recognition as Joyce's fiction.

Pomes Penyeach

Even as Joyce was producing some of the most innovative and powerful fiction of the twentieth century, he continued to write poetry. Between 1912 and 1924, he composed the 13 selections that are printed in this slim volume of 24 pages. The collection first appeared in 1927 when it was published by Sylvia Beach's bookstore, Shakespeare and Company, much as she had published *Ulysses* five years earlier. Like the verses in *Chamber Music*, these poems were adapted to music.

Opinions on the choice of title vary from speculation that it is the slurred cry of a street hawker selling verse for a penny to the idea that it is a multilingual pun—pomes (Fr. apple)/poems. Although the poems express a range of sentiments and experiences that shaped Joyce over the years of their composition, when they appeared they were generally ignored by critics and the

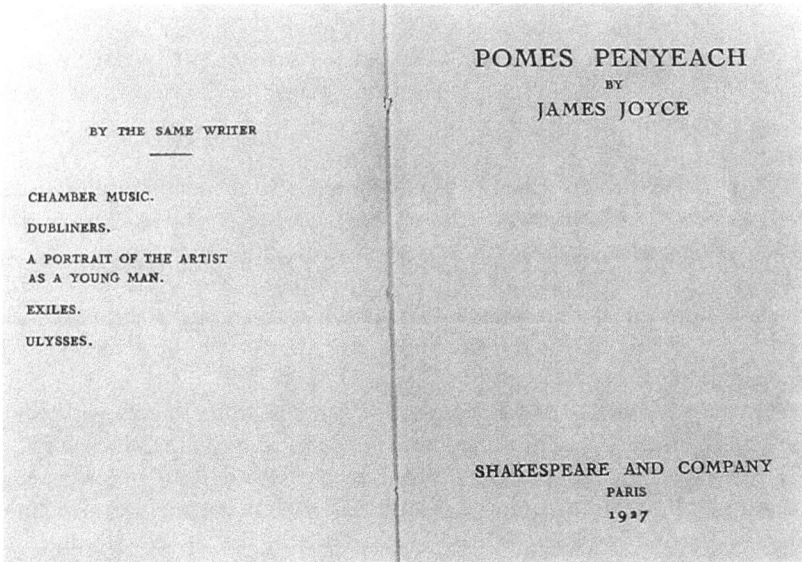

Figure 6.2 Card page and title page of *Pomes Penyeach*, Joyce's second volume of poetry. (Courtesy of C.W. Post Library of Long Island)

reading public. One can certainly argue that they have historic interest to students of Joyce's writing, and there is a measure of merit in each that many writers would envy. However, as is the case with *Chamber Music*, when read today, their literary achievements do not match those of Joyce's fiction. In a 1927 letter, Joyce mentioned that at his request Ezra Pound read two poems from *Pomes Penyeach* and concluded that the verses "belong in the bible or the family album with the portraits" (*Letters* III.155).

The following brief summary lists the poems in the order of their appearance in *Pomes Penyeach*. Of the 13, 11 were previously published, and the dates given in the volume are not always accurate. The rhyme scheme of each stanza, when Joyce uses rhyme, is normally a b a b. The recurring theme of loss throughout *Pomes Penyeach* becomes apparent to readers.

"Tilly," dated Dublin, 1904, contains three stanzas of four lines each with the first and second stanzas setting the somber tone of a cattle driver on a winter's night leading his beasts home. The third stanza heightens the somber mood as he laments his torn bough, which was once the "flowering branch" in the second stanza. The sense of loss, as Joyce's biographer Richard Ellmann speculates, may express the emotions Joyce himself was feeling when he wrote this poem shortly after his mother's death in 1903. "Cabra" was the poem's original title before Joyce changed it first to "Ruminants" and then to "Tilly." The word *tilly* means an extra amount of something, the thirteenth in a baker's dozen, for example.

"Watching the Needleboats at San Sabba," dated Trieste, 1912, contains two stanzas of four lines each. The exact origin of the name *needleboat* is uncertain. The last line of each stanza forms a refrain declaiming the sadness of passing moments in life never to return. The poem may also be expressing Joyce's acute awareness of the passing of his youth.

"A Flower Given to My daughter," dated Trieste, 1913, contains two stanzas of four lines each with the dominant imagery of frailness, the frailness of the flower, of the hands of the giver, and the recipient (the speaker's daughter).

"She Weeps over Rahoon," dated Trieste, 1913, contains three stanzas with four lines each, and was written after Joyce accompanied Nora to the gravesite of her teenage boyfriend, Michael Bodkin, in Rahoon, Ireland, who served as the model for Michael Fury in the *Dubliner*'s last story, "The Dead." Capturing the sentiments of a grown woman, the poem expresses both her sorrow and blunt recognition that death will come to the two lovers standing there.

"Tutto è Sciolto," dated Trieste, 1914, contains three stanzas with four lines each. Its title is taken from an aria in Vincenzo Bellini's *La Sonnambula* (*The Sleepwalker*); in English the phrase means "All is lost." In the opera, Elvino sees his finacée, Amina, in Count Rodolfo's bedroom but does not know she is sleepwalking; distraught, he believes he has lost everything.

"On the Beach at Fontana," dated Trieste, 1914, composed of three stanzas with four lines each, focuses on the deep paternal affection Joyce experienced toward his son, Giorgio, when they were together on an outing.

"Simples," dated Trieste, 1915, contains three stanzas with four lines each, and, like the previous poem of fatherly love, this poem focuses on Joyce's paternal affection toward his daughter, Lucia, who is gathering "simple salad leaves" in a garden.

"Flood" dated Trieste, 1915, contains three stanzas with four lines each. Its main theme is the incertitude of love that thwarts the passions.

"Nightpiece," dated Trieste, 1915, is composed of three stanzas with six lines each. The idea for the poem came from a dream that Joyce wrote down in *Giacomo Joyce*. As Joyce explains in *Giacomo Joyce*, the idea for this poem came from a dream he had of attending Good Friday services at Notre Dame in 1903 and the erotic feelings he experienced toward one of his female language students in Trieste. The poem articulates the frustrated sense of barrenness that emerges from the experience.

"Alone," dated Zurich, 1916, contains two stanzas of four lines each and conveys a sense of sensual pleasure the speaker is secretly experiencing.

"A Memory of the Players in a Mirror at Midnight," dated Zurich, 1917, composed of two stanzas with seven lines each, is a reflection Joyce's personal experience with the amateur acting group, the English Players, with which he was actively involved when living in Zurich during World War I.

"Bahnhofstrasse," dated Zurich, 1918, is one of Joyce's most personal poems. While on Zurich's Bahnhofstrasse in August of 1917, Joyce experienced for the first time a severe attack of glaucoma. The poem is composed of four short stanzas of two lines each that concisely expresses his worries of losing sight and his youth.

"A Prayer," dated Paris, 1924, is composed of three stanzas with six lines each. As its title implies, the poem is a lover's petition to surrender and be surrendered to in the joy and anguish of love.

"Ecce Puer"

This is an occasional poem with a dual focus. It was written by Joyce to commemorate the birth of his grandson, Stephen James Joyce, on 15 February 1932, and to mark the sense of sadness that he still felt over the death of his father, John Stanislas Joyce, on 29 December 1931. The poem's first two stanzas celebrate the joy that the birth of a grandson has brought the poet, and the last two lament the loss of his father. The poem was published in the January 1933 issue of the journal *Criterion* and subsequently appeared in *Collected Poems* in 1936.

The Critical Writings of James Joyce

The Critical Writings of James Joyce, published in 1959 nearly 20 years after the author's death, is a scholarly compilation rather than an artistic creation. Two academics, Ellsworth Mason and Richard Ellmann, brought together 57 pieces of nonfiction written by Joyce between 1896 and 1937. Their edition contains essays written while Joyce was still in school, book reviews, lectures, newspaper articles, broadsides in verse, letters to editors, and program notes. Most were produced during the first 21 years of the period covered, and often written before Joyce had achieved general acclaim for his fiction. Given the 41-year span covered by the writings and the fact that Joyce himself did not initiate its appearance, the unevenness of the collection can hardly be surprising. As is the case with his poetry and his play, most of the themes touched on in these essays were addressed more effectively and with greater sophistication in the fiction and even in selected correspondence. This collection of disparate pieces also contains Joyce's political works, all of which were written in Italian. Between 1907 and 1912, as Giorgio Melchiori has observed, the language of Joyce's politics was Italian. *The Critical Writings* provides both contextual and biographical background for a period of four decades during which Joyce's most intensive artistic development occurred.

Exiles

Joyce's only extant play, *Exiles* was written in Trieste between 1914 and 1915. Copies of two previous plays—*A Brilliant Career* and *Dream Stuff*—composed around 1900 have not survived, and, unfortunately, they cannot shed light on his development as a playwright or on the themes he explored. *Exiles* was first published on 25 May 1918, an appearance purposely delayed by Joyce until after *A Portrait of the Artist as a Young Man* had come out as a book in 1916. The play's structure and its themes reflect the influence of the works of Henrik Ibsen, a dramatist whom Joyce greatly admired, and it may offer insights into how Joyce felt about what life might have been for himself and his family had he chosen to return to Dublin around this time. The play also reveals in its last act Joyce's disappointment in Ireland's inability to secure Home Rule. Nonetheless, *Exiles* remains a work of fiction and so such speculation should proceed with caution.

The play is set in south suburban Dublin, primarily in Merrion, a fictitious location similar to Sandymount, and, in act two, in Ranelagh. It opens in a rented home in Merrion where **Beatrice Justice** and **Richard Rowan** speak of their personal lives in a form of exposition that tells the audience that Richard has been living in Rome with his common-law wife **Bertha** and their son **Archie**. Viewers also learn of Beatrice's love for her cousin, **Robert Hand**, a longtime friend of Richard's, and of the attitude of Richard's recently deceased mother toward Bertha.

Richard leaves to avoid meeting Robert who has come with roses for Bertha. Robert has an awkward exchange with Beatrice before she leaves to give Archie, who arrives with his mother, a piano lesson. Bertha and Robert speak of their affection for each other. However, despite embracing and kissing, the scene remains ambiguous whether Bertha will go to Robert's cottage as he has requested.

In a scene after Robert leaves, the voyeuristic motif that underlies the drama emerges. It becomes clear from their conversation that Bertha has told Richard all of the details of Robert's attempts to seduce her. She seems uncomfortable by the arrangement, particularly when Richard rebuffs her suggestions that he should forbid her to meet Robert. In his refusal to intervene, Richard seems to be acting the part of a detached onlooker. What remains unclear, however, is the sort of relationship that Richard and Bertha, who has accused Richard of loving Beatrice, have.

Act 2 takes place in Robert Hand's Ranelagh cottage, the place of his arranged rendezvous with Bertha. However, while he is waiting for her, Richard arrives instead. The scene is predictably awkward, but Richard seems to be taking a good bit of satisfaction from that. The two men speak of in generalities of fidelity, friendship, and freedom, but resolve nothing. When they hear Bertha arriving, Robert steps into the garden leaving Richard to confront her. After a lengthy discussion, he leaves and Bertha calls Robert in from the garden. Another unresolved discussion—on love, freedom, and friendship—takes place, and the act ends with the audience having no clear sense of what ultimately transpires. A comment Joyce made in his notes on the play is particularly revealing and an apt description of the second act. Joyce stated, "The play is three cat and mouse acts."

Act 3 begins early next morning in Merrion. Beatrice Justice, bringing a copy of the morning newspaper with a column on Richard's life written by Robert, comes in on Bertha. The awkwardness of the situation is apparent as the two discuss Richard's return to Ireland. As in nearly every conversation in the play, it ends without the speakers coming to any sort of resolution. As Beatrice leaves, Bertha offers her friendship, though it seems unclear what that entails. Richard then enters the drawing room, and he and Bertha attempt to resolve the conflict in their attitudes toward freedom and fidelity. Richard leaves and Robert enters. Calling Richard back, she tries to effect a reconciliation between Robert and Richard. Though Robert tries to present his efforts as a failure, after he has left Richard speaks of a "wound of doubt," and the play ends with Bertha trying to console him.

Exiles is every bit as melodramatic as the synopsis suggests, which goes a long way toward explaining why it is performed so infrequently despite the notoriety of its author. While it foregrounds a great deal of Joyce's favorite issues regarding the relationships of men and women, it does so in a histrionic, wooden fashion that one never finds in discussions of similar topics in his fiction. If nothing else, *Exiles* confirms the sense that a distinguished novelist is not necessarily capable of similarly great writing in other genres.

A Glossary of Characters

Bertha—one of the play's central figures. Her surname is not given, and she is acknowledged to be Richard Rowan's common-law wife and mother to their son Archie. She is identified as being from a lower social class than Richard, but she remains an unintimidated character in her struggles with him. Their relationship as well as her commitment to traditional values stand as difficult to discern, particularly because the details of her relationship with Robert Hand, tacitly endorsed by Richard, remain crucially ambiguous.

Robert Hand—a prominent Dublin journalist and longtime friend of Richard Rowan. He is also the cousin and former fiancée of Beatrice Justice. He stands as the antithesis of Richard, having remained in Ireland to lead a relatively conventional life. His attempted seduction of Bertha serves as a catalyst for bringing deeper issues on fidelity, friendship, and possession to the foreground in the play, but his motivation for it is never clearly articulated.

Beatrice Justice—a friend of Richard's who gives Archie piano lessons. Richard has corresponded with her while living abroad, and she emerges as more his intellectual equal than is Bertha. Though their affection for one another is clear, she and Richard maintain a platonic bond.

Archie Rowan—the son of Richard and Bertha. He is more a placeholder than a character since both parents seem to see his as a demonstration of the physical attachment rather than anything more.

Richard Rowan—the pivotal figure in the play. As a successful artist returning to Ireland, he seems to embody a life that Joyce might have chosen. While his affection for Bertha, Robert, and Beatrice is clear, he nonetheless manipulates each for his own self-gratification. Self-absorption dominates his relationships, and despite his supposed suffering, his egoism, selfishness, and cruelty come across as his most pronounced traits.

Giacomo Joyce

This is a journal and collection of short sketches that Joyce kept in a notebook while in Trieste between 1911 and 1914. The title by which it is known appears on the cover, though there is scholarly debate over its origin. The collection itself consists of a series of personal accounts seemingly documenting Joyce's infatuation—observations often expressively erotic—toward one of his younger female language students. There is no evidence that Joyce wrote it for publication, and one might argue whether it is more accurately classified as fiction or as memoir. After its composition, Joyce apparently mined it for material that he used in subsequent writings, further blurring the distinction between autobiography and fiction. *Giacomo Joyce* was published in 1968 by the Viking Press with an Introduction and notes by Richard Ellmann, an academic, and one of Joyce's biographers, always willing to bring portions of Joyce's life and creative process before the public.

The Letters of James Joyce

This is the collective title of the three volumes of James Joyce's letters. The first volume, edited by Stuart Gilbert, that appeared in 1957 covered letters from 1901 to 1940. With the discovery of additional letters, and of course an eye on merchandizing Joyce memorabilia, Richard Ellmann edited two additional volumes that appeared in 1966. Volume Two printed letters written between 1900 and 1920, and volume three covered the period from 1920 to 1940. The second volume also contains an invaluable listing of Joyce's addresses. In 1975, Ellman published a collection entitled *Selected Letters of James Joyce*. There was little new in this edition, but Ellmann did choose to print several explicit letters from Joyce to Nora with graphic sexually explicit material. The letters had previously appeared expurgated versions. Whether or not readers needed to see them in their unabridged form remains open to debate, but they certainly proved a lucrative endeavor for Ellmann and the publishers. (They were also the only work by Joyce ever reviewed in *Playboy Magazine*.)

A digital edition of Joyce's letters under the title of *James Joyce's Correspondence* is currently being produced at the University of Antwerp.

Chronology

1882	Virginia Woolf born (25 January) James Joyce born (2 February)
1884	"Love's Old Sweet Song" composed by James Lyman Molloy, lyrics by C. Clifton Bingham
1885	Ezra Pound born (30 October) D.H. Lawrence born (11 September)
1888	T.S. Eliot born (26 September) Joyce enters Clongowes Wood College (September)
1891	Joyce Writes "Et Tu, Healy," poem on Parnell's betrayal (nonextant) For financial reasons, Joyce withdrawn from Clongowes Wood College
1893	Joyce enters Belvedere College
1898	Joyce graduates from Belvedere College, enrolls in University College Dublin
1900	Joyce's first publication: "Ibsen's New Drama" in *Fortnightly Review* (1 April); Joyce writes *A Brilliant Career* (a play that has not survived)
1901	Joyce publishes "The Day of the Rabblement," an essay attacking Irish Literary Theatre
1902	Joyce graduates from University College Dublin, with a degree in modern languages; he leaves for Paris, ostensibly to study medicine
1903	Joyce's mother, Mary Jane "May" Joyce, dies (13 August)
1904	Joyce meets Nora Barnacle (10 June); goes walking with her (16 June); they elope to the Continent (October)
1905	Joyce and Nora settle in Trieste; son, George, is born (27 July)
1906	Samuel Beckett born (13 April) Joyce, Nora, and George move to Rome for six months
1907	Joyce, Nora, and George return to Trieste (March); *Chamber Music* published; daughter, Lucia, born (26 July)

1909	Joyce visits Ireland twice during the year; second time, opens Volta cinema in Dublin
1910	Volta cinema Dublin, which Joyce had helped establish while on a visit to Ireland, fails
1912	Joyce visits Ireland with his family (Galway and Dublin), his last trip to his homeland; he writes "Gas from a Burner" after the *Dubliners* sheets are destroyed by the printer, John Falconer
1914	*A Portrait of the Artist as a Young Man* is serialized (through 1915) in *The Egoist*; *Dubliners* is published by Grant Richards; Joyce begins writing *Ulysses* and *Exiles*
1915	Joyce and his family move to Switzerland with his family; *Exiles* is completed
1916	The Easter Rebellion takes place in Ireland B.W. Huebsch publishes *A Portrait of the Artist as a Young Man* in America to avoid the harsh penalties that could be imposed on British printers for material found to be scandalous or libelous
1917	Joyce undergoes first eye operation; publishes poems in *Poetry*
1918	*Ulysses* begins serialization in *Little Review* (through 1920); *Exiles* published in New York by B.W. Huebsch
1919	Irish War of Independence begins Five installments of *Ulysses* serialized in *The Egoist*; first stage production of *Exiles*, in German at the Münchener Theater (September); Joyce, Nora, George, and Lucia return to Trieste (October)
1920	Joyce and his family move to Paris (July); *The Little Review* is ordered to cease publishing installments of *Ulysses*
1921	The Anglo-Irish Treaty ends War of Independence
1922	Ireland partitioned; Irish Free State proclaimed, given dominion status by Britain; the Irish Civil War begins *Ulysses* published by Shakespeare and Company, Paris; the United States Post Office destroys copies on arrival
1923	Joyce begins work on *Finnegans Wake*
1924	Herbert Gorman publishes Joyce's first biography, *James Joyce: His First Forty Years* First fragment of Work in Progress appears in transAppendic review
1925	Fragments of *Work in Progress* continue to appear
1926	Joyce's *Ulysses* pirated and published serially in *Two Worlds Monthly* (through 1927)
1927	Joyce's *Work in Progress* begins to appear in regular installments in *transition*, 17 in all (through 1938); *Pomes Penyeach* is published by Shakespeare and Company, Paris

1928	Joyce publishes *Work in Progress Volume I* (*FW* 3–216) in book form to protect copyrights
1929	*Ulysses* translated into French; *Our Exagmination Round His Factification for Incamination of Work in Progress* published by Shakespeare and Company; with Nicoló Vidacovich, Joyce translates Synge's *Riders to the Sea* into Italian
1930	Stuart Gilbert publishes *James Joyce's* **Ulysses**, a book length critical study of the novel
	Joyce begins his promotion of Irish tenor John Sullivan (continuing until 1934)
1931	James and Nora marry in London (4 July) to protect the inheritance rights of the children; Joyce's father dies (December)
1932	Joyce's grandson, Stephen James Joyce, born; Joyce writes "Ecce Puer"; Joyce's daughter, Lucia, has her first mental breakdown
1933	Judge John M. Woolsey of U.S. District Court at New York rules that *Ulysses* is not pornographic and that it can be published in the United States
1934	Frank Budgen publishes *James Joyce and the Making of Ulysses*
	First American edition of *Ulysses* published by Random House
1936	First British edition of *Ulysses* published (The Bodley Head); the Black Sun Press publishes the *Collected Poems*
1939	World War II begins
	Faber and Faber, London, publishes *Finnegans Wake*
1940	Herbert Gorman's expanded biography, *James Joyce* is published
	Joyce and Nora leave Saint-Gérand-le-Puy, where Lucia is hospitalized, for Zurich
1941	Joyce dies in Zurich (13 January); buried at Fluntern Cemetery (15 January)

Bibliography

Primary Works

The Critical Writings of James Joyce. Ed. Ellsworth Mason and Richard Ellmann. New York: The Viking Press, 1959.
Dubliners. Ed. Margot Norris. New York: W.W. Norton, 2006.
Dubliners: Text, Criticism, and Notes. Ed. Robert Scholes and A. Walton Litz. New York: The Viking Press, 1996.
Exiles: A Critical Edition. Eds. A. Nicholas Fargnoli and Michael Patrick Gillespie. Gainesville: University Press of Florida, 2016.
Finnegans Wake. New York: The Viking Press, 1939.
Giacomo Joyce. New York: The Viking Press, 1968.
James Joyce: Poems and Shorter Writings. Eds. Richard Ellmann, A. Walton Litz, and John Whittier-Ferguson. London: Faber and Faber, 2001.
Letters of James Joyce. Vol. I. Ed. Stuart Gilbert. New York: The Viking Press, 1957.
Letters of James Joyce, Vols. II and III. Ed. Richard Ellmann. New York: The Viking Press, 1966.
A Portrait of the Artist as a Young Man. Ed. John Paul Riquelme. New York: W.W. Norton, 2007.
Selected Letters of James Joyce. Ed. Richard Ellmann. New York: The Viking Press, 1977.
Stephen Hero. Ed. Theodore Spencer. New Directions, New York, 1944.
Ulysses. New York: Random House, 1986.

Biographical Sources

Anderson, Chester G. *James Joyce and His World*. London: Thames and Hudson, Ltd., 1967.
Beja, Morris. *James Joyce: A Literary Life*. Columbus: Ohio State University Press, 1992.
Benco, Silvio. "James Joyce in Trieste." *The Bookman* 72(December 1930): 375–380.
Berrone, Louis. *James Joyce in Padua*. New York: Random House, 1977.
Bowker, Gordon. *James Joyce: A New Biography*. New York: Farrar, Straus and Giroux, 2011.
Bradley, Bruce, S.J. *James Joyce's Schooldays*. Dublin: Gill and Macmillan, 1982; New York: St. Martin's, 1982.
Colum, Mary, and Padraic Colum. *Our Friend James Joyce*. Garden City, N.Y.: Doubleday, 1958.
Costello, Peter. *James Joyce*. Dublin: Gill & Macmillan Ltd., 1998.
———. *James Joyce: The Years of Growth 1882–1915*. New York: Pantheon Books, 1992.

———. *Leopold Bloom: A Biography.* Dublin: Gill and Macmillan, 1981.
Crivelli, Renzo S. *Itinerari Triestini James Joyce Triestine Itinaries.* Trieste: Casa Editrice/Publishing House, 1996.
Curran, Constantine. *James Joyce Remembered.* New York and London: Oxford University Press, 1968.
Ellmann, Richard. *James Joyce.* New York: Oxford University Press, 1982.
———. (ed.) *Giacomo Joyce.* New York: The Viking Press, 1968.
Faerber, Thomas, and Markus Luchsinger. *Joyce in Zurich.* Zurich: Unionsverlag, 1988.
Gorman, Herbert S. *James Joyce: A Definitive Biography.* 1941; rpt. London: John Lane, The Bodley Head, 1949.
———. *James Joyce: His First Forty Years.* London: Geoffrey Bles, 1926.
Igoe, Vivien. *James Joyce's Dublin Houses & Nora Barnacle's Galway.* London: Mandarin, 1990.
———. *The Real People of Joyce's* **Ulysses**: *A Biographical Guide.* Dublin: University College Dublin Press, 2016.
Joyce, Stanislaus. *The Dublin Diary of Stanislaus Joyce.* Ed. George H. Healy. London: Faber and Faber, 1962; Ithaca, N.Y.: Cornell University Press, 1962. Revised and published as *The Complete Dublin Diary of Stanislaus Joyce.* Ithaca, N.Y.: Cornell University Press, 1971.
———. *My Brother's Keeper: James Joyce's Early Years.* Ed. With an introduction and notes by Richard Ellmann. Preface T.S. Eliot. New York: Viking, 1958.
Lidderdale, Jane, and Mary Nicholson. *Dear Miss Weaver: Harriet Shaw Weaver, 1876–1961.* London: Faber and Faber, 1970.
Maddox, Brenda. *Nora: The Real Life of Molly Bloom.* Boston: Houghton Mifflin, 1988.
McCourt, John. *The Years of Bloom: James Joyce in Trieste, 1904-1920.* Madison, WI: University of Wisconsin Press, 2000.
Magalaner, Marvin, and Richard M. Kain. *Joyce: The Man, The Work, The Reputation.* New York: New York University Press, [1965] 1956.
Noel, Lucie. *James Joyce and Paul L. Léon: The Story of a Friendship.* New York: Gotham Book Mart, 1950.
O'Brien, Edna. *James Joyce.* New York: Viking, 1999.
O'Connor, Ulick, ed. *The Joyce We Knew: Memories by Eugene Sheehy, Will G. Fallon, Padraic Colum, Arthur Power.* Cork: The Mercier Press, 1967.
Potts, Willard, ed. *Portraits of the Artist in Exile: Recollections of James Joyce by Europeans.* Seattle: University of Washington Press, 1979; rpt. New York: Harcourt Brace, 1986.
———. *Conversations with James Joyce.* Ed. Clive Hart. London: Millington Books, 1974.
Pound, Ezra. *Conversations with James Joyce.* Ed. Clive Hart. London: Millington Books, 1974.
———. *Pound/Joyce: The Letters of Ezra Pound to James Joyce.* Ed. By Forrest Read. London: Faber and Faber, 1967 (also published by New Directions in 1970).
Power, Arthur. *Conversations with James Joyce.* Ed. Clive Hart. New York: Barnes and Noble, 1974.
Staley, Thomas F., and Randolph Lewis, eds. *Reflections on James Joyce: Stuart Gilbert's Paris Journal.* Austin: University of Texas Press, 1993.
Sullivan, Kevin. *Joyce among the Jesuits.* New York: Columbia University Press, 1958.
Tindall, William York. *The Joyce Country.* Enlarged edition. New York: Schocken Books, 1966.

General

Adams, Robert M. *James Joyce: Common Sense and Beyond*. New York: Random House, 1966.
Attridge, Derek. *Joyce Effects: On Language, Theory, and History*. Cambridge, England: Cambridge University Press, 2000.
Bauerle, Ruth, ed. *The James Joyce Songbook*. New York: Garland Publishing, 1982.
———. *Shakespeare & Company*. Lincoln: University of Nebraska Press, 1991.
Beach, Sylvia. *Shakespeare & Company*. Lincoln: University of Nebraska Press, 1991.
———. *Catalogue of a Collection Containing Manuscripts and Rare Editions of James Joyce, etc*. Paris: Shakespeare and Co., 1935.
Benstock, Bernard. *James Joyce: The Undiscovered Country*. New York: Barnes and Noble; Dublin: Gill and Macmillan, 1977.
Benstock, Bernard, and Shari Benstock. *Who's He When He's At Home. A James Joyce Directory*. Urbana: University of Illinois Press, 1980.
Bérard, Victor. *Les Phéneciens dans l'Odyssée*. Paris, 1902.
Boheemen-Saaf, Christine van. *Joyce, Derrida, Lacan, and the Trauma of History: Reading, Narrative and Postcolonialism*. Cambridge, England: Cambridge University Press, 1999.
Bowen, Zack. *Bloom's Old Sweet Song: Essays on Joyce and Music*. Gainesville, FL: University Press of Florida, 1995.
——— and James F. Carens, eds. *A Companion to Joyce Studies*. Westport, CT: Greenwood Press, 1984.
Brannigan, John, Geoff Ward, and Julian Wolfreys, eds. *Re: Joyce: Text, Culture, Politics*. Basingstoke, England: Macmillan; New York: St. Martin's, 1998.
Bristow, Daniel. *Joyce and Lacan: Reading, Writing, and Psychoanalysis*. New York: Routledge, 2017.
Brivic, Sheldon. *The Veil of Signs: Joyce, Lacan, and Perception*. Chicago and Urbana: University of Illinois Press, 1991.
Brivic, Sheldon. *Joyce the Creator*. Madison: University of Wisconsin Press, 1985.
———. *Joyce between Freud and Jung*. Port Washington, N.Y., and London: Kennikaat Press, 1980.
Brown, Richard. *James Joyce and Sexuality*. Cambridge, New York: Cambridge University Press, 1985.
Burns, Christy L. *Gestural Politics: Stereotype and Parody in Joyce*. Albany, NY: State University of New York Press, 2000.
Cheng, Vincent J. *Joyce, Race, and Empire*. Cambridge, England: Cambridge University Press, 1995.
Cixous, Hélène. *L'Exil de James Joyce*. Paris: Bernard Grasset, 1968. Translated as *The Exile of James Joyce*. New York: David Lewis, 1972.
Connolly, Thomas E., comp. *The Personal Library of James Joyce: Descriptive Bibliography*. 2d edition. Buffalo: University Bookstore, University of Buffalo, 1957.
Cope, Jackson I. *Joyce's Cities: Archaeologies of the Soul*. Baltimore and London: The Johns Hopkins University Press, 1981.
Creasy, Matthew ed. *Errears and Erroriboose: Joyce and Error*. European Joyce Studies 20 Amsterdam: Rodopi, 2011.
Dunleavy, Janet E., ed. *Reviewing Classics of Joyce Criticism*. Urbana and Chicago: University of Illinois Press, 1991.
Eco, Umberto. *The Aesthetics of Chaosmos: The Middle Ages of James Joyce*. Trans. Ellen Esrock. Tulsa: University of Tulsa Press, 1982.

Eide, Marian. *Ethical Joyce*. Cambridge, England: Cambridge University Press, 2002.
Ellmann, Richard. *The Consciousness of Joyce*. New York: Oxford University Press, 1977.
Fahy, Catherine. *The James Joyce—Paul Léon Papers in The National Library of Ireland, A Catalogue*. Dublin: National Library of Ireland, 1992.
Fargnoli, A. Nicholas, ed. *James Joyce: A Literary Reference*. New York: Carroll & Graf, 2003.
Fargnoli, A. Nicholas, and Michael Patrick Gillespie. *Critical Companion to James Joyce: A Literary Reference to His Life and Work*. New York: Facts On File, 2006.
Fish, Stanley. "What is Stylistics and Why are They Saying Such Terrible Things About It." In *Is There a Text in This Class?: The Authority of Interpretative Communities*. Cambridge, MA.: Harvard University Press, 1980, 68–96.
Froula, Appendice. *Modernism's Body: Sex, Culture and Joyce*. New York: Columbia University Press, 1996.
Garvin, John. *James Joyce's Disunited Kingdom*. New York: Barnes and Noble, 1977.
Gibson, Andrew. *Joyce's Revenge: History, Politics, and Aesthetics in Ulysses*. New York: Oxford University Press, 2002
Gillespie, Michael Patrick. *James Joyce and the Exilic Imagination*. Gainesville, FL: University Press of Florida, 2015.
———, ed. *Joyce Through the Ages: A Nonlinear View*. Gainesville, FL: University Press of Florida, 1999.
———. *Reading the Book of Himself: Narrative Strategies in the Works of James Joyce*. Columbus: Ohio State University Press, 1989.
———. *James Joyce's Trieste Library: A Catalogue of Materials*. Austin: Humanities Research Center/University of Texas, 1986.
Givens, Seon, ed. *James Joyce: Two Decades of Criticism*. New York: The Vanguard Press, 1963.
Goldman, Arnold. *The Joyce Paradox*. London: Routledge & Kegan Paul, 1966.
Goldman, Jonathan, ed. *Joyce and the Law*. Gainesville, FL: University Press of Florida, 2017.
Gordon, John. *Joyce and Reality: The Empirical Strikes Back*. Syracuse: Syracuse University Press, 2004.
Gottfried, Roy. *Joyce's Comic Portrait*. Gainesville, FL: University Press of Florida, 2000.
Hart, Clive, et al. *Images of Joyce*. Gerrards Cross, England: Smythe, 1998.
Hayman, David, and Sam Slote, eds. *Genetic Studies in Joyce*. Amsterdam, Netherlands: Rodopi, 1995.
Heller, Vivian. *Joyce, Decadence, and Emancipation*. Urbana: University of Illinois Press, 1995.
Henke, Suzette A. *James Joyce and the Politics of Desire*. New York and London: Routledge, 1990.
Henke, Suzette A, and Elaine Unkeless, eds. *Women in Joyce*. Urbana and Chicago: University of Illinois Press, 1982.
Herr, Cheryl . (ed.) *Cultural Studies of James Joyce*. European Joyce Studies Vol. 15 (2003).
———. *Joyce's Anatomy of Culture*. Urbana and Chicago: University of Illinois Press, 1986.
Herring, Phillip F. *Joyce's Uncertainty Principle*. Princeton: Princeton University Press, 1987.
Hulle, Dirk van, ed. *James Joyce: The Study of Languages*. Brussels, Belgium: Peter Lang, 2002.
Hutchins, Patricia . *James Joyce's World*. London: Methuen, 1957.
———. *James Joyce's Dublin*. London: The Grey Walls Press, 1950.

Igoe, Vivien. *A Literary Guide to Dublin*. London: Methuen, 1994.
Jaurretche, Colleen. *The Sensual Philosophy: Joyce and the Aesthetics f Mysticism*. Madison, WI: University of Wisconsin Press, 1997.
Kelly, Joseph. *Our Joyce: From Outcast to Icon*. Austin, TX: University of Texas Press, 1998.
Kenner, Hugh. *Joyce's Voices*. Berkeley, Los Angeles, London: University of California Press, 1978.
———. *The Stoic Comedians: Flaubert, Joyce, and Beckett*. Berkeley, Los Angeles and London: University of California Press, 1974.
———. *Dublin's Joyce*. London: Chatto and Windus, 1956.
Kershner, R.B. *Joyce, Bakhtin, and Popular Literature: Chronicles of Disorder*. Chapel Hill and London: The University of North Carolina Press, 1989.
Knowles, Sebastian D.G., ed. *Bronze by Gold: The Music of Joyce*. New York: Garland, 1999.
Knowlton, Eloise. *Joyce, Joyceans, and the Rhetoric of Citation*. Gainesville, FL: University Press of Florida, 1998.
Lernout, Geert. *The French Joyce*. Ann Arbor: The University of Michigan Press, 1990.
Leonard, Garry M. *Advertising and Commodity Culture in Joyce*. Gainesville, FL: University Press of Florida, 1998.
Levin, Harry. *James Joyce: A Critical Introduction*. London: Faber and Faber, 1944; New York: New Directions, 1960.
Levitt, Morton P., ed. *Joyce and the Joyceans*. Syracuse: Syracuse University Press, 2002.
Lobner, Corinna del Greco. *James Joyce's Italian Connection*. Iowa City: University of Iowa Press, 1989.
Lowe-Evans, Mary. *Crimes Against Fecundity: Joyce and Population Control*. Syracuse: Syracuse University Press, 1989.
Lyons, J.B. *James Joyce and Medicine*. Dublin: The Dolmen Press, 1973.
MacCabe, Colin. *James Joyce and the Revolution of the Word*. New York: Barnes and Noble, 1979; Basingstoke, England: Palgrave Macmillan, 2003.
Mackey, Peter Francis. *Chaos Theory and James Joyce's Everyman*. Gainesville, FL: University Press of Florida, 1999.
Magalaner, Marvin. *Time of Apprenticeship: The Fiction of the Young James Joyce*. New York and Toronto: Abelard-Schumann, 1959.
Magalaner, Marvin and Richard M. Kain. *Joyce: The Man, the Work, the Reputation*. New York: New York University Press, 1956; London: John Calder, 1957.
Mahaffey, Vicki. *Reauthorizing Joyce*. Cambridge: Cambridge University Press, 1988.
Manganiello, Dominic. *Joyce's Politics*. London: Routledge & Kegan Paul, 1980.
Martin, Timothy. *Joyce and Wagner: A Study of Influence*. Cambridge: Cambridge University Press, 1991.
McCarthy, Patrick A., ed. *Critical Essays on James Joyce's **Finnegans Wake***. New York: G. K. Halland Company, 1992.
McCormack, W.J. and Alistair Stead. *James Joyce & Modern Literature*. London: Routledge & Kegan Paul, 1982.
McMorran, Ciaran. *Joyce and Geometry*. Gainesville, FL: The University Press of Florida, 2020.
Melchiori, Giorgio. *Joyce's Feast of Languages: Seven Essays and Ten Notes*. Rome: Bulzoni Editore, 1995.
Mitchell, Andrew J. and Sam Sloate (eds.). *Derrida and Joyce: Texts and Contexts*. Albany: State University of New York Press, 2013.
Morse, J. Mitchell. *The Sympathetic Alien, James Joyce and Catholicism*. New York: New York University Press, 1959.

Mullin, Katherine. *James Joyce, Sexuality and Social Purity*. Cambridge, England: Cambridge University Press, 2003.

Nadel, Ira B. *Joyce and the Jews: Culture and Texts*. Iowa City: University of Iowa Press, 1989.

Nolan, Emer. *James Joyce and Nationalism*. London: Routledge, 1995.

Noon, William T. *Joyce and Aquinas*. New Haven: Yale University Press, 1957.

O'Rourke, Fran. *Joyce, Aristotle, and Aquinas*. Gainesville: University Press of Florida, 2022.

Parrinder, Patrick. *James Joyce*. London: Cambridge University Press, 1984.

Peake, Charles. *James Joyce: The Citizen and the Artist*. Stanford: Stanford University Press, 1977.

Peterson, Richard F. *James Joyce Revisited*. New York: Twayne, 1992.

Potts, Willard. *Joyce and the Two Irelands*. Austin, TX: University of Texas Press, 2000.

Rabaté, Jean-Michel. *James Joyce and the Politics of Egoism*. Cambridge: Cambridge University Press, 2001.

Reizbaum, Marilyn. *James Joyce's Judaic Other*. Stanford: Stanford University Press, 1999.

Reynolds, Mary T., ed. *James Joyce: A Collection of Critical Essays*. Englewood Cliffs, NJ: Prentice Hall, 1993.

———. *Joyce and Dante: The Shaping Imagination*. Princeton: Princeton University Press, 1981.

Rice, Thomas Jackson. *Joyce, Chaos, and Complexity*. Urbana, IL: University of Illinois Press, 1997.

Riquelme, John Paul. *Teller and Tale in Joyce's Fiction: Oscillating Perspectives*. Baltimore: Johns Hopkins University Press, 1983.

Roughly, Alan. *James Joyce and Critical Theory*. Ann Arbor: The University of Michigan Press, 1991.

Scholes, Robert E. *In Search of James Joyce*. Urban: University of Illinois Press, 1992.

———. *The Cornell Joyce Collection: a Catalogue*. Ithaca, N.Y.: Cornell University Press, 1961.

Schlossman, Beryl. *Joyce's Catholic Comedy of Language*. Madison: University of Wisconsin Press, 1985.

Schork, R.J. *Joyce and Hagiography: Saints Above!* Gainesville, FL: University Press of Florida, 2000.

———. *Greek and Hellenic Culture in Joyce*. Gainesville, FL: University Press of Florida, 1998.

———. *Latin and Roman Culture in Joyce*. Gainesville, FL: University Press of Florida, 1997.

Schwarze, Tracey Teets. *Joyce and the Victorians*. Gainesville, FL: University Press of Florida, 2002.

Scott, Bonnie Kime. *Joyce and Feminism*. Bloomington: Indiana UP, 1984.

Spielberg, Peter. *James Joyce's Manuscripts and Letters at the University of Buffalo*. Buffalo: University of Buffalo Press, 1962.

Spoo, Robert. *Modernism and the Law*. London: Bloomsbury Academic, 2018.

Spurr, David. *Joyce and the Scene of Modernity*. Gainesville, FL: University Press of Florida, 2002.

Staley, Thomas F. *An Annotated Critical Bibliography of James Joyce*. New York: St. Martin's Press, 1989.

Steppe, Wolfhard. "The Merry Greeks (With a Farewell to *epicleti*)." *James Joyce Quarterly*, 32 (Spring-Summer, 1995): 597–617.

Sultan, Stanley. *Joyce's Metamorphosis*. Gainesville, FL: University Press of Florida, 2001.
———. *Eliot, Joyce & Company*. New York, Oxford: Oxford University Press, 1987.
Thurston, Luke. *James Joyce and the Problem of Psychoanalysis*. Cambridge, England: Cambridge University Press, 2004.
Tindall, William York. *A Reader's Guide to James Joyce*. New York: The Noonday Press, 1976.
Tysdahl, B.J. *Joyce and Ibsen: A Study in Literary Influence*. Oslo: Norwegian Universities Press; New York: Humanities Press, 1968.
Valente, Joseph, ed. *Quare Joyce*. Ann Arbor: University of Michigan Press, 1998.
Wales, Katie. *The Language of James Joyce*. New York: St. Martin's Press, 1992.
Wawrzycka, Jolanta W., and Marlena G. Corcoran, eds. *Gender in Joyce*. Gainesville, FL: University Press of Florida, 1997.
Weaver, Jack W. *Joyce's Music and Noise: Theme and Variation in His Writings*. Gainesville, FL: University Press of Florida, 1998.
Whittier-Ferguson, John. *Framing Pieces: Designs of the Gloss in Joyce, Woolf, and Pound*. New York: Oxford University Press, 1996.
Williams, Trevor L. *Reading Joyce Politically*. Gainesville, FL: University Press of Florida, 1997.

Dubliners

Baker, James R. and Staley, Thomas F., eds. *James Joyce's **Dubliners**: A Critical Handbook*. Belmont, Calif.: Wadsworth, 1969.
Beck, Warren. *Joyce's **Dubliners**: Substance, Vision, and Art*. Durham, N.C.: Duke University Press, 1969.
Bollettieri Bosinelli, Rosa M., and Harold F. Mosher, Jr., eds. *ReJoycing: New Readings of **Dubliners***. Lexington, KY: University Press of Kentucky, 1998.
Brandabur, Edward. *A Scrupulous Meanness: A Study of Joyce's Early Work*. Urbana: University of Illinois Press, 1971.
Brown, Terence. ***Dubliners***. New York: Penguin, 1992.
Garrett, Peter, ed. *Twentieth-Century Interpretations of **Dubliners**: A Collection of Critical Essays*. Englewood Cliffs, N.J.: Prentice-Hall, 1968.
Gifford, Don, and Robert J. Seidman. *Joyce Annotated: Notes for **Dubliners** and **A Portrait of The Artist as a Young Man***. 1967; 2nd edition, Berkeley, Los Angeles and London: University of California Press, 1982.
Ingersoll, Earl G. *Engendered Trope in Joyce's **Dubliners***. Carbondale: Southern Illinois University Press, 1996.
Jackson, John Wyse, and Bernard McGinley, *James Joyce's **Dubliners**: An Illustrated Edition with Annotations*. New York: St. Martin's Press, 1993.
Leonard, Garry M. *Reading **Dubliners** Again: A Lacanian Perspective*. Syracuse, N.Y.: Syracuse UP, 1993.
Norris, Margot. *Suspicious Readings of Joyce's **Dubliners***. Philadelphia, PA: University of Pennsylvania Press, 2003.
San Juan, Epifano, Jr. *James Joyce and the Craft of Fiction: An Interpretation of **Dubliners***. Rutherford, N.J.: Fairleigh Dickinson University Press, 1972.
Schwarz, Daniel R, ed. *James Joyce: The Dead*. Boston: Bedford, 1994.
Torchiana, Donald T. *Backgrounds for Joyce's **Dubliners***. Boston: Allen & Unwin, 1986.
Vesala-Varttala, Tanja. *Sympathy and Joyce's **Dubliners**: Ethical Probing of Reading, Narrative, and Textuality*. Tampere, Finland: Tampere University Press, 1999.

Wright, Charles D. "Melancholy Duffy and Sanguine Sinico: Humors in 'A Painful Case.'" *James Joyce Quarterly*, 3(Spring 1966): 171–180.

A Portrait of the Artist as a Young Man

Anderson, Chester G., ed. *A Portrait of the Artist as a Young Man: Text, Criticism, and Notes*. New York: Viking, 1968.

Beja, Morris, ed. *James Joyce: **Dubliners** and **A Portrait of the Artist as a Young Man**: a Casebook*. London: Macmillan, 1973.

Bidwell, Bruce, and Linda Heffer. *The Joycean Way. A Topographic Guide To **Dubliners** and **A Portrait of the Artist as a Young Man***. Baltimore: Johns Hopkins University Press, 1982.

Brown, Homer Obed. *James Joyce's Early Fiction: The Biography of Form*. Cleveland: Case Western Reserve University, 1972.

Buttigieg, Joseph A. *A Portrait of the Artist in Different Perspective*. Athens: Ohio University Press, 1987.

Connolly, Thomas E. (ed.). *Joyce's Portrait: Criticism and Critiques*. New York: Appleton-Century-Crofts, 1962.

Deane, Seamus, ed. *A Portrait of the Artist as a Young Man*. New York: Penguin, 1992.

Epstein, Edmund L. *The Ordeal of Stephen Dedalus: The Conflict of the Generations in James Joyce's A Portrait of the Artist as a Young Man*. Carbondale: Southern Illinois University Press, 1971.

Gifford, Don, and Robert J. Seidman. *Joyce Annotated: Notes for **Dubliners** and **A Portrait of The Artist as a Young Man**.* 1967; 2nd edition, Berkeley, Los Angeles and London: University of California Press, 1982.

Halper, Nathan. *The Early James Joyce*. New York: Columbia University Press, 1973.

Hancock, Leslie. *Word Index to James Joyce's Portrait of the Artist*. Carbondale: Southern Illinois University Press, 1967.

Kershner, R.B. ed. *A Portrait of the Artist as a Young Man: The Complete, Authoritative Text with Biographical and Historical Contexts, Critical History, and Essays from Five Contemporary Critical Perspectives*. New York: Bedford Books of St. Martin's Press, 1993.

Ryf, Robert S. *A New Approach to Joyce: The Portrait of the Artist as a Guide Book*. Berkeley and Los Angeles: University of California Press, 1962.

Scholes, Robert, and Richard M. Kain, eds. *The Workshop of Daedalus: James Joyce and the Raw Materials for **A Portrait of the Artist as a Young Man***. Evanston, Ill.: Northwestern University Press, 1965.

Schutte, William M., ed. *Twentieth Century Interpretations of A Portrait of the Artist as a Young Man: A Collection of Critical Essays*. Englewood Cliffs, N J.: Prentice, Spectrum, 1968.

Staley, Thomas F., and Bernard Benstock, eds. *Approach to Joyce's Portrait: Ten Essays*. Pittsburgh: University of Pittsburgh Press, 1976.

Swisher, Claire, ed. *Readings on **A Portrait of the Artist as a Young Man***. San Diego, CA: Greenhaven, 2000.

Thornton, Weldon. *The Antimodernism of Joyce's Portrait of the Artist as a Young Man*. Syracuse: Syracuse University Press, 1994.

Exiles

Bauerle, Ruth. *A Word List to James Joyce's **Exiles***. New York and London: Garland, 1981.

Evans, Simon. *The Penetration of* **Exiles**. A *Wake Newsletter* Monograph no. 9. Colchester, Essex, England: A Wake Newsletter Press, 1984.
MacNicholas, John. *James Joyce's* **Exiles**: *A Textual Companion*. New York and London: Garland, 1979.
Watt, Stephen. *Joyce, O'Casey and the Irish Popular Theatre*. Syracuse University Press, 1991.

Ulysses

Adams, Robert Martin. *Surface and Symbol: The Consistency of James Joyce's* **Ulysses**. New York: Oxford University Press, 1962.
Bell, Robert H. *Jocoserious Joyce: The Fate of Folly in* **Ulysses**. Gainesville, FL: University Press of Florida, 1996.
Benstock, Bernard. *Narrative Con/Texts in* **Ulysses**. Urbana and Chicago: University of Illinois Press, 1991.
Blamires, Harry. *The New Bloomsday Book*. Revised Edition. London: Routledge, 1988.
Bowen, Zack. *Bloom's Old Sweet Song: Essays on Joyce and Music*. Gainesville, FL: University Press of Florida, 1995.
———. **Ulysses** *as a Comic Novel*. Syracuse, N.Y.: Syracuse University Press, 1989.
Budgen, Frank. *James Joyce and the Making of* **Ulysses**. Bloomington: Indiana University Press, 1960.
Caspel, Paul P. J. van. *Bloomers on the Liffey: Eisegetical Readings of James Joyce's* **Ulysses**, *Part II*. Groningen, Netherlands: Veenstra Visser, 1980; revised and enlarged edition, Baltimore: Johns Hopkins University Press, 1986.
Cheng, Vincent. *Joyce, Race, and Empire*. Cambridge: Cambridge University Press, 1995.
Delaney, Frank. *James Joyce's Odyssey: A Guide to the Dublin of* **Ulysses**. London: Hodder and Stoughton, 1981; New York: Holt, Rinehart and Winston, 1981.
Dent, R. W. *Colloquial Language in* **Ulysses**: *A Reference Tool*. Newark: University of Delaware Press; London: Associated University Press, 1994.
Devlin, Kimberly J., *James Joyce's "Fraudstuff."* Gainesville: University Press of Florida, 2002.
Duffy, Enda. *The Subaltern Ulysses*. Minneapolis: University of Minnesota, 1994.
Fuller, David. *James Joyce's* **Ulysses**. New York: St. Martin's Press, 1992.
Gabler, Hans Walter. "On Textual Criticism and Editing: the Case of *Ulysses*." In *Palimpsest: Editorial Theory in the Humanities*. Eds. George Bornstein and Ralph Williams. Ann Arbor: University of Michigan Press, 1993, 195–224.
Gifford, Don, with Robert J. Seidman. **Ulysses** *Annotated*. Second edition (of *Notes for Joyce*). Berkeley: University of California Press, 1988.
Gilbert, Stuart. *James Joyce's* **Ulysses**: *A Study*. London: Faber and Faber, 1930; 2nd edn., New York: Knopf, 1952.
Gillespie, Michael Patrick, and A. Nicholas Fargnoli (eds.). **Ulysses** *in Critical Perspective*. Gainesville: University Press of Florida, 2006.
Gose, Elliott B., Jr. *The Transformation Process in Joyce's* **Ulysses**. Toronto: University of Toronto Press, 1980.
Gottfried, Roy K . Joyce's *Iritis and the Irritated Text: The Dis-Lexic* **Ulysses**. Gainesville, FL: University Press of Florida, 1995.
———. *The Art of Joyce's Syntax in* **Ulysses**. Athens: University of Georgia Press, 1980.
Groden, Michael. **Ulysses** *in Progress*. Princeton: Princeton University Press, 1977.
Harkness, Marguerite. *The Aesthetics of Dedalus and Bloom*. Lewisburg: Bucknell University Press; London and Toronto: Associated University Presses, 1984.

Hart, Clive, and A.M. Leo Knuth. *A Topographical Guide to James Joyce's* **Ulysses**, 2 vols. Colchester, England: *Wake Newslitter* Press, 1975. For an expanded version, see Gunn, Ian and Clive Hart. *James Joyce's Dublin: A Topographical Guide to the Dublin of* **Ulysses**. London: Thames and Hudson, 2004.

Hart, Clive, and David Hayman, eds. *James Joyce's* **Ulysses**: *Critical Essays*. Berkeley and Los Angeles: University of California Press, 1974.

Hayman, David. **Ulysses**: *The Mechanics of Meaning*. Englewood Cliffs, N.J.: Prentice Hall, 1970; rev. and expanded edition, Madison: University of Wisconsin Press, 1982.

Henke, Suzette. *Joyce's Moraculous Sindbook: A Study of* **Ulysses**. Columbus: Ohio State University Press, 1978.

Kenner, Hugh. **Ulysses**. London: Allen & Unwin, 1980. Revised edition, Baltimore and London: Johns Hopkins University Press, 1987.

Kiberd, Declan, ed. **Ulysses**. New York: Penguin, 1992.

Killeen, Terence. **Ulysses** *Unbound: A Reader's Companion to James Joyce's* **Ulysses**. Bray: Wordwell, 2004

Kimball, Jean. *Odyssey of the Psyche: Jungian Patterns in Joyce's* **Ulysses**. Carbondale, IL: Southern Illinois University Press, 1997.

Kitcher, Phillip (ed.). *Joyce's* **Ulysses**: *Philosophical Perspectives*. Oxford: Oxford University Press, 2021.

Knowles, Sebastian D.G. *The Dublin Helix: The Life of Language in Joyce's* **Ulysses**. Gainesville, FL: University Press of Florida, 2001.

Lawrence, Karen. *The Odyssey of Style in* **Ulysses**. Princeton: Princeton University Press, 1981.

Litz, A. Walton. *The Art of James Joyce: Method and Design in* **Ulysses** *and* **Finnegans Wake**. London: Oxford University Press, 1961.

Maddox, James H., Jr. *Joyce's* **Ulysses** *and the Assault upon Character*. New Brunswick, N.J.: Rutgers University Press, 1978.

McCarthy, Patrick A. **Ulysses**: *Portals of Discovery*. Boston: Twayne Publishers, 1990.

McGee, Patrick. *Paperspace: Style as Ideology in Joyce's* **Ulysses**. Lincoln and London: University of Nebraska Press, 1988.

McMichael, James. **Ulysses** *and Justice*. Princeton: Princeton University Press, 1991.

Murphy, Michael. *Ulysses in West Britain: James Joyce's Dublin &* **Dubliners**. Brooklyn: Conal and Gavin, 2018.

Newman, Robert A., and Weldon Thornton, eds. *Joyce's* **Ulysses**: *the Larger Perspective*. Newark: University of Delaware Press; London and Toronto: Associated University Presses, 1987.

Norris, Margot, ed. *Virgin and Veteran Readings of* **Ulysses**. New York: Palgrave Macmillan, 2011.

———. *A Companion to James Joyce's* **Ulysses**. Boston: Bedford, 1998.

Osteen, Mark. *The Economy of* **Ulysses**: *Making Both Ends Meet*. Syracuse, NY: Syracuse University Press, 1995.

Raleigh, John Henry. *The Chronicle of Leopold and Molly Bloom:* **Ulysses** *as Narrative*. Berkeley and Los Angeles: University of California Press, 1977.

Rickard, John S. *Joyce's Book of Memory: The Mnemotechnic of* **Ulysses**. Durham, NC: Duke University Press, 1998.

Sandulescu, C. George, and Clive Hart, eds. *Assessing the 1984* **Ulysses**. Gerrards Cross, Buckinghamshire: Colin Smythe; Totowa, New Jersey: Barnes and Noble, 1986.

Schutte, William. *Joyce and Shakespeare: A Study in the Meaning of* **Ulysses**. New Haven: Yale University Press, 1957.

Seidel, Michael. *Epic Geography: James Joyce's* **Ulysses**. Princeton: Princeton University Press, 1976.
Schwaber, Paul. *The Cast of Characters: A Reading of* **Ulysses**. New Haven: Yale University Press, 1999.
Schechner, Mark. *Joyce in Nighttown: A Psychoanalytic Inquiry into* **Ulysses**. Berkeley and Los Angeles: University of California Press, 1974.
Sherry, Vincent. *James Joyce/***Ulysses**. Cambridge, England: Cambridge University Press, 1994.
Sultan, Stanley. *The Argument of* **Ulysses**. Columbus: Ohio State University Press, 1964.
Thomas, Brook. *James Joyce's* **Ulysses**: *A Book of Many Happy Returns*. Baton Rouge: Louisiana State University Press, 1982.
Thornton, Weldon. *Voices and Values in Joyce's* **Ulysses**. Gainesville, FL: UP of Florida, 2000.
———. *Allusions in* **Ulysses**: *An Annotated List*. Chapel Hill: University of North Carolina Press, 1968.
Tymczko, Maria. *The Irish* **Ulysses**. Berkeley: University of California P, 1994.
Van Caspel, Paul P.J. *Bloomers on the Liffey: Eisegetical Readings of James Joyce's* **Ulysses**. Baltimore: Johns Hopkins University Press, 1986.
Vanderham, Paul. *James Joyce and Censorship: The Trials of* **Ulysses**. New York: New York University Press, 1998.

Finnegans Wake

Atherton, James S. *The Books at the Wake: A Study of Literary Allusions in James Joyce's* **Finnegans Wake**. New York: Viking Press, 1960.
Beckett, Samuel, et al. *Our Exagmination Round His Factification for Incamination of Work in Progress*. Paris: Shakespeare and Co., 1929; 2nd edn. New York: New Directions, 1972.
Begnal, Michael H., and Fritz Senn, eds. *A Conceptual Guide to* **Finnegans Wake**. University Park: Pennsylvania State University Press, 1974.
Benstock, Bernard. *Joyce-Again's Wake: An Analysis of* **Finnegans Wake**. Seattle: University of Washington Press, 1965.
Bishop, John. *Joyce's Book of the Dark:* **Finnegans Wake**. Madison, Wisconsin: The University of Wisconsin Press, 1986.
Boyle, Robert, SJ. *James Joyce's Pauline Vision: A Catholic Exposition*. Carbondale and Edwardsville: Southern Illinois University Press, 1978.
Brivic, Sheldon. *Joyce's Waking Women: An Introduction to* **Finnegans Wake**. Madison: University of Wisconsin Press, 1995.
Burrell, Harry. *Narrative Design in* **Finnegans Wake**: *The Wake Lock Picked*. Gainesville, FL: University Press of Florida, 1996.
Campbell, Joseph, and Henry Morton Robinson. *A Skeleton Key to* **Finnegans Wake**. 1944; rpt. N.Y.: Viking Press, 1966.
Cheng, Vincent John. *Shakespeare and Joyce: A Study of* **Finnegans Wake**. University Park and London: Pennsylvania State University Press, 1984.
Connolly, Thomas E., ed. *James Joyce's Scribbledehobble: The Ur-Workbook for* **Finnegans Wake**. Evanston, Ill.: Northwestern University Press, 1961.
Crispi, Luca, and Sam Slote, ed. *How Joyce Wrote* **Finnegans Wake**: *A Chapter-by-Chapter Genetic Guide*. Madison: University of Wisconsin Press, 2008.
Deane, Seamus, ed. **Finnegans Wake**. New York: Penguin, 1992.

Devlin, Kimberly J. *Wandering and Return in* **Finnegans Wake**. Princeton: Princeton University Press, 1990.
DiBernard, Barbara. *Alchemy and* **Finnegans Wake**. Albany: State University of New York Press, 1980.
Epstein, E.L., ed. *A Starchamber Quiry: A James Joyce Centennial Volume 1882-1982*. New York: Methuen, 1982.
Epstein, Edmund Lloyd. *A Guide through* **Finnegans Wake**. Gainesville, FL: University Press of Florida, 2009.
Fordham, Finn. *Lots of Fun at* **Finnegans Wake***: Unravelling Universals*. New York: Oxford University Press, 2007.
Glasheen, Adaline. *A Third Census of* **Finnegans Wake***: An Index of the Characters and Their Roles*. Berkeley: University of California Press, 1977.
Gordon, John. **Finnegans Wake:** *a Plot Summary*. Syracuse: Syracuse University Press, 1986.
Hart, Clive. *Structure and Motif in* **Finnegans Wake**. London: Faber and Faber, 1962.
Hayman, David. *The "Wake" in Transit*. Ithaca: Cornell University Press, 1990.
Hodgart, Matthew J.C., and Ruth Bauerle. *Joyce's Grand Operoar: Opera in* **Finnegans Wake**. Urbana: University of Illinois Press, 1997.
Litz, A. Walton. *The Art of James Joyce: Method and Design in* **Ulysses** *and* **Finnegans Wake**. New York: Oxford University Press, 1961.
McCarthy, Patrick A. *The Riddles of* **Finnegans Wake**. Rutherford, Madison and Teaneck, N.J.: Fairleigh Dickinson University Press; London and Toronto: Associated University Presses, 1980.
McHugh, Roland. *Annotations to* **Finnegans Wake**. Revised edn. Baltimore and London: Johns Hopkins University Press, 1991.
———. *The* **Finnegans Wake** *Experience*. Berkeley, CA.: University of California Press, 1981.
———. *The Sigla of* **Finnegans Wake**. London: Edward Arnold, 1976.
McLuhan, Eric. *The Role of Thunder in* **Finnegans Wake**. Toronto: University of Toronto Press, 1997.
Mink, Louis O. *A* **Finnegans Wake** *Gazetteer*. Bloomington: Indiana University Press, 1978.
Norris, Margot. *The Decentered Universe of* **Finnegans Wake***: A Structuralist Analysis*. Baltimore: Johns Hopkins University Press, 1974.
O Hehir, Brendan. *A Gaelic Lexicon for* **Finnegans Wake**. Berkeley: University of California Press, 1967.
O Hehir, Brendan, and John Dillon. *A Classical Lexicon for* **Finnegans Wake**. Berkeley: University of California Press, 1977.
Rose, Danis. *The Textual Diaries of James Joyce* Edinburgh: Split Pea Press, 1995.
Rose, Danis, and John O'Hanlon. *Understanding* **Finnegans Wake***: A Guide to the Narrative of James Joyce's Masterpiece*. New York: Garland Publishing, 1982.
Sandulescu, C. George. *The Language of the Devil: Texture and Archetype in* **Finnegans Wake**. Gerrads Cross, England: Colin Smythe; Chester Springs, Penn.: Dufour Editions, 1987.
Solomon, Margaret C. *Eternal Geomater: The Sexual Universe of* **Finnegans Wake**. Carbondale and Edwardsville: Southern Illinois University Press, 1969.
Tindall, William York. *A Reader's Guide to* **Finnegans Wake**. New York: Farrar, Straus & Giroux, 1969.

Miscellaneous: Joyce Foundations and Journals

Groden, Michael. *The James Joyce Archive*. 63 vols. New York: Garland Publishing, 1977.
The International James Joyce Foundation
The Zurich James Joyce Foundation
Abiko Quarterly (Literary Rag), The James Joyce Broadsheet
James Joyce Literary Supplement (online publication as of 2022)
James Joyce Newestlatter
James Joyce Review (no longer being published)
James Joyce Quarterly
Joyce Studies Annual
The James Joyce Centre
The James Joyce Museum
James Joyce Tower
The James Joyce Society
Joyce Museum Trieste

Libraries with Major Holdings of Joyce's Works

British Library
Buffalo, the State University of New York)
Cornell University
Harvard University
Huntington Library, San Marino, CA
Princeton University
Rosenbach Museum and Library, Philadelphia
University of Texas at Austin
Yale University

Appendices
Appendix I: The Uncle Charles Principle

Throughout his academic career, Hugh Kenner was one of the foremost close readers of the works of James Joyce. When Kenner made a pronouncement about some aspect of the canon, it was usually given the status of a pope speaking *ex cathedra*. The vast majority of the time, such deference was well-deserved. In lucid, concise, and thought-provoking turns of phrases, Kenner would emphasize key moments in Joyce's writing that would clarify both the passage and the large context in which it appeared. However, on occasion, this trust and Kenner's own idiosyncratic approach could produce misleading impressions. That has become true of "The Uncle Charles Principle," a term that Kenner made popular decades ago.

In 1987 in his book *Joyce's Voices*, Kenner asserted quite correctly that throughout Joyce's narratives numerous instances exist in which the elements denoting the perspective of a particular individual are integrated into an otherwise detached account by a third-person narrator. This amalgamation gives the passage a unique dual perspective, both detached and subjective, and provokes the reader to see these multiple points of view informing the single description. Kenner identified a stylist technique, that of insinuating a character's perspective into a piece of third-person narration, as "The Uncle Charles Principle," names after an instance in *A Portrait of the Artist as a Young Man* when the feelings of that particular character appear in an otherwise unaffiliated exposition.[1]

Kenner is perfectly correct in noting this occurrence in a range of instances from passages in *Dubliners* to portions of *Ulysses*. However, he goes too far when, like Columbus landing on Guanahani and naming it San Salvador, he claims this discovery of a stylistic technique as his own. In fact, what Kenner describes has been known for over a century as Free Indirect Discourse, a term introduced as *style indirect libre* by the Swiss linguist, Charles Bally, in 1912.[2] Over the twentieth century, a number of critics took up the idea, and have made illuminating comments about its use by a wide range of authors from the eighteenth century to the present.[3]

Kenner's work has always been distinguished by its brilliance, but it also is often shaped by the author's unwillingness to consult or even acknowledge secondary sources. It would be nothing more than a minor misappropriation had not so many other students of Joyce unquestionably adopted the term at face value.[4] Linking the idea to Joyce, who introduced so many stylistic innovations in his fiction, will seem like a logical interpretive strategy. It does no immediate harm in terms of understanding Joyce's writings, but it does impose a parochialism that threatens to blunt an awareness of the technique in the works of other authors.

Notes

1 Hugh Kenner. *Joyce's Voices* (Berkley: University of California Press, 1987), pp. 16–38.
2 Charles Bally. "Le style indirect libre en français modern." *Germanisch-Romanische Monatsschrift* 4 (1912), 549–556 & 597–606.
3 For a good overview of the work in the area that preceded Kenner's, see Brian McHale. "Free Indirect Discourse: a Survey of Recent Accounts." *PTL: a Journal for Descriptive Poetics and Theory of Literature* 3 (1978): 249–278.
4 Michael Mayo stands as an exception to this trend, but he too hesitates to point to the anachronistic quality of Kenner's term. See Michael Mayo's "Beyond the Uncle Charles Principle." *James Joyce Quarterly* 56.3–4 (Summer-Fall 2019): 245–266.

Appendix II: The Love Life of Leopold and Molly Bloom

Erotic images of Molly Bloom fill her husband's consciousness from the time readers first see him on June 16th until he falls asleep early the following morning. Equally, over the course of her rambling monologue in the final chapter of *Ulysses*, Molly presents graphic and ecstatic recollections of physical intimacies that she has enjoyed. However, despite the frankness of their reveries, a clear sense of the status of their intimacy is more difficult for readers to discern. Pointing to a few revelatory moments can provide a clearer sense of the physical side of their marriage and will dispel some reductive generalizations about their most intimate behavior.

Like his spouse, Bloom is a highly sensuous individual. Beginning with his ogling of his next-door neighbor's servant girl in the Calypso chapter, we see that Bloom is always on the alert for glimpses of the female form. In Lotus Eaters, he takes great pleasure in reading a titillating letter, the latest addition to his correspondence with Martha Clifford, and then silently curses a tram driver for blocking his view when a young woman lifts her skirt while entering a carriage in front of the Grosvenor Hotel. And although he remains a model of restraint when he visits Bella Cohen's whorehouse in the Circe chapter, who can forget that a few hours earlier Bloom had masturbated on Sandymount Strand while watching Gerty McDowell exhibit herself.

Equally true, early impressions of Molly give readers the sense that she has a strong and not necessarily discerning sexual appetite. A number of most Dublin males convey this view directly or indirectly over the course of the novel. When Bloom speaks of the concert tour that Boylan is arranging, listing the participants, Jack Power archly reminds him of his wife's inclusion:"and *madam* ... Last but not least" (6.224, author's italics). Lenehan, always ready to deal in salacious innuendo, in one of the vignettes of Wandering Rocks bluntly claims her openness to his fondling in a carriage coming back from the Glencree Dinner (10.545–576). And, in his typical sardonic fashion, punning on the fact that the Blooms at one time sold secondhand garments, sums up the views of many by noting that "Marion Bloom has left-off clothes of all descriptions" (11.496–497). Bloom's hallucinations in the Circe chapter offer graphic illustrations of Molly's promiscuousness, and his list of her possible lovers, compiled in the Ithaca chapter, suggests an insatiable appetite.

A great many readers have proven all too quick to fall into line with Lenehan, Simon Dedalus and have accepted Bloom's subconscious fears—often relying on assumptions based upon partial truths or outright falsehoods—to make assumptions about Molly's nature.[1] However, a closer inspection of available information in the Penelope chapter undermines many of these assertions. There, Molly's dismissal of Jack Power with an invalid wife and a barmaid he is keeping undermines his view of women. Earlier, the reaction of the barmaids in the Ormond Hotel to Lenehan's feeble attempt at flirtation shows his ineffectuality with women. And Simon Dedalus' willingness to sacrifice even a small degree of factual accuracy for the benefit of a funny remark makes anything he says suspect. Finally, the telling list of Molly's loves compiled by Bloom are filled with so many unlikely candidates as to invalidate it all. As Hugh Kenner aptly puts it, "this is a list of past occasions for twinges of Bloomian jealousy, and there is no ground for supposing that the hospitality of Molly's bed has been extended to anyone but her husband and Boylan."[2]

When Molly talks about her love life, her tangled reminiscences both clarify some matters and make others more ambiguous. Her specific recollections of her early sexual experience with time she spent with Mulvey, the young Royal Navy lieutenant on Gibraltar, including masturbating him into a handkerchief give a sense of precociousness. By the same token, the vagueness of her memories of encounters with the young Army officer, Stanley Gardner in Dublin, suggests that fervor did not translate into consummation. Even when thinking of something as recent as her assignation that afternoon with Blazes Boylan, Molly has difficulty settling on the number of times that they had intercourse. On the other hand, memories of lovemaking with Bloom, while not entirely uncritical, are vivid and exact. In the end, as with so much in the novel, Joyce leaves matters to his readers to sort out.

In fact, the sex life of Leopold and Molly Bloom is not truncated by prudishness or abhorrence of one another but by a fear of the consequences of another pregnancy. As noted in the Ithaca chapter, since the death of Rudy "there remained a period of 10 years, 5 months and 18 days during which carnal intercourse had been incomplete, without ejaculation of semen within the natural female organ" (17.2282–2284). The key word being "incomplete," coinciding with Molly's remark in Penelope about "the last time he came on my bottom" (18.77).

Leopold and Molly Bloom continue to have strong sexual appetites. At the same time, they remain haunted by the memories of the pain that they felt over the sudden death of their son Rudy. Given the information that the narrator provides about their sexual activity, it seems most logical to presume that while they still seek to satisfy sexual cravings, both are afraid to do anything that would cause Molly again to become pregnant by Bloom.

Notes

1 For a survey of such views see Valérie Bénéjam's essay "Molly inside and outside 'Penelope'." *European Joyce Studies* (2006): 63–74. Luca Crispi makes some subsequent interesting observations about Joyce's composition process in laying out Molly's sexual experiences. See, "Revisiting Molly's Lovers." *James Joyce Quarterly* 51.2–3 (Winter-Spring): 489–493.
2 The point Kenner makes is worth dwelling upon, particularly in light of our criticism of him in Appendix I. There is no definitive evidence to justify the salacious inuendoes of males throughout the narrative. Given the clarity of the information relating to Molly's liaison with Boylan, it seems an extrapolation beyond Joyce's text to make more of Molly than the facts support. Hugh Kenner, *Ulysses* rev. ed. (Baltimore: Johns Hopkins University Press, 1987), pp. 142–144.

Appendix III: The Dream of *Finnegans Wake*

The dream narrative is nothing new in English literature. Chaucer's *The Book of the Duchess* and Bunyan's *Pilgrim's Progress* may be two titles that immediately come to mind. The idea of applying a significantly modified version of this convention to *Finnegans Wake* seems to have been the brainchild of the American writer and literary critic Edmund Wilson, first in a 1929 essay on Joyce and then again ten years later in his review of *Finnegans Wake*. In the essay, "James Joyce,"[1] Wilson speculated that Joyce's new work (fragments of which were being published in *transition* at the time) "is apparently to occupy itself with the single night's sleep of a single character" (p. 91). In his review of the published novel in 1939, "The Dream of H. C. Earwicker,"[2] Wilson expanded upon this assumption that over the next several decades became the standard point of entry into the chaosmos of *Finnegans Wake*. Though the dream framework gave early readers a workable interpretative strategy, some critics by the late 1950s and early 1960s seriously questioned the validity of this approach.

In his study of literary allusions in the *Wake*, James S. Atherton quotes a remark that Joyce's benefactor Harriet Shaw Weaver made in a letter he received from her in which she dismisses the notion that *Finnegans Wake* is a dream:

> My view is that Mr. Joyce did not intend the book to be looked upon as the dream of any one character, but that he regarded the dream form with its shiftings and changes and chances as a convenient device, allowing the freest scope to introduce any material he wished – and suited to a night piece.[3]

Clive Hart, in his chapter on the *Wake*'s dream-structure, observes that identifying the dreamer has "met with little success" and that Wilson in his review of the novel "made the unwarranted assumption that Earwicker himself is the Dreamer."[4] Many critics, however, long after these early objections appeared, continued approaching *Finnegans Wake* as a dream and continued making valuable contributions to *Wake* studies. Asserting that the novel is a dream, cautions Patrick Parrinder, is much easier than proving it.[5] But dismissing it unilaterally can diminish creative and ingenious readings of the text not circumscribed by Joyce's own narrative intentions. In his extended examination of the *Wake*'s dream framework, Derek Attridge suggests that it may be "one among a number of such contexts which, though incompatible with one another, all have some potential value."[6] Joyce's writings are not one-dimensional and continually entreat readers to uncover and critically articulate their perceptions of his works.

Some critics offered alternative possibilities as to who the dreamer is from Finn MacCool to Shakespeare to L. Boom (the misprint of Leopold Bloom's name as it appeared in the *Evening Telegraph*) to Joyce to the reader and to Joyce and the reader combined.[7] Atherton himself later declared that the various theories identifying the dreamer "are all true up to a point" and that the *Wake* "is everyone's dream, the dream of all the living and the dead."[8] The question, then, of whether someone like Earwicker, a pub owner, can possess such vast knowledge of history, philosophy, languages, literature, and other disciplines referenced throughout the *Wake* becomes a moot point. Answering it one way or another does not minimize the complexity of the narrative or the burden of exegesis. The voices of Shem and Shaun, of the Ondt and the Gracehoper, of Issy and her multiple personalities, of HCE, of ALP, and of any other character are still heard whether through the medium of Earwicker's dream or the omniscient narrator.

Identifying or even claiming the existence of a dreamer may ultimately be irrelevant to the *Wake*'s fictional universe, a preview of which Joyce presents to us in *Ulysses*. The hallucinatory transformations in the Circe episode, chapter 15, one may argue, provide a prelude to the *Wake*'s narrative and linguistic transformations readily to be grasped through an oneiric metaphor. In his book *The Theatre of the Absurd*, Martin Esslin touches upon a point relevant to our discussion here. Circe, "written in the form of a dream play," Esslin explains, "is one of the great early examples of the Theatre of the Absurd," and the *Wake* "also anticipates the Theatre of the Absurd's preoccupation with language, its attempt to penetrate to a deeper layer of the mind, closer to the subconscious matrix of thought."[9]

In composing *Finnegans Wake* in the form of a dream language, a language individual yet universal, Joyce succeeded so well that the language itself conjures up a dreamer and the logical necessity of having one: "What can't be coded can be decorded if an ear aye sieze what no eye ere grieved for" (*FW* 482.34–36). However defined or however decorded, this dream space that is *Finnegans Wake*, like the Medieval image of the circle professing the boundlessness of God, professes its dream center everywhere, circumference nowhere for all readers living and dead. To paraphrase Bottom in *A Midsummer Night's Dream* (IV.1), readers of *Finnegans Wake* have a most rare vision and be past our wit to say what dream it is.

Notes

1 Edmund Wilson, "James Joyce," *The New Republic*, 61 (18 December 1929), 84–93. In the essay, Wilson does not refer to the title *Work in Progress* that Joyce gave to the fragments as they were being published.

2 Edmund Wilson, "The Dream of H.C. Earwicker," *The New Republic*, 91 (12 July 1939): 270–274. This review is republished in Wilson's *The Wound and the Bow: Seven Studies in Literature* (Boston: Houghton Mifflin, 1941), pp. 243–271 and again in Seon Givens, ed., *James Joyce: Two Decades of Criticism* (New York: Vanguard Press, 1963), pp. 319–342.

3 James S. Atherton, *The Books at the Wake: A Study of Literary Allusions in James Joyce's* **Finnegans Wake** (Carbondale: Southern Illinois University Press, 1959), p. 17.

4 Clive Hart, *Structure and Motif in* **Finnegans Wake** (Evanston, IL: Northwestern University Press, 1962), p. 78.

5 Patrick Parrinder, *James Joyce* (New York: Cambridge University Press, 1984), p. 215.

6 Derek Attridge, "Finnegans Awake: The Dream of Interpretation." *James Joyce Quarterly* 27.1 (Fall 1989): 26.

7 See Robert Boyle, *James Joyce's Pauline Vision: A Catholic Exposition* (Carbondale, IL: Southern Illinois University Press, 1978), pp. 57, 82.

8 James S. Atherton, "The Identity of the Sleeper," *A Wake Newslitter* IV.5 (October 1967): 83.

9 Martin Esslin, *The Theatre of the Absurd* (Garden City, NY: Anchor Books, 1961), pp. 252–253.

Appendix IV: Definitions of Modernism and Postmodernism

There are any number of definitions of Modernism and Postmodernism, and one often finds both terms used without any clear delineation of the author's sense of either. We offer here a general explanation of what we mean when we use either term.

Modernism—Although as a literary designation, it is generally associated with twentieth-century writing that came to prominence after World War I, one finds elements of it throughout the nineteenth century from the works of Jane Austen onward. It posits broad skepticism regarding the communal elements that shape one's behavior. Specifically, Modernist thought questions the legitimacy of social groups—family, church, state, for example—as institutions that nurture, protect, and guide one. Instead, Modernist thinking sees the individual as the sole source of moral judgment.

Postmodernism—Like Modernism, it is often seen as a perspective arising from the shock of World War II. However, one finds postmodern views in the book of Job, in *King Lear*, and at various other points in literary history. Like Modernism, it rejects the primacy of social institutions as arbiters of moral values, but Postmodernism goes even further. It rejects the concept of morality completely. Rather, it sees humans as purely material creatures without any metaphysical attributes. Good and evil, for example, have no more significance to humans than they do to dogs, cats, or any other animals.

Appendix V: Epiphanies, Epicleti, and Epiclets

Epiphanies

One of the most common terms associated with Joyce's writings and especially with *Dubliners* is *epiphany*, a transliteration of the Greek word *epiphaneia*, which means a momentary revelation, a showing forth. The term has both a theological and literary meaning. Theologically, it refers to a divine manifestation and the uncovering of a hidden truth. On January 6th, Christians celebrate the Feast of the Epiphany to commemorate the revelation of Christ's divinity to the world. As Joyce did with many theological and philosophical terms that he learned in his Jesuit education and Catholic upbringing, he employed the idea behind epiphany to portray a character's true identity, without directly having to state it in the narrative. This practice stayed with him throughout his life and was very much in the forefront of his mind when writing *Ulysses*. In *James Joyce and the Making of **Ulysses***, Frank Budgen, Joyce's Zurich friend and contributor to *Our Exagmination Round His Factification for Incamination of Work in Progress*, recorded a comment Joyce made that underscores the lasting effect the notion of epiphany had on his writings: "I want the reader to understand always through suggestion rather than direct statement" (p. 21). The epiphany or showing forth of a character's true self can go unnoticed by the inattentive readers.

Joyce's first obvious use of the term can be seen in *Stephen Hero* where the narrator clearly defines the way Stephen Daedalus understands the word term:

> By an epiphany he meant a sudden spiritual manifestation, whether in the vulgarity of speech or of gesture or in a memorable phase of the mind itself. He believed that it was for the man of letters to record these epiphanies with extreme care, seeing that they themselves are the most delicate and evanescent of moments.
>
> (*SH* 211)

The epiphanic moment reveals a truth about a character that is as subtle as it is profound.

Joyce was writing epiphanies before he went to Paris and while he was there in 1903. In a 9 March letter of that year, he mentioned to his brother Stanislaus that up to that point he had written 15 (*Letters II*, 35). In the Proteus episode of *Ulysses*, Stephen Dedalus recalls his "epiphanies written on green oval leaves, deeply deep" and believes that if he dies copies should be sent "to all the great libraries of the world" (3.141–142). Joyce carried with him a notebook in which he jotted down his epiphanies, and a few of them found their way into *Stephen Hero* and *A Portrait of the Artist as a Young Man*. The concept of epiphany became part of the evolution of Joyce's narrative techniques and in some respects can serve a role similar to free indirect discourse.

In addition to learning about epiphany from his Catholic education, Joyce may also have been encouraged to use the term in a literary sense after having read *Il Fuoco* by the Italian writer Gabrielle D'Annunzio. Borrowing from the Joyce critic, Umberto Eco, Giorgio Melchiori (cited in our general bibliography) argues that in 1900 Joyce read this two-part novel. Melchiori points out that the first part "bears the title *L'Epifania del Fuoco*. The words 'epiphany of fire' impressed Joyce, who was at the time looking for a definition of that moment of sudden revelation which was for him the core of poetic creation" (*Joyce's Feast of Languages*, p. 101).

Joyce's epiphanies have been published in Robert Scholes and Richard M. Kain's *The Workshop of Daedalus: James Joyce and the Raw Materials for **A Portrait of the Artist as a Young Man***, and in Richard Ellmann, A. Walton Litz, and John Whittier-Ferguson's *James Joyce: Poems and Shorter Writings*; both works are cited in the bibliography.

Epicleti vs Epiclets

The term *epicleti* may be a misreading of *epiclets* (little epics). In August of 1904, Joyce informed Constantine P. Curran, a former University College Dublin classmate, that he was "writing a series of epicleti—ten—for a paper" and had "written one ["The Sisters"]." He went on to say that he calls "the series *Dubliners* to betray the soul of that hemiplegia or paralysis which many consider a city" (*Letters*, I.55). According to the German textual critic and contributor to *Ulysses: A Critical and Synoptic Edition*, Wolfhard Steppe (cited in our general bibliography), Joyce's handwriting was misread; he wrote *epiclets* and not *epicleti*.

But here's the rub. Whether a misreading or not, the word and the idea behind *epicleti* actually make sense and perfectly fit the context of what Joyce may have actually intended. Relevant here may be the comment Stephen Dedalus says to his listeners in Scylla and Charybdis, the library episode in *Ulysses*: "A man of genius makes no mistakes. His errors are volitional and are the portals of discovery" (9.228–229). Even Joyce's handwriting is a portal of discovery for those who may misread it.

Epicleti looks like a Latin word derived from the Greek *epicletos*, an adjectival form of the noun *epiclesis*, a word meaning invocation. Though the term in its theological sense is not part of the Roman Catholic liturgy, it is used to this day by the Greek Orthodox Church to identify that moment during the Eucharistic consecration when the Holy Spirit is called upon (invoked) to transform the bread and wine into the body and blood of Christ. The terms *epiclesis* and *epicletos* can, respectively, refer to someone against whom an accusation has been leveled and the accused who is summoned to appear in court. In this respect, the intent in his letter to Curran indicates that those in Dublin are Joyce's accused and summoned by him to appear in the court of his writings for the world to judge. In an around about way, the term *epicleti*, whether a misreading or not, is in fact a portal of discovery.

Epicleses, however, is not "another name for J's epiphanies" as incorrectly stated in the index of Richard Ellmann's *James Joyce*. The two terms derive from different Greek words and are radically different.

Appendix VI: Satiric and Serious Joyce: "The Holy Office," "Gas from a Burner," and "A Curious History"

By the time Joyce reached his late teens and early twenties, he had a strong belief in his own abilities to write poetry, drama, and prose, but, for various reasons, he never became part of the established Dublin literati. He dissociated himself from this cenacle, which at the time consisted of George Russell (Æ), William Butler Yeats, Lady Gregory, Edward Martyn, Padraic Colum, and others. "The Holy Office" is a satirical broadside of 96 lines attacking these members. It was distributed by his brother Stanislaus in June of 1905 when Joyce was living in Trieste. Joyce thought the piece was clever (*Letters II*, 73) as it provided a clear juxtaposition between his conception of the artist and theirs. In the opening two lines, he names himself Katharsis-Purgative, the one who purges the waste found in literature by cleansing it with a purpose direct and uncompromising. He closes the satire with a minatory statement that some may consider he made good on:

> Though they may labour to the grave
> My spirit shall they never have
> Nor make my soul with theirs at one
> Till the Mahamanvantara be done:
> And though they spurn me from their door
> My soul shall spurn them evermore.

The satire takes its name from Church's Congregation of the Holy Office which has its roots in the twelfth century but was not designated an official congregation until the mid-sixteenth century. Its main duty is to protect the teachings of the Church against false doctrines. By titling his piece "The Holy Office," Joyce, who would have been aware of the existence of this office in the Church, is positioning himself not only as the defender of what is or is not literary but also as its most promising contributor.

By 1912, Joyce's conviction in the quality of his writings was even more pronounced when he wrote the 98-line satiric broadside, "Gas from a Burner." He condemns both publisher and printer for breaking the contract to publish *Dubliners*, which he had signed in 1909 when he opened and operated the Volta, the first cinema in Dublin. Over the three years that elapsed from the time Joyce signed the contract to the time he penned this invective broadside, the publisher George Roberts of Maunsel and Company began to find issues with the stories and demanded that certain passages be altered and that one of the stories be taken out. (See "A Curious History" below.) Though the printer, John Falconer, destroyed the sheets he produced, Joyce managed to acquire a complete set that he took with him to Trieste in September 1912. This date marks the last time Joyce would ever be in Ireland. On the way back to Trieste, he wrote the broadside which satirizes George Roberts in his own voice. Once in Trieste, he had the piece printed and then mailed it to his brother Charles in Dublin to distribute.

Joyce's account of the delay in publishing *Dubliners* is titled "A Curious History." It first appeared in *The Egoist* on 15 January 1914, and again as a promotional piece by B.W. Huebsch, the New York publisher of *Dubliners*, in 1917. Ezra Pound wrote a preface.[1]

The delay in publishing the short stories went on for a little more than eight years, from April 1906 to June 1914, before Grant Richards finally came out with the collection in 1914. In the two letters that comprise "A Curious History," the first written in August 1911 and the second in November 1913 (*Letters II*, 291–293, 324–325), Joyce reviews specific objections the publishers had. He sent copies of the August letter to several Irish newspapers; an excerpt of the letter appeared in The *Northern Whig* on August 26th. The newspaper *Sinn Féin* published the whole letter on September 2nd. The November letter expands upon the one Joyce wrote in August. Joyce's biographer, Richard Ellmann, records that Joyce wanted the expanded letter published as a preface to *Dubliners*, but Grant Richards nixed that idea (*James Joyce*, p. 353). "A Curious History" is also published in *Pound/Joyce: The Letters of Ezra Pound to James Joyce* (cited in our bibliography).

As a form of oppression, censorship is an extension of the abuse of power by a state and runs contrary to the modernist objectives someone like Joyce would hold. Ten months after Joyce signed a contract with the London publisher Grant Richards in 1906, Richards insisted that the story "Two Gallants" be removed from the collection and passages in other stories be edited. Joyce, of course, refused to amend what he submitted and strongly stated that "for the most part" he wrote the stories "in a style of scrupulous meanness and with the conviction that he is a very bold man who dares to alter in the presentment, still more to deform, whatever he has seen and heard" (*Letters* I.134). The idea here is an extension of the forthright honesty the writer is to achieve that Joyce anticipated in 1904 when he wrote "The Holy Office." Toward the end of 1906, Richards cancelled the contract after an extended period of negotiations between him and Joyce.

A new contract in 1909 with Maunsel and Company, a Dublin publisher, gave Joyce high hopes that *Dubliners* would finally appear. In the early months of 1910, George Roberts, the managing director and co-founder of the publishing firm, disapproved of passages in "Ivy Day in the Committee Room" that he found disparaging toward King Edward VII. He also objected to passages that named actual people and streets. Joyce was adamant that he would not make any changes and prohibited from including the disclaimer he wanted to add. His persistence, however, was to no avail, even after seeking legal advice and the judgment of King George V, King Edward VII's successor. In August of 1911, the king's private secretary acknowledged receipt of Joyce's correspondence and returned the material Joyce sent with the comment that "it is inconsistent with rule for His Majesty to express his opinion in such cases" (*Letters II*, 292–293).

Wanting *Dubliners* published, Joyce begrudgingly complied with Roberts' demands: The second story in the collection, "An Encounter," was to be deleted, real names were to be removed, and other passages modified. Joyce was also required to pay a security deposit of £1000, which he refused to do, but instead he was willing to cover 60% of the printing costs, which he expected to recoup after the collection was on the market. Roberts accepted the offer, but in the summer of 1912 when Joyce was in Dublin to sign the new contract, John Falconer, the printer, refused to hand copies over to him. Joyce returned to Trieste in September of 1912, and in a letter to William Butler, Yeats explained what happened:

> I suppose you will have heard of the fate of my book *Dubliners*. Roberts refused to publish it and finally agreed to sell me the first edition for £30 so that I might publish it myself. Then the printer refused to hand over the 1000 copies which he had printed either to me or to anyone else and actually broke up the type and burned the whole first edition.
> (*Letters I*, 71–72)

During this time in Ireland and England, printers as well as publishers and authors were liable for what they published.

After several attempts with other publishers, in March 1914 Joyce signed a second contract with Grant Richards, the very first publisher to whom he sent the manuscript, and, on 15 June 1914, *Dubliners* was published.[2]

Notes

1 Joyce's correspondence to Grant Richards can be found in *Letters I*, 55 and 60–64; and in *Letters II*, 122–123, 132–144, 324–325, 327–329, 332, and 340–341. For more information regarding the publication of *Dubliners*, also see Robert Scholes, "Grant Richards to James Joyce" published in *Studies in Bibliography*, edited by Fredson Bowers, Vol. XVI, pp. 139–160 (Charlottesville, VA: Bibliographical Society of the University of Virginia, 1963).
2 The full text of "A Curious History" can be found in Robert Scholes and A. Walton Litz's *Dubliners: Text, Criticism and Notes*, cited under primary sources in our bibliography. Also, see the relevant section on the publication history of *Dubliners* in Michael Groden's "A Textual and Publishing History" in *A Companion to Joyce Studies*, edited by Zack Bowen and James F. Carens, cited in under general sources in our bibliography.

Appendix VII: Currency Terms with Selected Examples from Joyce's Literary Works

bob: Slang for a shilling; a bob can be singular or plural (one bob or six bob). An example from Joyce is when Bloom reflects on the third hint he has given Hynes to repay a loan: "Three bob I lent him in Meagher's. Three weeks. Third hint" (*U* 7.119).

crown: Abbreviated cr., a crown is equivalent to 5s (five shillings). In one respect, the term may apply to any coin with an imprint of a crown on it. In the Cyclops episode of *Ulysses*, the publican, Terry, mentioned to the patrons at Barney Kiernan's that he wagered money on one of the horses in the Ascot Gold Cup race that took place on the day of the novel's setting: "'I had half a crown myself,' says Terry, on *Zinfandel* that Mr Flynn gave me" (*U* 12.1224–1225).

farthing: A fourth or a quarter of a unit, a fourth of a penny in British currency written as 1/4d. Thus 2 farthings would equal a halfpenny (1/2d) and 4 farthings a penny (1d). Farthings were last minted in 1956 and taken out of circulation in 1960. When Stephen Dedalus confesses his sins at the end of chapter III of *A Portrait of the Artist as a Young Man*, the priest uses the imagery of this currency to emphasize the heinousness of fornication and his worthlessness in committing it: "As long as you commit that sin, my poor child, you will never be worth one farthing to God" (p. 145).

florin: A gold coin worth two shillings whose name comes from the image of a lily stamped on it. According to the *Oxford English Dictionary*, the florin, derived from the Latin word for flower (*florem*), was first issued in 1252 at Florence. An example from Joyce can be seen with the unnamed narrator in "Araby": "I held a florin tightly in my hand as I strode down Buckingham Street towards the station" (p. 34).

groat: Once worth 4 pence, a groat has been out of circulation since the mid-seventeenth century. Its insignificant sum is alluded to by Stephen Dedalus in the Proteus episode, chapter 3 of *Ulysses*, when he reflects on his time in Paris: "Eating your groatsworth of *mou en civet*" (*U* 3.177).

guinea: A gold coin once worth 21 shillings (1£ 1s) before it ceased to be minted in 1813. The term, however, remained in use to refer to an equivalent worth reserved for expensive items. The *Oxford English*

Dictionary explains: "The guinea is the ordinary unit for a professional fee and for a subscription to a society or institution; the prices obtained for works of art, racehorses, and sometimes landed property, are also stated in guineas."

Toward the end of the Nestor episode, chapter 2 of *Ulysses*, when Garrett Deasy is paying Stephen Dedalus his wages, Stephen thinks of the guineas and other amounts he owes: "Mulligan, nine pounds, three pairs of socks, one pair brogues, ties. Curran, ten guineas. McCann, one guinea. Fred Ryan, two shillings. Temple, two lunches. Russell, one guinea, Cousins, ten shillings, Bob Reynolds, half a guinea, Koehler, three guineas, Mrs MacKernan, five weeks' board. The lump I have is useless" (*U* 2.255–259). This section of the Nestor episode where Deasy and Stephen are speaking with one another contains the most concentrated references to currencies in Joyce's works.

half crown: Once worth two shillings sixpence (2s 6d), a half crown by 1970 was no longer legal tender. In the same section of Nestor where we refer to the use of the term guinea, Deasy explains to Stephen the usefulness of having a savings box: "These are handy things to have. . . . This is for shillings. Sixpences, halfcrowns" (*U* 2.219–220).

halfpenny: A halfpenny, pronounced ha'penny and written 1/2d, is an amount equivalent to 2 farthings. The halfpenny was last minted in 1967 and its use discontinued in 1984. The plural of the halfpenny (a single coin) is halfpence (more than one coin). In "Two Gallants," the narrator indicates the condition of the financially strapped Lenehan as he pays for a plate of peas at a cheap restaurant: "He paid twopence halfpenny to the slatternly girl and went out of the shop to begin his wandering again" (p. 58).

half sovereign: A gold coin that is valued at ten shillings. In the Circe episode, chapter 15 of *Ulysses*, the narrative (or stage directions) has Bloom place this amount of money on a table between Bella and Florry: "(*quietly* [Bloom] *lays a half sovereign on the table between Bella and Florry*)" (*U* 15.3583).

£ s d: Symbols for pound, shilling, and penny, and not LSD (Lysergic Acid Diethylamide) or *Lucy in the Sky with Diamonds* (the Beatles' song). Examples: £5 (five pounds), 2/- or 2s (two shillings), and 1d, 3d, ¼d, and ½d (one penny, three pence, a quarter of a penny or a farthing, and a halfpenny).

penny: Symbolized by the letter d, an abbreviation of the ancient Roman coin denarius, a penny is equivalent to 4 farthings or 2 halfpence. Its plural is pence. The penny is written as 1d and its related minted coins as 3d (threepence) and 6d (sixpence). In "Counterparts," the main character Farrington, who finds relief in the comfort of a pub, is desperate for money and decides to pawn his watch because "he had spent his last penny for the g.p. [glass of porter] and soon it would be too late for getting money anywhere" (p. 92).

pound: From the Latin word for a pound of silver, *libra*, a pound is equivalent to 20 shillings or 240 pence and abbreviated by the symbol £. In the Ithaca episode, chapter 17 of *Ulysses*, one question and answer segment of the narrative refers to the money that the host (Bloom) was, since the Circe episode, safekeeping for the guest (Stephen):

What exchange of money took place between host and guest?
The former returned to the latter, without interest, a sum of money (£1–7-0), one pound seven shillings sterling, advanced by the latter to the former. (U 17.956–959)

quid: This term is slang for one pound sterling or a sovereign and is used for both the singular and plural (one quid, four quid). In the Cyclops episode, chapter 12 of *Ulysses*, one of the two narrators (here the first person singular) arrives with Joe Hynes at Barney Kiernan's for a drink and is shocked that Hynes stood the round: "So anyhow Terry brought the three pints Joe was standing and begob the sight nearly left my eyes when I saw him land out a quid. O, as true as I'm telling you. A goodlooking sovereign" (U 12.206–208).

shilling: A coin worth 12d (12 pence). Though the derivation of the term is questionable, it may come from *solidus*, a Latin word conveying the meaning of that which is solid. The abbreviation for shilling appears in several ways: as the letter s or the forward slash / and less frequently as sh. or shil. The forward slash or the letter s usually follows the specific amount: 3/ or 3s for three shillings. If the specific amount includes a penny or pence, it appears as 3/1 (3s 1d) or 3/3 (3s 3d). The coin remained in circulation for a while after decimalization in 1971, and eventually it ceased to be used. In "The Dead," Gabriel Conroy in the spirit of the Christmas season generously tips the cabdriver: "When the cab drew up before the hotel Gabriel jumped out and, in spite of Mr Bartell D'Arcy's protest, paid the driver. He gave the man a shilling over his fare" (pp. 214–215).

sovereign: Equivalent to 1 £, a sovereign is a gold coin worth 20 shillings. In the opening chapter of *Ulysses*, the Telemachus episode, when Buck Mulligan finds out that Stephen will be paid in the morning, he exclaims: "'Four shining sovereigns,' Buck Mulligan cried with delight. 'We'll have a glorious drunk to astonish the druidy druids. Four omnipotent sovereigns'" (U 1.296–297).

tanner: A sixpence silver coin first minted in 1551 whose etymology is uncertain. No longer in use, a tanner refers to a small amount. In the Lestrygonians episode, chapter 8 of *Ulysses*, Bloom momentarily compares the ambrosia of the gods with the food humans eat: "Not like a tanner lunch we have, boiled mutton, carrots and turnips, bottle of Allsop" (U 8.926–927).

Index

Note: Page numbers in *italics* refer to figures.

Addison, Joseph 4
After the Race 37–38
alcoholism: in *Dubliners* 27, 40, 41, 43, 45; in *Ulysses* 102, 104, 105, 106
alienation feeling, in *Dubliners* 27–28, 38, 42–44
ambiguity portrayal: in *Portrait of the Artist as a Young Man, A* 64–65, 66; in *Ulysses* 86–87
Anderson, Margret 81, 82
Anderson, Sherwood 21
anti-Semitism, in *Ulysses* 86, 96
Aquinas, St. Thomas 16
Araby 35–36
Art of James Joyce, The (Litz) 6
Atherton, James S. 197, 198
Attridge, Derek 126, 197
Austen, Jane 28, 31

Bally, Charles 192
Barnacle, Nora 13, 18
Beach, Sylvia 21, 82, 165, 169
Beckett, Samuel 21, 22
Beja, Morris 6
Benstock, Bernard 126, 129
biographical criticism 5–6
Bishop, Joseph 126
Boarding House, The 39–40
Brilliant Career, A 16
Bristow, Daniel 7
Brivic, Sheldon 7
Bruno, Giordano 16, 133
Budgen, Frank 3, 19–20, 130, 146, 201

cadenza and musicality, in *Ulysses* 113–115
Campbell, Joseph 126, 129
Carleton, William 33
Carr, Henry 20

Catholicism: in *Dubliners* 28, 46; in minor works 166; in *Portrait of the Artist as a Young Man, A* 60–61, 67–68, 70–71, 73–74, 75–76; in *Ulysses* 85, 96–97, 106
Chamber Music 16, 17, 56, 164, 167–169, 170
Cheng, Vincent 9
Clay 41–42
Clongwes Wood College 67
conjunction and polarity of opposites, in *Finnegans Wake* 133–135, 138, 159–160
Conrad, Joseph 31
Corcoran, Marlena G. 8
Couterparts 40–41
creativity portrayal, in *Dubliners* 28
Crispi, Luca 7
Criterion (journal) 171
critical theory 4–5
Critical Writings of James Joyce 171–172
cultural studies 8
Cultural Studies of James Joyce (Herr) 8
"Curious History, A" 205
Curran, Constantine P. 202, 203
cyclical nature of life, in *Finnegans Wake* 130, 133, 137, 155, 160

Dana (journal) 56, 164
D'Annunzio, Gabrielle 202
Darantiere, Maurice 21, 83, 126
Dead, The 19, 32, 46–47; nostalgia and rancor at the Gresham Hotel in 47–49; thematic summation in 49–50
deconstruction 7, 126
deferral of closure feature, in *Dubliners* 31
Derrida, Jacques 5, 7
Derrida and Joyce (Mitchell and Sloate) 7
Dickens, Charles 28, 33

"Dream of H.C. Earwicker, The" (Wilson) 126, 197
Dream Stuff 16
Dubliners 13, 18, 19, 26, 126, 165, 205–206; *After the Race* in 37–38; alcoholism in 27, 40, 41, 43, 45; alienation feeling in 27–28, 38, 42–44; alternative readings in 47–50; *Araby* in 35–36; *Boarding House, The*, in 39–40; Catholicism in 28, 46; *Clay* in 41–42; *Counterparts* in 40–41; creativity portrayal in 28; *Dead, The*, in 46–50; deferral of closure feature in 31; duty sense in 28–29; *Encounter, An*, in 35; *Eveline* in 36–37; free indirect discourse in 31, 37, 38, 39, 50; gender portrayal in 29; *Grace* in 45–46; identity in 29; importance of 26–27; irony depiction in 31, 33; *Ivy Day in the Committee Room* in 43–44, 85; *Little Cloud, A*, in 40; *Mother, A*, in 44–45; nationalism in 29, 43; overview of stories in 31–33; *Painful Case, A*, in 42–43; paralysis as theme in 29–30, 34, 50; realism in 30; relationships in 30; self-esteem in 40–41; sex and sexuality in 30, 48; *Sisters, The*, in 33–35; style of 30–31; *Two Gallants* in 38–39
Duffy, Enda 9

Ecce Puer 171
Eco, Umberto 202
Egoist, The (magazine) 21, 26, 56, 82, 205
Eliot, T.S. 21, 22
Ellmann, Richard 12, 15, 131, 148–149, 151, 170, 171, 203, 205
emptiness, in *Dubliners* 41, 42, 47, 48
Encounter, An 35
epicleti and epiclets, comparison of 202–203
epiphany 201–202
episodic incidents, in *Portrait of the Artist as a Young Man, A* 63
episodic narration, in *Ulysses* 87
Epstein, Edmund Lloyd 129, 146
"Essay on Criticism, An" (Pope) 148
Esslin, Martin 198
Eveline 36–37
Exiles 19, 163, 172–173

Falconer, John 205, 206
family relations: in minor works 163; in *Portrait of the Artist as a Young Man, A* 60; in *Ulysses* 84–85
feminist criticism 7–8

Finnegans Wake 22, 23–24, 125–126, 167; Book of Parents, The, section of 137–145; Book of Sons, The, section of 145–150; Book of the People, The, section of 150–154; conjunction and polarity of opposites in 133–135, 138, 159–160; cylical nature of life in 130, 133, 137, 155, 160; dream of 197–198; evolution, and published excerpts 126–128; frustrated love and lovemaking in 135–136; historical repetition as motif in 133; identity in 160; journals involved in publishing excerpts of 127–128; language variability in 135, 138–139; lapsarian theme in 133; letters as motif in 138, 141, 147; organizational approaches to 129–130; passage referencing in 128–129, 147; polarity of twins in 141–142; rebirth motif in 132, 146, 152, 154; recorso section of 154; renewal as theme in 133, 137, 140, 144, 154; riddles in 135, 138, 143, 146, 158–161; sexuality in 135–136, 152, 153; sigla (signs) to compose 130–131; title significance of 131–133
Fish, Stanley 6
Fitzgerald, F. Scott 21
Ford, Ford Madox 131
formal experimentation 6
Fortnightly Review (journal) 16
Fournier, Henry 37
free indirect discourse 192; in *Dubliners* 31, 37, 38, 39, 50; *Portrait of the Artist as a Young Man, A* 62, 65–66; in *Ulysses* 81, 86–87, 103
Freud, Sigmund 7, 8
Fuoco, Il (D'Annunzio) 202

Gabler, Hans Walter 6, 165
"Gas from a Burner" 204
gender: portrayal, in *Dubliners* 29; studies 8
genetic criticism 7
Giacomo Joyce 163, 171
Glasheen, Adaline 129
Gorman, Herbert 167
Grace 45–46
Groden, Michael 126
Guide through Finnegans Wake, A (Epstein) 129, 146

hallucinations, in *Ulysses* 105–106
Hart, Clive 147, 197
Hauptmann, Gerhart 16
Hayman, David 127

Heap, Jane 81, 82
Hemingway, Ernest 21
Herr, Cherly 8
historical repetition, as motif in *Finnegans Wake* 133
Hoarth, Herbert 169
"Holy Office" 204, 205
How Joyce Wrote Finnegans Wake (Crispi and Sloate) 7
Huebsch, B. W. 205

"Ibsen's New Drama" 16
identity: in *Dubliners* 29; in *Finnegans Wake* 160; in minor works 162–163; in *Ulysses* 83–84
Imagistes, Des (Pound) 56
Importance of Being Earnest, The (Wilde) 20
incertitude feature, in *Ulysses* 88
Irish experience 8–9, 33
Irish Homestead (newspaper) 26, 33, 36, 37
Irish nationalism, in *Portrait of the Artist as a Young Man, A* 61, 68, 72, 75, 76
Irish Times 37
irony: in *Dubliners* 31, 33; in *Portrait of the Artist as a Young Man, A* 62–63
Is There a Text in This Class (Fish) 6
Ivy Day in the Committee Room 43–44, 85

James, Henry 31
James Joyce (Beja) 6
James Joyce (Ellman) 149, 203
"James Joyce" (Wilson) 197
James Joyce and Nationalism (Nolan) 9
James Joyce and the Making of Ulysses (Budgen) 130, 201
James Joyce Archive, The 6
Johnson, Samuel 4
Jolas, Eugene 131
Joyce, James: biography of 11–25; birthplace of 12; death of 25; Dublin experiences of 12–14; election, as prefect of Sodality of the Blessed Virgin Mary 14; health condition of 21–22; Jesuit influence on 16; Nora Barnacle as life partner of 18–19; original death mask of 24; in Paris 21; school education of 13, 15; in Trieste 18–19, 20; in Zurich 19, 25
Joyce, John 13
Joyce, May 16–17
Joyce, Race, and Empire (Cheng) 9
Joyce, Stanislaus 18–19, 20–21, 22, 32, 40, 41, 125, 167
Joyce-Again's Wake (Benstock) 129
Joyce and Feminism (Scott) 8
Joyce and Lacan (Bristow) 7
Joyce between Freud and Jung (Brivic) 7
Joyce's Voices (Kenner) 192

Kain, Richard M. 202
Kenner, Hugh 192, 195, 196n2

Lacan, Jacques 7
language variability, in *Finnegans Wake* 135, 138–139
lapsarian theme, in *Finnegans Wake* 133
Lawrence, D. H. 63
Léon, Paul 165
Letters 32, 163–164
letters, as motif in *Finnegans Wake* 138, 141, 147
Lewis, Wyndham 143, 151
literary theories, importance of 5
Little Cloud, A 40
Little Review, The (journal) 21, 81
Litz, Walton 6

Magee, W. K. 56, 164
Mason, Ellsworth 171
Mathews, Elkin 167
Maupassant, Guy de 33
McCormick, Mrs. Harold 19
McHugh, Roland 150
Melchiori, Giorgio 172, 202
Michael Kramer (Hauptmann) 16
minor works 162; Catholicism in 166; *Chamber Music* as 167–169; *Critical writings of James Joyce* as 171–172; *Ecce Puer* as 171; *Exiles* as 172–173; familial relations in 163; identity in 162–163; nationalism in 163; *Pomes Penyeach* as 169–171; *Portrait of the Artist, A*, as 164; sexuality in 163–164; *Stephen Hero* as 165–166
Mitchell, Andrew 7
Modernist fiction 33, 57
modulating quality, in *Portrait of the Artist as a Young Man, A* 63
Moods 16
Mother, A 44–45
Murray, Josephine 21

nationalism: in *Dubliners* 29, 43; in minor works 163; in *Ulysses* 85–86
National Library, Dublin 73
New York Review of Books (journal) 6
Nolan, Emer 9
Northern Whig (newspaper) 205

O'Hanlon, John 132
Owenson, Sydney 33

Painful Case, A 42–43
paralysis as theme, in *Dubliners* 29–30, 34, 50
Parrinder, Patrick 126, 197
Piccola della Sera, Il (newspaper) 19
polarity of twins, in *Finnegans Wake* 141–142
Pomes Penyeach 169–171
Pope, Alexander 148
Portrait of the Artist as a Young Man, A 11, 13, 14, 18, 19, 29, 31, 33, 56–57, 126, 159, 160, 165; alternative readings in 74–76; ambiguity portrayal in 64–65, 66; Catholicism in 60–61, 67–68, 70–71, 73–74, 75–76; culture in 61–62; episodic incidents in 63; family relationships in 60; free indirect discourse in 62, 65–66; identity in 59; Irish nationalism in 61, 68, 72, 75, 76; irony in 62–63; issues in 58–62; modulating quality in 63; thematic inconclusiveness in 63; view of Ireland in 59–60
postcolonial studies 9
Pound, Ezra 19, 21, 22, 26, 56, 81, 82, 94, 125, 164, 170, 205
Pound/Joyce (Pound) 205
Power, Arthur 27
Pride and Prejudice (Austen) 31
psychoanalytic assessments 7

Quare Joyce (Valente) 8
queer studies 8
Quinet, Edgar 147

Rabelais 4
Ratio Studiorum 16
Reader's Guide to James Joyce, A (Tindall) 129, 136, 147
Real Charlotte, The (Somerville and Ross) 33
realism, in *Dubliners* 30
rebirth, as motif in *Finnegans Wake* 132, 146, 152, 154
relationships, in *Dubliners* 30
renewal, as theme in *Finnegans Wake* 133, 137, 140, 144, 154
Richards, Grant 26, 31, 205, 206
riddles, in *Finnegans Wake* 135, 138, 143, 146, 158–161
Roberts, George 205
Robinson, Henry Morton 126, 129
Rose, Danis 131, 132
Ross 33
Russell, George 26

"Scandal of Ulysses, The" 6
Scholes, Robert 202
Scott, Bonnie 8
Scotus, Duns 160
Selected Letters (Ellman) 151
self-esteem, in *Dubliners* 40–41
sexuality: in *Finnegans Wake* 135–136, 152, 153; in minor works 163–164; in *Ulysses* 86, 103–104, 110–111, 112, 114–115; sex and, in *Dubliners* 30, 48
Shine and Dark 16
Sigla of Finnegans Wake, The (McHugh) 150
Silhouettes 16
Sinn Féin (newspaper) 205
Sisters, The 33–35
Skeleton Key, A (Robinson) 126, 129
Sloate, Sam 7
Smart Set, The (magazine) 39, 40
Somerville 33
Sons and Lovers (Lawrence) 63
Spencer, Theodore 165
Steele, Richard 4
Stephen Hero 56–57, 165–166, 201
Steppe, Wolfhard 202
stream of consciousness, in *Ulysses* 86, 99, 104
Structure and Motif in Finnegans Wake (Hart) 147
stylistic criticism 6
Subaltern Ulysses, The (Duffy) 9
Suter, August 130
Sykes, Claude 20
Symons, Arthur 167, 169

textual criticism 6–7
textual studies 6
Theatre of the Absurd, The (Esslin) 198
thematic inconclusiveness, in *Portrait of the Artist as a Young Man, A* 63
Third Census of Finnegans Wake (Glasheen) 129
Time and Western Man (Lewis) 143
Tindall, William York 129, 136, 147
Traits and Stories of the Irish Peasantry (Carleton) 33
transaccidentation 135, 144, 160
transatlantic review 125, 127
transition (magazine) 131
Two Gallants 38–39

Ulysses 11, 18, 19, 21, 23, 38, 81–83, 126; Aeolus chapter in 97–98; alcoholism in 102, 104, 105, 106; alternative readings in 112–115; ambiguity portrayal in 86–87; anti-Semitism in 86, 96; cadenza and musicality in 113–115; Calypso chapter in 91–94; Catholicism in 85, 96–97, 106; chapter structures in 87–88; Circe chapter in 105–107; Cyclops chapter in 101–103; episodic narration in 87; Eumaeus in 107–108; family relationships, in 84–85; free indirect discourse in 81, 86–87, 103; Hades chapter in 95–97; hallucinations in 105–106; identity in 83–84; incertitude feature in 88; Ithaca chapter in 108–109; Lestrygonians chapter in 98–99; Lotus Eaters chapter in 94–95; love life of Leopold and Molly Bloom in 194–195; Molly's Lulabye in 112–113; nationalism in 85–86; Nausikaa chapter in 103–104; Nestor chapter in 90; Oxen of the Sun chapter in 104–105; Penelope chapter in 109–111; Proteus chapter in 91; Scylla and Charybdis chapter in 99–100; sexuality in 86, 103–104, 110–111, 112, 114–115; Sirens chapter in 101; stream of consciousness in 86, 99, 104; Telemachus chapter in 88–90; Wandering Rocks chapter in 100–101

Ulysses in Progress (Groden) 126
University College 72
Uncle Charles Principle 192–193

Valente, Joseph 8
Vico, Giambettista 129, 137, 160
Vor Sonnenaufgang (*Before Sunrise*) (Hauptmann) 16
Voyage Out, The (Woolf) 57

"Wake" in Transit, The (Hayman) 127
Wawrzycka, Jolanta W. 8
Weaver, Harriet Shaw 21, 22, 56, 82, 125, 130, 131, 137, 143, 144, 145, 197
Wilde, Oscar 20
Wild Irish Girl, The (Owenson) 33
Wilson, Edmund 126, 197
Woolf, Virginia 57, 86
Woolsey, John M. 23
Work in Progress (journal) 131
Work in Progress 22–23, 125–126, 201
Workshop of Daedalus, The (Scholes and Kain) 202

Yeats, W.B. 19, 206

For Product Safety Concerns and Information please contact our EU representative GPSR@taylorandfrancis.com
Taylor & Francis Verlag GmbH, Kaufingerstraße 24, 80331 München, Germany

www.ingramcontent.com/pod-product-compliance
Lightning Source LLC
Chambersburg PA
CBHW051357290426
44108CB00015B/2045